Message Post

February 1990   One issue $1

Portable Dwelling Info-letter
POB 190, Philomath, OR 97370
Six issues $5 cash; $5½ check

Primitive Trap for Birds Does Not Harm Them

My great grandfather used this during the depression to help feed his family. It will catch quail and many other ground-feeding birds - a dozen or more at one time. It does not harm them; the birds not wanted can be released.

slope

The trap is made of sticks. Birds feed down a slope to the entrance, come up thru the hole, and when ready to leave always look up and go round and round the sides, over the small board, hunting a way out.

A portable version can be made of hardware cloth (wire mesh). It's a box about 20" long, 12" wide and 8" high. An 8" long tunnel leads in from the entrance. When trying to leave, the birds go up and over the tunnel. Roger, Alabama, November

small board
bait
bait
bait

Tools Useful When Camping - Part I

Air Force Survival Knife. Use to shave, cut, shape wood. Use butt to hammer stakes, small nails. Attach sharpening stone to back of sheath with epoxy glue. Use pocket to carry flint or magnesium stick.

Hammer/axe/nail puller combination. Made in Taiwan.

Machette with 12" or 18" blade length. Good one made in El Salvador. Cut/chop brush and small trees. Dig holes in ground and ice. Use for defense. 8-10" machine file resharpens.

Small files for resharpening. Small stone, arransan(?) type, fine-medium grain. Sharpens sizzors, knives, chisels, etc., even razor blades.

Bow saws. Use to cut trees, trim dead wood. Buy a good one with an extra blade.

Pulley and rope set. Useful for picking up or dragging heavy objects.

Additional tools for bikes: chain tool, pressure gauge, tire tools, air pump, patch kit, 6" adjustable wrench, and valve tool helps in basic maintenance.

Additional tools for small engines: socket tube wrench for spark plugs, gap & wire tool, 120 volt neon tester with clips (checks spark safely when cranking), and 4" adjustable wrench helps in basic maintenance.

For appliances, generators, batteries, bulbs, radios, etc., a basic VOM can be used. Also check line voltages. If utility is lowering them ("brownouts"), that can damage electrical items hooked into the line. Wildflower, CT, April

A Way to Do Errands in Town

My m⸱ther, a confirmed city dweller, insists it's cheaper to use t⸱⸱⸱⸱⸱⸱⸱⸱⸱⸱⸱⸱⸱⸱s than to own a car. She rents a ⸱⸱⸱⸱⸱⸱⸱⸱e a year to do a well planned ⸱et-to places. Anne, CA

● This

6 pages done during 1990s.

1

Message Post

Portable Dwelling Info-letter
POB 190, Philomath, OR 97370

May 1990 #26   One issue $1   Six issues $5 cash; $5½ check

Head Strap on Flashlight Leaves Both Hands Free

I sometimes hold a penlight in my mouth
but not when hiking. (I might trip and
ram it against my teeth or into my
throat.) Instead, to my pen-light
I tie a rubber strap (cut from an
inner tube) or a piece of elastic.
The penlight goes along the side
of my head above my ear and the
rubber strap goes around my head.
Julie Summers, Oregon, March

To Revive Weak Batteries

I rub each end vigorously back
and forth on a taut piece of cloth
(such as on my pants when my thigh is
bent). If an eraser is handy I first
clean the ends with it. Both these actions
remove invisible corrosion. If a flashlight is seldom used,
this cleaning before each use brightens the beam.

Warming batteries next to my body, inside my clothes or
sleeping bag, also helps. Don't heat with flame - batteries
may explode if they get hot enough. Julie Summers, March

Tools Useful for Camping - Part II

Vise grip pliers. I carry two 5 WR size in my traveling
tool bag (old camera case). I use them to grip nuts, bolts,
and nails; to cut wire; to clamp wires to battery terminals;
as vise; as handle for 6" saber saw blades, sewing awl needles,
and xacto razor blades. I prefer the name brand.

Rachet head. I prefer one with a magnetic socket that
takes various ¼" hex-based bits, including screwdrivers (for
Phillips, straight, hex, tork, etc.) and drills (for wood,
plastic and light metals). Also, with a ¼" adapter, it can
drive sockets (for nuts and bolts, metric and standard).

Paramedic sizzors. These have their handles at an angle
to the blades so your hand stays out of the slit. They can
cut canvas, screen, light metals, leather, rubber, etc. Buy
them at local medical supplier. Beware of cheap imitations.

Folding shovel. In addition to digging holes, removing
fire ash and preparing garden beds, by sharpening one side it
can be used as an axe or for defense.

Web belt, alice harness, or alice pack. These military
surplus items are useful for carrying machette, shovel, and
other tools. Wildflower, CT, April & Oct. (Part I, in Feb'90
MP, mentioned survival knife, hammer/axe combo, machette,
files/stones, bow saw, pulley, and bike & small engine tools.)

No Special Tool Carried for Pocketknife Sharpening

In the woods I can usually find a rock or pebble that
suffices. It needn't be flat, merely without bumps. In town
I use any convenient concrete edge, such as a step or low wall.

On a regular sharpening stone with uniform fine grains,
I move the blade edge-first, to avoid getting a feather edge.
But on a rock with rough grain, or on concrete, I move the
blade edge-last so that it can ride up over any protruding
grains: better a feather edge than a knick.

Hand holding a small stone for sharpening can be dangerous - keep eyes and mind on your task. If unsure of yourself, try to use a rock heavy enough to stay in place by itself, or wear a stout glove. Julie Summers, Oregon, March

Pump-Spray Bottles and Squeeze Bottles Have Many Uses

I use pump-spray bottles to spray cooking oil on pans, kerosene on rusty bolts, light oil on gears, ammonia on pests (including any two-legged types), and sterile water or hydrogen peroxide on wounds, scrapes and cuts. Various sizes, from very small to two-quart, are available in discount, hardware, and drug stores. Wildflower, Connecticut, October

(We use squeeze bottles as water dispensers when washing things that won't fit under a Portable Faucet. We find many discarded (originally contained shampoo, flavorings, etc.) Squeeze bottles are even simpler and lighter than pump-spray bottles, and better when a stream is wanted. Pump-spray bottles are better when a fine spray is wanted. Holly & Bert)

Degradable Plastics Waste Money and Hinder Recycling

Some plastic recyclers have stopped recycling bags because degradable bags get mixed in and cause problems. We've called for a boycott of degradables. (Degradable materials are also less reusable. Once you have something, the best disposal is to reuse it yourself. Better than recycling, which requires collection, transport, sorting, cleaning, refining, etc.)

When shopping, the best thing is to bring your own reuseable bag. If you don't have it along, then choose either paper or plastic, depending on which you can recycle or reuse. Jeanne Wirka (condensed from Nutrition Action, April 1990)

Fire Black Need Not Be Removed From Pots

If you wish, you can go thru the coating-the-outside-with-soap-before-cooking routine to ease soot removal from a pot which is used over an open fire. But I find it much easier to simply wash the pot's inside and leave the outside alone. I let the pot air dry, then double bag it in a couple of large bags. (I like the large plastic bags used at supermarket checkouts. Paper bags are bulkier and tend to fall apart if they get wet.) I close the bags tightly with a couple of rubber bands. The bags keep the pot from soiling other things in my pack. Julie Summers, Oregon, March

We Use Skunk Cabbage Quite Extensively in Our Cooking

But as a flavoring agent, not as a main course. It imparts an excellent flavor to rice, noodles, or stews. It is dried and saved for use. When harvesting the heart, bring the leaves home and wrap your cheese in it to age. I learned these uses from a friend who learned it from Nisqually Indians with who he grew up. Gary Cropper, POB 864, Snoqualmie,WA 98065; July

After 15 Years Storage, 95% of Wheat Germinated

I reported (in June'89 MP) a sprouting test of 12-year-old wheat. Recently some even older wheat gave an even higher rate of germination: 371 out of 392 kernels showed sprouts $\frac{1}{4}$" or longer after four days. (A random sample of 400 had been counted out but 8 were broken or crushed and not included in test.)

This wheat, purchased in 1974, was not sprouted as it normally would be for eating. Instead, after soaking about 12 hours, it was drained, then distributed on a cotton cloth which was rolled up and placed on its side in a small plastic container left open. The cloth was kept moistened.

Thinking that the different sprouting method or the warmer
temperatures (later in spring) might be responsible for the
greater germination, some of the 1978 wheat was tested with
that method and 86% germinated (versus 76% with earlier method).

Why did the 1974 wheat sprout better than the 1978? Was
the 1974 wheat actually younger? (The dates are when we
purchased; we don't know when the grain was grown.) Or was it
stored better (cooler) prior to our acquisition? Or was it of
better quality for stor age (higher in vitamin E)?

Both kinds were stored by us in similar conditions: in
sealed metal containers with no special atmosphere (as I
recall), outside, in shady areas. Carl DeSilva, OR, July

Raw Watercress May Contain Liver Flukes

Liver flukes are parasites of ruminants (cattle, sheep,
goats, deer, elk) and occasionally of humans. Aquatic snails
are the intermediate hosts. After leaving the snail, the
fluke forms a cyst around itself. This form is found on vegetation or in water. Barely visible to the naked eye (small
pin-point tan colored spots), it can be identified only thru
a microscope. Humans have reportedly become infected by eating contaminated watercress. Cooking should destroy the cysts.
Gary Zimmerman, DVM, Col.of Vet.Med.,OSU; May'89 (reply to JS)

Poison Oak Most Dangerous if Smoke is Breathed

The letters in Message Post (Sept'86, Feb'87, June'87,
June'88 & Dec'88) are interesting.

The mucus membranes of the mouth, esophagus, stomach and
intestines are less penetrable to the oil than is the surface
skin. That is why Robin got a rash on his/her anus - the oil
came out in the feces and caused a reaction on surface skin.

Julie's point (that if anaphylactic shock were likely,
manufacturers wouldn't sell the oil over the counter) is good.

A bigger danger is breathing the smoke of a poison oak
fire into your lungs along with tiny droplets of the oil. In
my research that is the only cause of death I have heard about.

For people who are highly allergic to poison oak, I suggest
eating a small piece of mango skin every day - then every week.
It has the same oil as poison oak. My son, just back from
Australia, mentioned "mango rash" around people's mouths.
(Have you heard of anybody dying from eating a mango? I have
not, so I think it would be safe to eat a little skin.) The
oil does not degrade, so you can dry the skin and it will keep
for years. To keep up a tolerance, it is necessary to continue
to expose yourself to the oil, or your sensitivity will return.

In my book Poison Oak & Poison Ivy (reviewed in May'82 MP),
I tell the possible risks - because Jon Seaver is right: "You
oughta know something of the risks you face." Sandra Baker, CA

We Had a Lot of Trouble With Ticks Last Spring

One visitor got Lyme disease; we aren't sure from her home
ticks or from ours. The best control measure for us has been
to keep the grass cut short wherever we spend much time.

We got some info on non-pesticide control and traps from:
Bio-Integral Resource Center, POB 7474, Berkeley, CA 94707.
It cost about $3½. Please put everything you can find on
ticks in Message Post. Anne Callaway, California, March

Cat Flea/Tick Collars Worn on Ankles Repel Ticks

Nancy Sturhan, in WA, wore them over her work boots but
under her jeans. (Sci.News,29April'89)

Large Tents are Versatile

Our group lived and worked in southern Nevada for 12 years before moving to Washington. During that time we accumulated equipment for manufacturing almost anything we might want (as well as lots of just plain stuff) and hauled it north in old travel trailers. After arrival we needed storage for the stuff so that we could utilize the trailers. We spotted an ad for 16x32' military tents and bought two. As we get more permanent facilities constructed, we'll move the equipment in from the tents and set it up, but that'll take time.

Meanwhile we're getting our biosystems started. We've got 52 diary goats, 32 steers, 9 sheep, 2 cows, chickens, rabbits, and a pony. All these critters require space and storage, and the tents have played an important part. We're doing our milking and our intensive bottle feeding in an 18x52' we call the barn tent, and we have a second large tent that we're setting up to handle meals during the summer. Additionally we've picked up a few 16'-wide octagonal tents that are handy for various purposes.

The tents allow us maximum versatility in layout, both within the tent and in the selection of a place for the tent. There are a hundred ways to lay out a barn, milk parlor or workshop, and with the tents, we don't have to be locked into any one way. We're constantly shifting things around to meet our current needs or the latest insight into how things can be done better. For example, because of the embryonic state of our electrical system, we presently cluster our pens and facilities. Later we'll be able to spread out into a more dispersed format. When we no longer need the tents for year-round operations, we plan on using them for gatherings we will host from May until September, and for hay and equipment storage fall and winter.

A surprising side effect is the image the tents convey to visitors. So many people have enjoyed the M*A*S*H series that a group with lots of army tents is not all that strange. On the other hand, it is a different setting. Windward operates by the consensus process which differs from the competitive system in subtle but powerful ways. If people are in surroundings that resemble what they are used to, on a fundamental level, they presume that "things" work in the usual ways. In unusual surroundings, that presumption isn't so strong. Walt Patrick The Windward Foundation, POB 51, Klickitat, WA 98628; (509) 369-2448; March (Notes from Windward describe their daily activities. Sample $2. (22p.8x11))

For Fire Safety, Make Exits Easy

In 1967 two children died when unprotected interior foam insulation caught fire in a garage where they were playing. "There was just no chance of getting to them", said their father. "When the insulation was burning, the flames were so red hot you could hear the fire roar."

Though plastic on fire will sometimes go out when blown on (unlike wood), under certain conditions polyurethane foam (even "non-burning" types) has a "very high flame spread, high early heat output, and produces large quantities of dense black smoke.... Ironically, flame inhibitors usually increase toxic gases or greatly increase amount of smoke." (Refried Domes, review on page 8.)

Most other plastics burn, including polyethylene (bags, tarps) and styrofoam (packing, cups), as do most natural materials (straw, leaves, thin wood.) Most materials that won't burn (adobe, rocks) are heavy and dangerous in earthquakes. So, the best advice may be:

Be careful using flames. And build your shelter so all occupants can get out quickly if it does catch fire.

The safest entrance covering may be a curtain which you can simply duck under or pull up. (If wind's a problem, anchor the lower corners with elastic straps.) A zipper may jam. So may a door if warped by heat, or in the smoke a child might not find the latch. B & H

Ventilation Vital Where Flame Used

In answer to Anne's question, use of any flame appliance (including catalytic utensils) in an enclosed space mandates absolutely reliable ventilation. Carbon monoxide poisoning may manifest as either acute poisoning (one exposure produced symptoms) or chronic (you lose neurons to hypoxia, your children become intellectually stunted). Also, children raised in homes with flame appliances therein, seem to fall prey to more frequent respiratory infections, and to more often develop asthma. This problem may be more pronounced with wick appliances which, I imagine, provide less complete combustion than a mantle can. Jon Seaver RN, Michigan, March

Always Use a "Full-Spectrum" Light

if you use fluorescents. It warns the iris to close so the retina is not "burned". Paul Doerr, Calif., November

Kenwood Amateur Radios Fail in Salt Air

Our Kenwood 140-S has been repaired five times in the year we've owned it, and has never worked for more than 14 days. Kenwood personnel have advised that their radios, even properly and professionally installed, are not suitable aboard boats. Fred & Lori (from Dec'89 Seven Seas, address on page C)

Skate Usable on Rail or Road?

I'm looking for a skate/scooter I can use for cross-country travel, going between cities on railroads, then using side roads/streets to detour around rail yards. Any made? Or kits? Or plans? One foot rests on the skate, the other pushes (like with a skate board). When one leg tires, change off.

The skate may have two main wheels, front and rear, and two or four auxiliary wheels which flip down for rail use (to keep the skate on the rail) and up for road use. I'd like main wheels that are fairly large (kiddy bike size?) for low resistance and so they don't catch in holes, and rubber tired for quiet operation (to hear approaching trains).

Yurt Spacious But Hard to Find Places For Near City

We have lived for most of five years in our 16-foot yurt.
We are now a family of six. The largest group we've had in
our yurt at one time, for a party, was 22 - 14 children and 8
adults. It was crowded but everyone had a lot of fun.

We've never had any trouble entertaining friends during
good weather as long as we are in a place where the owners of
the place want to join in the party (i.e. we have the same
circle of friends). We just throw a barbeque party, pull out
the guitar, and sit around and sing.

While living in a house last winter, all of us were home-
sick for our yurt - except for our oldest boy because he
likes cooking with the electric kitchen gadgets. Once I read
that some Mongolians obtained a castle in which to live.
They put their animals in the castle and pitched their yurts
outside the wall. Now I feel the same way.

The hardest part of portable living has been finding
places to put our yurt where we are welcome. We have always
traded work for a camping site, but it's never been easy to
find people who want that, so we are frequently stuck someplace longer than we want to be, or forced to move by circumstances we're not responsible for. It would feel much more
comfortable if we were the ones to choose to move on.

We can't get too far from the Bay Area because that's
where my husband works (8 days a month) to feed us all (four
children). Otherwise we'd head for the wilderness. As it is
now, I think we are going to try living out of our VW bus in
the city this summer. We've been able to stay off welfare for
3 years and don't want to get back into that again.   Anne

Inner City People Pleasanter to Camp Near

We never had any hassle until we moved to this more-rural
area last year. The houses are mostly on 3+ acre lots. We
had a chores-for-rent exchange with friends who own vacation
property here. But someone complained to the building
inspector, and we had to take our yurt down. Fortunately we
were able to use the house for the winter, because the owners
never come here then. The neighbors said they hadn't
complained, so we think it was the meter reader, mail man, or
fire inspector - all of whom have been here.

In retrospect I see we didn't pay enough attention to
camoflage. The yurt is covered with blue tarps - perfect for
the city where every few houses there's some junk under a blue
tarp. But here in the future, we'll use camoflage or dark
green tarps, and we'll hide the yurt from view of the driveway
(it was already hidden from neighbors and from the street).

This past year has been our first experience camping
rurally. The previous four years our yurt was set up in the
city (San Francisco Bay Area) in various friends' back yards.
Although we really appreciate the beautiful trees, clean air,
peace and quiet, etc., we've found the inner city people
easier to live with. It would seem that with so much space
the country folks would not notice us so much. But the city
neighbors were much more live-and-let-live types.

I'm coming to the opinion that the more people own, the
more they get locked into the social pressures which don't
let them do what they want with what they own. In other
words, they don't really own their property; it owns them.

Everyone we know has a house and privately or not so privately wonders what's wrong with us that we don't have one too.
I'm always glad to get your newsletter. It encourages me just

to know there are others like us out there facing similar problems. Anne Callaway, California, September & March

Yurt Survives Strong Wind and Heavy Snow

Last winter we experienced hurricane-force winds in the yurt. The whole structure was moving and distorting. Things hanging from the rafters were swinging for 24 hours. But the yurt stayed put. It was tied down to six tent pegs - nothing special. My husband threw two extra ropes over the clear plastic we use to cover the opening in the ceiling. (The clear plastic slides off for ventilation, using ropes attached by Lexan clips to the plastic. The Lexan clips work very well.)

A few ropes had to be tightened, a few pieces of plastic pushed in under the leaks, and the blankets we use to insulate the ceiling had to be pushed back in place in a few spots, then we were back in business again, good as new.

Around the neighborhood there were fences blown down, porches blown off, windows broken, screens blown away, plus lots of broken branches. Next door there were circular marks worn in a wooden fence by dead weeds whipping back and forth.

This winter was the first time we "camped" in snow. That big storm in February dumped three feet of wet, sticky snow on this area. The yurt handled the weight - no problem. But a wickiup-shaped tent collapsed.

Lots of trees and branches fell due to the heavy snow build up. The top of a tree (8" diameter) fell and crushed our entryway tent set-up. It brushed against our oldest boy. He wasn't hurt, but pretty scared. We believe that even that large a branch wouldn't have hurt anyone inside the yurt, though it would wreck the tent. Our yurt is strong. (We built it using Chuck & Laurel Cox's plans for the frame, and covered by lashing on old blankets and cheap plastic tarps.)

The entry porch needed a new plastic cover, but the PVC pipe arches just sprang back into shape once the weight was removed. We had no choice about where to put the tent on this property, and knew it was too close to the trees for comfort.

Except for this deep snow, we've found the colder, drier weather in the Sierra foothills more comfortable than the warmer, damper winters near the coast. The deep snow was just plain hard work shoveling paths. Rain goes away by itself, but leaves all that mud. Anne Callaway, CA, Sept. & March

I May Soon Be Living in a Tipi With a Young Child

Or perhaps in a twipi, a yurt, or a wickiup - investigating possibilities. I'm also interested in connecting with other portable shelter dwellers. Chris White, 157 Woodland Avenue, Lexington, KY 40502; November

Suggestions for Adding Insulation to Portable Shelter

I live in a canvas yurt and also a dome. This is my fourth Oregon winter coming up and I'm not looking forward to the cold and dampness - tho it usually isn't bad enough to get me back into the suburbs. I have thought about lining the yurt with wool felt - though I haven't gathered that much together yet. I'd like to see other yurt set-ups. Jao, OR, August

(Reply) Any lining material will help insulate. Even plastic. If there isn't much wind, I believe several thin liners would insulate more than would one thick liner. On the other hand, if the yurt is buffeted by wind a lot, then something heavy like wool felt might insulate more. Try to space the liner(s) ½" to 1" from the yurt (and from each other) for most warmth.

Quite often I find a lightweight white foam, sort of closed cell, about 1/8" thick, thrown out at furniture stores (used to pad shipments). Several layers of it gives good insulation on a ceiling or wall (but <u>not</u> on a floor - we tried some once for bed padding and it soon crushed paper thin.) It also tears easily, so I'd cover it with something tougher.

I wonder if you've tried suspending a tarp above the yurt and extending out a foot or so beyond it. By keeping the rain off the roof, it might make the yurt drier and warmer. Space the tarp a few inches above the yurt's roof. (If just layed on, it will hold moisture in the yurt's roof.) Bert, Sept.

Techniques for Working and Walking in the Rain

For working I wait until it lets up and wear as few clothes as possible. It's a lot easier to dry wet skin and warm up, than to take off piles of wet clothes that are hard to get dry again in wet weather.

For walking I prefer the good old umbrella. It doesn't make you sweat and it's not noisy like a raincoat or poncho. It's also faster to put on, so to speak. I wish there were a way to make an umbrella since they are so fragile and not always available in stores. Anne Callaway, Calif., September

Condos Condemned

Condominiums combine all the worst features of owning a home with all of the worst features of apartment life, with the unique and added annoyance of a "condominium board" consisting of little tyrants who call tow trucks on other people's cars in in the parking lot and write official-sounding "notices" about having "scruffy-looking" guests.

Condos were the biggest fast-buck scam around for someone with the money to buy a building, sell it unit by unit, and then get the hell out with the money. Some condo high-rise buildings along Chicago's lakefront strip were built as quickly as possible during a construction frenzy about 25 years ago, and built so close to the lake that huge waves were crashing through the lobby windows during a period of high water levels a few years ago. The cracks in these cheap concrete structures are now becoming more and more evident, and I have seen them weaken to the point that shoring crews were holding up the corners of a building with huge jacks and timbers while they patched it up. What an investment!

A person would be out of their mind to buy a home in this city, as doing so would place them squarely in the crosshairs of politicians looking for more and more tax dollars from fewer and fewer working people. Property taxes are rising all the time, and the homeowner is being milked dry; largely to support the sort of people who are going to lower the value of his property until he will only be able to get out at a loss.

Of course, a property "owner" actually only rents his property from the government, which can seize it for failure to pay taxes. And an apartment dweller is actually paying as much as a homeowner, in many cases, except for a down payment.

As I look around me, I notice how society "conspires" to keep us chained down to rent or house payments. Did you notice how, as more women started working, the price of everything increased to the point that it now takes two people working full-time to support the same household that one person could support before? Of course, people with too much "disposable income" could be dangerous, because they'd be able to lift their noses from the grindstone long enough to see what was happening around them. J. Wieser, Illinois, January

Message Post

Portable Dwelling Info-letter
POB 190, Philomath, OR 97370
July 1990   One issue $1   Six issues $5 cash; $5½ check

When Walking a Bicycle That Has a Flat

valve stem at
bad angle

A partly or fully deflated tube and tire will gradually rotate on the rim. But the valve stem is held by its hole in the rim and cannot follow. This may eventually tear the valve stem from the tube, resulting in an unpatchable leak.

rotate tire and tube this way to reposition valve stem

To avoid this, I can carry the bike, of course. But that will be tiring if I'm going a long distance with a loaded bike.

If I decide to walk the bike, I first transfer most of the load, if necessary, so it rides on the unflat wheel. Then periodically I stop and check the tire, and if necessary rotate the tire and tube to put the valve stem back in its proper unstressed position. This is easiest if the tube is deflated as completely as possible and the wheel is off the ground. With one hand I hold on to the rim and push, while with the other hand I jiggle and pull the tire in the opposite direction. Then I move my hands a few inches along the rim and do the same thing. I repeat, working my way around the wheel, until the valve stem is perpendicular to the rim. Julie Summers, 1986

valve stem at
proper angle

I Intended to Bicycle Around Last Summer

But rides with friends and hitch-hiking seemed to happen easier. I haven't got a real touring bicycle yet. I like the new lightweight mountain bikes (except for the prices). Aarran, British Columbia, March

Some Day I'm Going to Have a Fold-Up Bicycle

It will pull a fold-up trailer carrying a fold-up boat. I saw your ad in Messing About in Boats. Paul, NH, March

A Friend and I are Leaving Home to Travel the USA by Foot

Julie and I have back packs, sleeping bags, and a small tent. Jenn, New York, February

Walking Plus Occasional Taxi Saves Money

My car was getting old and I was spending a lot keeping it in shape. So I got rid of it. I live four miles from town and found walking wasn't bad at all and I feel so much better. I usually walk in, stay over night with a friend, next day do what I have to, then go back home. I can always take a taxi when I bring groceries back, if I don't catch a ride.

I'm still planning to get a tipi but not sure when. I have to get new flooring on my deck this year. That's where I'll put my tipi. I want to get a good one as I would like to live in it for 8 or 9 months a year. Until I get one, I'll use my camper and the two tents I have. Gloria Orr, NY, April

Camping Out Near Towns or in Large City Parks

The piece about using a camo net (June'87 MP) is good. Other ideas in this field? Ellis Weinberger, Exeter, U.K., Apr

I Am Reducing My Possessions to Travel Lighter and Faster

I have a mini van so I want to condense what I have to fit in it. It's 6 cylinder so could pull a small storage trailer like a U-haul. I am contemplating tipi living in a community during June and July, and am trying to decide how.

I plan to keep two file cabinets (letter size, 2 drawer), which I will use with a board across the top as my work station. I make jewelry and don't know if my gold and sterling silver wire will be protected in a tipi. (I know how clothes are hung up inside but that's all.) Samie, AL, April

On the Road Three Months

Enjoying the excitement of new horizons, places to explore, and interesting, friendly folks. Few mechanical problems; most I can deal with. Gas our major expense, at 5-7 mpg. Overnight stops not difficult: we use reststops on the freeway (except Calif.); mall parking lots (dark corner), industrial areas and church parking lots in town; any out-of-the-way spot. High-use agricultural areas are most difficult. One contact with police was positive - brake lights out, guided us to nearby church parking lot. Travel slow (40-50) and make lots of stops for food prep, exercise, exploring, junk stores. When we meet new folks, we tell them we are looking for homeschoolers interested in community and simple living, and they generally refer us to friends with similar interests.

Food is a bit tricky for us, as we are vegetarians without refrigeration. We stock up on organic vegies at the co-ops, and store them in insulated areas low in the bus. It has generally been cool enough (Jan-Apr) to get away with this. Sometimes we must resort to mainstream produce. We haul lots of grains, beans and dried fruit in square 5 gal buckets. We stock up on bulk foods through Nutrasource in the northwest and Tucson Co-op Warehouse in southwest. We cook on a propane one-burner (would like two) and our "tin" wood stove. Use a dish-pan. Water in plastic 5 gal (spring water when available, or hook our purifier to public water). No plumbing in our bus.

To bathe we heat water and sponge it, visit hotsprings often (have done considerable research on locations). We dig holes or roll rocks to poop; plastic bucket with lid for town/emergency use.

We make sure the boys, who are very social, get plenty of time with other kids. We trade off with other parents when-ever possible. When in town, we visit parks. Our land search and homeschool interest connects us with people. We never pass a bulletin board, especially in co-ops, peace centers, used bookstores, country stores, etc., without looking at it.

So far, we like the Gila National Forest best, especially the southwest section. Silver City is a great small town with alternative schools (including high school), co-op, small uni-versity. 3.3 million acres of forest are nearby, including the Gila Wilderness Area, inhabited for thousands of years, now saved from development. The canyons are filled with the presence of the ancient ones. Jai, New Mexico, April

I'd Like to Retain a Low Rent Home While Traveling

Do you have any advice on this? I'm presently renting a room in a large home (I'm a Humbolt State University student), but will be away overseas on a low budget journey across Africa for at least a year. I'd like to have a "home" to come back to when I return. I'm particularly interested in small cabins, trailers, etc. I lived in a disabled VW van (no wheels) for two years. David Buck, CA, May

Message Post

October 1990   One issue $1

Portable Dwelling Info-letter
POB 190, Philomath, OR 97370
Six issues $5 cash; $5½ check

Hands-Free Magnifier Holder

In the 1990 Nature Company's catalog, is a stand which holds a low-power magnifying glass and alligator clips. It allows hand-free viewing of objects, which is very helpful when dissecting flowers to identify them or when removing a splinter from one's own hand. But rather than spend $15 (plus $4 postage) and encourage unnecessary use of resources, I came up with this free-from-salvaged-materials version.

rubber straps

The stand is improvised from a piece of drift wood, sculpture, book end, or whatever you have available. (I used a piece of junk machinery.)

For the arms I used clothes-hanger wire. (If my magnifier were heavier, I'd double the wire.) To bend wire at sharp angles, I hold it with pliers. After positioning the pliers, I move the wire **well away** from my face, and direct my force so that, if the pliers slip, nothing will move towards my face. Particularly if the wire is long, I'm careful not to whip the distant end into my face. I hold that end down with my foot.

A clothes pin, spring metal clip, or alligator clip is fastened to the wire arm with a rubber strap cut from a blown innertube (discarded at bike shops). Julie Summers, OR, May

I Would Like to Live Simply and Portably in the Wilderness

I am just beginning to learn the techniques of survival, so any help and references (human preferred) would be appreciated. I am a 43 year old woman. I saw your ad in Great Expeditions. Valerie Morgan, P.O.Box 9, Lion's Head, Ontario, Canada, NOH 1W0; August

We Are Selling Our Home and Plan to Travel Awhile

This is a **very** new experience for us. I saw your Home Education mag ad. Mary Aschenbrener, Wisconsin, July

Next Year, I Plan a Road Trip Across the U.S.

And maybe into Canada. I've got an old jalopy and very little cash. I'm originally from the D.C. area. Elio, VA, Aug

Comfortable Compact Car Camping. Part I: The Car

The last three summers, I've taken 12,000-mile-long trips with a friend, including one to Alaska and the Yukon, and another up the spectacular Dempster Highway over two mountain ranges and two ferry crossings to Inuvik, North West Territories. On both trips we camped out almost every night. I'd like to pass along tips and ideas from these trips and from many years of similar ones.

On our first trip, we had a used Volvo station wagon. This was very nice in terms of comfort and space. But the new Toyota Corolla hatchback we had on the later trips had almost as much room, twice the gas mileage, and was just as comfortable. A back seat that folds **flat**, doesn't have large wheel bases and doesn't have a space between it and the front seat, is preferable. Check for good clearance under the car, and if you carry a canoe, look for a roof with gutters and solid hooks under the car in front and rear for tie downs.

Service the car before you go, making sure the tires are in good condition (including the spare), the fluids are all topped up and you have new oil and air filters. If your car is foreign made, you may want to take extra filters as it may be hard to get non-US-made ones in some areas. Take time out on a long trip to have it serviced again after 4,000 or 5,000 miles. We've never needed (or taken) extra gas, fan belt, etc., or special tools, but make sure your jack is intact and you know how to use it, and take your car manual and registration. A screwdriver for tightening loose screws, some glass cleaner and rags or paper towels for wiping windows, and a pair of pliers for all sorts of things, completes your tool kit. Artificial sheepskin seat covers are great both for keeping cool in the summer and warm in the winter.

Our only addition to car care equipment was a large sponge, a necessity after thousands of miles on muddy dirt roads when no commercial car wash was available. And rain gear and waterproof boots came in handy when the car wash was a do-it-yourself high pressure hose!

If you are traveling with a "significant other" who is not a close legal relative, consider each of you getting a Medical Power of Attorney (technically, Power of Attorney and Temporary Guardianship) for the other. Then in case of a serious accident, there will be no hassle about hospital visiting, granting permission to operate, etc. Finally, check that your car insurance covers out-of-state accidents and Canada, if you plan to drive there. Jan Brown, Massachusetts, 1988 & 1989 (This article was published in Women Outdoors Magazine, v8n4,

For health, minimize exposure to solvents.

Kerosene is not used as widely as formerly, but should still be avoided. Dr Hulda Clark found many of the alcoholics in her clinic had a build up of beryllium from kerosene fumes of lamps previously used by the patients. Beryllium in the body causes depression by blocking normal pleasure centers.

Since lead was replaced by even more dangerous gas additives in California, hundreds of people have gotten toxic illnesses. Other states seem to have less toxic gasoline. Beware of breathing gas fumes continuously.

Most shampoos now have traces of propyl alcohol (same as rubbing alcohol) in them, and Clark found it in all breast cancer cases she treated. It slowly erodes and accumulates.

Almost all other solvents and additives commonly found in potions, lotions and cleansers bring on health problems. Clark's "Cure for All Diseases" is a testament to living without the usual packaged and processed products.

Most houses with their rugs, upholstered furniture, and other bacteria catchers are invitations to sickness. Persons who can adapt to a simple living plan have a much better chance for health. Al Fry, Idaho, April

Spit trick for silicone glue application.

Apply glue to item. Insert finger in mouth to moisten. Spread glue with finger. Silicone won't stick to wet finger. Water also works but not as well, and spit is always handy.

I don't think silicone is too toxic. The seams of fish tanks are sealed with it, and tropical fish die if you look at them sideways. Double Dorji

Message Post

Portable Dwelling Info-letter
POB 190, Philomath, OR 97370

Jan. 1991   #27   One issue $1   Six issues $5 cash; $5½ check

Spots a Few Miles Apart Have Quite Different Microclimates

We are only ten miles from last winter's spot. But we've had heavy frost every night for weeks, while our former neighbors had only one frost. We've seen 21° three mornings.

This is unexpected. Last summer was much hotter here than at our former spot "up the hill" (1000 feet higher).

The cause may be: we are camped on a ridge within a little valley. The valley bottom often gets frost.

This winter so far has been much colder than last. Today (Dec. 15) was our first snow. The boys were disappointed as rain soon melted it. 3 miles away and 200' up, 4" accumulated.

Fortunately we have plenty of warm clothes and a good propane heater. (Wood heat would attract attention.)   Anne, CA

My Family and I Now Live in TWO Tleantos

The new one is presently about 400 miles south of the first one. We migrate between, not so much for winter warmth (the southern spot isn't much warmer then), as for a sunnier spring and to be closer to the couple whose kids we board.

The new tleanto is much like the original (Sept'85 & Sept '86 MP) except longer: 36' total. (Actually there are two separate frames joined end-to-end with covers overlapping.) It contains two insulated rooms plus some uninsulated areas.

Usually two adults and three small children live in it; on occasion two additional adults. During the coldest weather for warmth we all crowd together into one room. (One morning I measured 22°F outside, 30° within the outer shell, and 48° in our room.) We don't want a heating stove with the fire hazard, fumes, smoke, work. During milder weather we spread out. The tleantos are warmest where there is little wind.

For ceiling insulation, I replaced the leaves with sheets of flexible foam, which are quicker to put on and easier to keep in place. I am now gradually replacing the foam with bubble plastic (as we find it) which has not been bothered much by animals (whereas the foam becomes nests if not protected). We take down each tleanto when we leave for the season, to avoid mouse/rat infestation.

Another change: I angle the south wall with the top farther out than the bottom, so the sun doesn't reflect far. (Once we were careless and attracted a hunter who was on the slope below. Luckily, he was friendly.)

I have now lived in tleantos for most of five years and am quite satisfied with them.   Wanda, California, August & Nov.

To Prevent Condensation, We Lined Our Yurt Ceiling With Plastic

Layer of plastic, lots of blankets, then the roof. It worked well last winter.   Anne, California, August

Two Pails Together Protect Long Objects

Round plastic pails are made in various widths. So a wide pail can be placed, inverted, over a narrow pail to protect objects too long for a single pail. The pails probably won't seal airtight, but will keep out rain and rodents. Last fall we stored some things this way. The pails fit so firmly that strapping didn't seem necessary. However a racoon or larger animal could probably work them apart.   Bert & Holly, Oregon, November

13

Materials Worth Accumulating for Long-Period Camping

These items are cheap when found new "on special" or used at garage sales - or free when found in dumpsters. Whereas they may be expensive or unobtainable if you're rushed.

PLASTIC PAILS for storing other things, and for use at a camp kitchen. In-store bakeries often sell them, 50¢-75¢ each. Unless free, check that lids and rims fit well and are undamaged. (Lids that are notched to open, may have excessive cuts that extend to the lid's top, sever the gasket, or even penetrate the pail. Also pails are sometimes badly scarred inside or even holed by sharp utensils used to dig or scrape out frozen contents.) Clean before using, outside as well as in, to remove any food remnants/odors which might attract animals. Larger containers, such as 55-gal barrels with heads that come off, are also useful, but harder to find, cost more per capacity, and harder to transport, especially by backpack or bike. So, before acquiring anything that needs protection but won't fit in one or two 5-gallon pails, we think thrice!

PLASTIC JUGS. Milk/juice jugs are fine for storing, but too flimsy for reliably hauling water. Bleach jugs (discarded at laudromats) and various other jugs are sturdier. Read label; but also sniff inside for unfamiliar odors. (The jug might have been reused for toxic chemicals that linger. Bleach seems to rinse out.) We put only wash water in a jug for a month or more, before using for drinking water or (after thoroughly drying) for storage of rice, beans, etc.

SHEET PLASTIC (polyethylene) for tarps and tents. We use both clear and black (and white if we find it), either new (on special) or salvaged (furniture store discards).

TWINE for tying out tarps, rigging clotheslines, etc. Much twine is discarded by many stores, but most of this is clear/white - okay inside but deteriorated outside by sunshine. Black, orange or pink twine, used for hay bailing, is more durable outside; black is best.

RESILIANT FOAM, for floor padding and mattresses. At rug store dumpsters, we sometimes have our choice of scraps of new foam or large sheets of old foam. The latter, removed during remodelings, smells of cigarette smoke, etc., so we place plastic over as well as under it. The least desirable foam is the kind that looks like fruit cake, with various colored fragments stuck together. It's heavier, lumpier, weaker.

CLOTH remainders and remnants. Some discount fabric shops sell unpopular patterns for 50¢ a yard or less. Piece together to form top tarps. Dark, drab blacks, greys, browns and greens "visually pollute" least. Synthetics are more durable in wet; cotton in sun; acrylic withstands both quite well. Netting, such as old window curtains, is useful for blocking bugs.

Not included above are items most readers will already have for short camping, hiking, car travel, or indoor living; such as lighters, flashlight, water sterilizer (iodine crystals or tincture), knife(s), needle & thread, utensils, etc. H & B

Footwear Made from Salvaged Materials is Warm and Dry

While sewing up snow pants from used rain coats (the executive type), and felting mittens from fleeces being thrown out at a Barter Faire, I devised an alternative to $90 Sorvel boots: I made a felted boot slip-in with cuff, which goes into vibram-soled galoshes; with gaters made from raincoats.

Since that moment, both Jai and I have not been tempted to buy things we wanted but could not afford. Going beyond recycling, we just don't bring the stuff in! Even our food comes in bulk bags we reuse. Beguin Z. Lapwing, WA, December

Aluminized Mylar "Space Blanket" Reduces Heat Loss

If suspended above you, it will reflect back 80% of your
body heat, adding to your warmth. It will also add to your
safety if ever a helicopter with an infrared sensor is night-
stalking you. Above the mylar, suspend camo netting or an
improvised burlap "shaggy". Wildflower, Connecticut, July

Bedding in the Bush

Cheap sleeping bags provide plenty of warmth if two or
more are used together. (A single cheap bag loses much heat
out its sewen-through seams; but with two together, most seams
are offset.) Cheap (light) bags are more versatile, easier
to dry, and not much heavier than is one expensive bag.

Synthetic (usually nylon) covers and liners are the most
durable in a damp climate; we acquire cotton-covered bags only
if free. A bag with defective zipper is usable as a quilt.
Blankets seem heavier for the warmth; we acquire only if free.

Used bags (or blankets) we seal up in pails for a few
months or put through a hot dryer to kill any vermin (details
in 1980m MP). We may leave extra bedding stashed in pails
near places we travel to often, rather than carrying it along.

At base camps we use several layers of foam under us.
But it's bulky and heavy, so when light camping, we take only
one thin piece and build a bed out of springy weeds.

When we camp together, we put opened sleeping bags over
us as quilts. On top we place an old sheet (if we have one)
to collect most of the moisture. The sheet is faster to dry,
less to rot if it doesn't dry, or lighter to carry along.

Our bedding would not favorably impress the staff of
Outdoor Fashions magazine, but it keeps us warm and comfy.

H & B, OR

We Often Have Large Quantities of Laundry to Dry

We let it drip outside for a day, and then hang it inside
for heat from the stove, lantern, or heater to finish off.
But this causes a lot more condensation on the walls. Our
yurt has some insulation. Maybe we need more.

We have the walls arranged so the condensation runs off
into the dirt, instead of dripping on our heads, which isn't
too bad. But we'd rather not have it at all. Anne, CA, Dec.

We Like Simple Showers Very Much

For simplicity, water conservation, and reliable temperature control (especially important for children who could
scald themselves with fauceted showers). A little practice
was needed before the motions became easy. Half-gallon jugs
with handles are easier for me to hold than are quart/liter
bottles lacking handles (as most do). If only gallon jugs are
available, I fill just half way for myself, less than a fourth
for the oldest child (who usually bathes herself; the younger
ones don't yet). Wanda, California, August

I Live on a 30' Houseboat in the Delta of Northern California

My neighbors include ducks and lots of other river-rats
(that's what we boaters are known as). We fish for crawdad,
catfish, etc. It is very easy to get 300 or 400 crawdads in
one hour using a slice of beef heart. No, they do not eat it;
they just grab on and hold. You can bring in 3 or 4 each time
you cast (sometimes just one). This is a great place to live
and fish. I'm looking for others, women especially, that like
boating and fishing. I'm 45. Richard Arndt, 333 Tuleburg
Levee #2, Stockton, CA 95203; September

● Most addresses and prices in here are out of date.

The Past Five Summers I Horse Trekked in the Pacific Northwest

I have two horses, both for riding and packstock. I have trekked, mostly solo, in the Coast Range, Cascades, and central and eastern Oregon. The High Plateau is where my heart belongs.

The sun and warmth and long days and fresh green make for easy living during summer. But I don't know enough yet to make it all year around in the backcountry. Another obstacle is a certain lostness in my loneliness. I would like other people (a tribe, so to speak) living a nomadic "horse-way-of-life" along with the appropriate philosophies and techniques to move lightly on the land.

This spring I plan a short trip back to Germany, to see my folks and to look at some alternative ways of living going on there. An old buddy is part of a group of 500 people who are about to start an "eco-village" in what was East Germany.

Upon coming back, I will move my outfit to a basecamp in the Ochoco's (east of Prineville), then drift from there over to the Steen Mtns, and later back north towards the Hell's Canyon of the Snake River. But I'm totally open to rerouting, as long as I'm able to make out a spot to spend the winter at.

I'm presently living in a camper with tarp-porch extension in the backyard of friends and do housesitting here and there. That is okay but it keeps me too far from the earth.

Other crafty skills include saddle and leathercraft, fine woodworking (for 15 years - trained in Germany), spontaneous street and vaudeville theatre performer, and photographer with equipment for both 35 mm still and 16 mm movie. I am currently producing a couple of slideshows about the use of horses in wilderness: one about backcountry access by alter-abled riders; the other about high plateau places for trekking and long camping.

I have found that grainsacks, as well as army surplus duffel bags, make excellent horsepacking gear.

The single one-front-foot hobble with 20 feet of soft rope to a screw-in stake (as sold in department stores for stake-outs of large dogs - but don't use the little dingy swivel to tie the rope to!) is the best way to allow for controlled grazing of the stock. Mine are rolling and resting and moving "free" on that device each morning and evening feed. I just have to be in sight.

Over night, the hitchline strung between two solid points well above horses' heads, does the job, without any entanglement.

On Forest Service land, I like to make contact with the FS people and offer myself as a volunteer. That way, I'll get accepted when spotted and usually left alone when dropping out of sight. To private landowners, I say I'm a backcountry photographer. Works well - and is part of the truth, too. Eberhard Eichner, POB 23433, Eugene, OR 97402; February

Info Wanted About Native American Living on the Oregon Coast

I noticed Julie's review in MP #27 of "Tillamook Indians of Oregon Coast". I'd like to learn more about living there and about foods and shelters there. Is it true that coastal Native Americans had a high standard of living compared to other groups? I'm currently living about half time in a small 30-year-old trailer in the woods east of Florence, and the rest of the time with a combination of truck/camper/bicycle mobility.

Also I like the idea of "confluential" living or "flowing together". As a way of relating, this seems to come closest to having the best of all worlds with the least structure, exposure, and other costs. Roy, Oregon, January

I Am Newly Moved Into a Converted Bus-Camper
Ms C. M., Arizona, November

I <u>Have a</u> <u>Chouinard</u> "<u>Megamid</u>" <u>Tent</u>
  It's 9x9' and weighs 3 lbs. I've
used it extensively in rain, snow, very
high winds, and desert. In spite of
having no floor (use poncho or tarp if
you want), my only weather-related
problems were during extreme downpours
and blowing powder snow.
  The original center pole was weak.
They now have a beefed-up pole that
should not fail. A design fault not
corrected is the #5 coil zipper. When
this fails you can get by with the full-
length velcro flap, but you may want to
replace it with a #7 coil zipper. (The
tent gets stuffed into a sack smaller
than a football, which could break teeth
off a toothed zipper.)
  Also this tent is too expensive.
It could be made much cheaper at home.
I'd like one twice as large (18x
18'). Do you know anyone who can make
this? The ripstop nylon used in my
original tent, is also used in cargo
parachutes that take huge loads, and so
should be satisfactory. Henry, AZ, Aug.

(Comment:) To withstand as much wind or
snow load, a tent twice as large must be
stronger. How much heavier? With the
span of the fabric double, it's strength
must be double - requiring twice as much
fiber per area and thus twice the weight
per area. And there's four times the
area, so the fabric might weigh <u>8 times</u>
as much. This assumes it never flaps in
the wind. If it flaps, loads are even
greater (Bert was told, when doing the
twipi). Also the center pole must be
stouter (16 times?). So, if your 9-foot
tent weighs 3 pounds, expect an 18-foot
tent with the same configuration and able
to withstand the same wind, to weigh
between 24 and 48 pounds. Of course, if
you'll never be in that strong a wind,
then the fabric in your 9-footer might
be adequate. (Bigness costs! Elephants
need stockier legs, proportional to body
size, than do mice or spiders.) B & H

<u>Comments</u> <u>on</u> LLL's <u>Shelter</u> <u>Plans</u>
  WOODLAND TENT. This is the only one
of your plans I've built, a 15x9x9.
  Structurally, it's been okay so far
except that set up is slow because of
the many tie-outs to adjust.
  Shelter-wise it's kept out the rain.
Sometimes there's a little condensation
inside. I haven't covered the entrance
to try to keep out insects, but instead
just hang netting over my bed.
  My biggest complaint is, the plastic
roof reflects any open sky to any passer-
by. Where that's undesirable, the tent
must be completely covered by foliage or
by a cloth over-tarp, which nullifies
its light-passing advantages.
  TWIPI. This seems rather complicated for what it is: essentially just an
insulated roof over a hole in the ground.
  Both the twipi and the woodland tent
have steep roofs - to shed snow, you say.
But, as you also point out, to leave them
set up and unattended, is to invite
rodents to foul them. If they are taken
down, they don't need to shed snow.
(While you're there, you can keep brush-
ing it off.) Could they be simplified,
or other features improved, by dispensing
with the steep roofs?

  BUG FREE. Net tents are fairly
inexpensive to buy. So collecting and
piecing together old curtains doesn't
seem a wise use of time, unless you need
a different shape than what's for sale.
Even then, it may be cost effective to
buy a roll of netting. Dave Drake, OR

(Reply:) Regarding the twipi, roof
insulation is very important. That's
where, otherwise, the most heat will be
lost. As for covering "a hole in the
ground": well, the earth is there so
why not use it, assuming it's firm
enough, well drained enough, easily dug,
and environmentally tolerable. Where
it's not, a twipi isn't recommended.
(Also see comments in Sept'85 MP, p.5.)
                                    Bert
<u>Comments</u> <u>on</u> <u>Arches</u> <u>Used</u> <u>for</u> <u>Storage</u>
  Regarding Dave Drake's idea (in
June'89 MP) for assembling a storage
structure out of plastic arches. Plastic
no heavier than that in trash cans will
deform under load and not provide
weather-proof and perhaps not even
mouse-proof joints. Corrugating the
plastic crosswise (like road culverts)
would help stabilize shape, but not
enough I think. To obtain weatherproof
joints would require heavier gauge
material, and/or a more complex shape
with ribs, and/or fastenings at many
points. If such arches were manufactured, I suspect the unit cost would be
more like $50-$100 than $5-$10.
  Regarding Dave Stewart's idea (in
August'89 MP) for forming arches out of
plywood sheets glued together. As soon
as the clamps are released, the plywood
will partially unbend and assume an
intermediate shape. And each arch will
be shaped differently (wood <u>not</u> being a
uniform material). Better, I think, to
glue together the arches out of individual veneers (plywood plys) - a technique
used for boat building. But even then,
a stable, consistent shape will require
ribs - as does a sizeable boat.
  The boat comparison is useful
because, what is wanted is much like the
hull of a long narrow boat turned upside
down (tho simpler because of constant
cross-section). Boat hulls have to
withstand water, waves and organisms for
long periods. So any technique good for
boat hulls might also be good for
storage arches. Luke Hoppingmole, Oct.

<u>Sexicosas</u> <u>Use</u> <u>Materials</u> <u>Efficiently</u>
  If building a portable dome, storage
container, den liner, or snow-cave liner
out of sheet materials such as plywood
or fiberglass-foam sandwich, the sexicosa
is a shape worth considering. Not one
of the regular geometric solids, the
sexicosa (short for sexicosahedron - 26
faces) consists of 18 square faces and
8 equilateral triangular faces.
  If a sexicosa with 4-foot edges is
built from 4x8' plywood, 11 sheets are
needed, with only 2½% scrap. Whereas
domes with all triangular faces have 10%
to 20% scrap (according to <u>Refried Domes</u>).
Furthermore, the sexicosa's "scrap" will
be two strips 8'x6¼" which will almost
certainly find uses. 24 of the faces
(6 triangles and all 18 squares) are sawn
directly; two of the triangles require

one join each (as shown →). If that's not feasible, 12 sheets will be needed, with 11% scrap. The resulting dome will be approx 9.6 feet diameter with 557 ft³ volume.

For comparison, an 8-foot cube would require 12 sheets of plywood and provide only 512 ft³ volume. Furthermore, its edges and faces are twice as long, requiring, for the same strength, much heavier plywood or more reinforcing.

A model sexicosa can be easily made by cutting two pieces of card stock as shown (below left), folding along the dashed lines (scoring them first with a dull edge helps), gluing/taping each tab to its adjacent edge, and then joining the two halves together. (Two 8½x11 sheets suffices for a model with all edges 2½".) The finished model shown ⌐

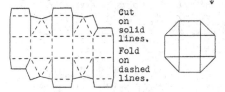

Cut on solid lines. Fold on dashed lines.

The card model is stable. A strut model will not be stable because, as Lloyd Kahn said, "triangles are necessary for stability." To stabilize, add two diagonal bracing cords to each face.

Ordinary plywood is weaker on the diagonal than parallel with the grain. If strength per weight is important, I would reinforce each square face along the diagonals by gluing on fiberglass ribbons. Some marine plywood includes plys with grain on the diagonal.

As with any structure built of sheets, the edges must be joined very well along their entire lengths to reinforce each other. Openings will weaken a sexicosa less if thru the triangular faces than if thru the square faces.

Many of the problems of all-triangular domes are shared by sexicosas: e.g., difficulty roofing by conventional techniques. So, with any structural form, think and test! Is it right for your application? Don't just fall in love with a "sexy" shape. Luke, NW, Oct.

Portable Housing IS Efficient

(The following is in response to Refried Domes, reviewed in May'90 MP p.8, which said: "Portable housing: bad idea. Once you build a floor (there are no portable floors), install plumbing and wiring and road or paths, it's very inefficient to move the building.")

We've lived in portable housing for over ten years and we disagree.

A floor for our 9-foot-diameter "Thing" costs no money and requires one hour to one day of labor (depending on how steep and rocky the site is). We: 1) clear, level and smooth the soil; 2) lay down a vapor barrier (we use big plastic wraps found in furniture store dumpsters); 3) lay down something soft and insulative such as moss, leaves or salvaged foam (from rug store dumpsters);

4) lay down another vapor barrier; 5) lay down rugs or whatever we'd like next to us. All but the soil is portable.

Plumbing and wiring we don't have. They, and the heavy appliances they feed, may be truly labor saving for a laudromat, restaurant, or big farm. But we can live more efficiently without them.

Consider water, for example. For cooking and washing we catch rain. For drinking we backpack water from a spring, often in the course of hikes for other purposes. If we piped water, we'd not only need plumbing; we'd probably also need a filter, a pump, and power. If you are far from existing utility lines, a pump is expensive to connect, or complicated to power with a windmill or PV system. Besides initial costs, there is maintenance, repair, and eventual replacement. Also freezing protection: keeping a heater going if you're away during winter. (Pails we can just empty.) Labor saving? I doubt it.

The same holds for most electrical appliances. Compared to simpler, lighter alternatives, they might save some time when you use them. But add up all the costs and they're usually labor wasting.

We aren't against all high tech. But we only want what's truly beneficial; not expensive, encumbering toys.

As for roads and paths, we don't need them. Our dwelling is small and light enough to backpack (in pieces).

Regarding efficiency, the bottom line is: How much time do you have for what you enjoy - versus time consumed by household chores and by outside employment (including not only time at work, but also time spent training for, searching for, priming for, commuting to, and recovering from work). By this measure, for us portable housing is highly efficient. Holly & Bert, OR

Exchanges Backwoods Child Care

I now have a baby girl - and a new companion. Also, for 8 or 9 months a year, we have been hosting two somewhat older kids of another couple who live and work in an urban area.

This has been a good arrangement for us, financially and otherwise. We are paid about as much as a conventional boarding school, but have much lower expenses. Also, on most weekends, the other couple relieves us; sometimes taking their kids with them; sometimes staying here and caring for ours along with theirs while we use their car.

Of course for this to work, the adults must agree on how kids should be treated, the hosts must get along with the kids, and the kids with each other. No major problems, so far.

One attraction for the parents: their kids are less exposed to other kids, who might have serious diseases without showing symptoms, and who often have crazy attitudes picked up from TV.

During summers, the other kids live with their parents, and we with our child live at our northern tleanto or travel with friends. (We no longer have a car of our own.)

My former companion and I broke up. He grew bored and restless living in the boonies, even though originally he had been the one most keen for it. Also, I wanted kids before I got any older whereas he wanted to wait. Wanda, Aug.

Comfortable Compact Car Camping.   Part II: The Tent

My friend and I are back from our 12,000-mile summer camping trip to Inuvik, North West Territories. Instead of turning left as Dawson City and going into Alaska as we did the summer before, we turned right and drove the spectacular Dempster Highway over three mountain ranges and two ferry crossings of the Peel and MacKenzie Rivers. We camped out almost every night. I'd like to pass along tips and ideas from these trips and from many years of similar ones.

For sleeping take a roomy tent with a waterproof floor that comes up a foot or so and a fly that extends almost to the ground. On previous trips we took an Eureka Sentinel which we liked as it has two doors. One tarp under the tent, and another on the floor inside, give extra moisture and puncture protection. Tuck the edges of the outside tarp under the tent so they don't collect rain. Bring the edges of inside tarp up around your air mattress and sleeping bags.

Free standing tents are much easier to set up than those requiring stakes. If you need stakes, invest in some 6" spikes from a hardware store; they are the only kind that will penetrate packed gravel sites. You'll need a hammer to drive them in. A little piece of string tied to the tent loops can then be wrapped around each nail to hold the loop in place. If you use regular tent stakes, a stake-puller really helps.

Have a roomy stuff bag in which all this will pack easily. Take some spare large trash bags for wet tarps and fly. (Often you can dry them in a few minutes on your car at lunch.)

On previous trips, for daytime comfort we also took a screen tent. A cheap one will do. It goes up in ten minutes. Be sure to take plenty of 6" spikes to hold it down. You can put the screen tent over a picnic table and cook and read, bug and rain free in the evening. Or you can set it up anywhere with your folding table and chairs inside, or even put your sleeping tent inside so that it doesn't get wet in a downpour.

On our latest trip, instead of separate sleeping and day-use tents, we tried a Camel model 2510 Sahara cabin screen tent that performs both functions. We found it very satisfactory. The 8 x 10' sleeping area has two full-length zipper doors and two large windows that zip closed from the inside. It provides ample room for two cots and could sleep 3 or 4 women. The floorless 6 x 10' screened area has enough room for two tables and chairs. It sets up easily in about 10 minutes and weighs less than 30 pounds with steel poles. This tent will not withstand driving rain or gale winds, but it held up well in the moderate weather we experienced.

Camel's latest catalog (5988 Peachtree Corners E, Norcross GA 30071) lists a new 2500 model for $249 which has a smaller screened area and a less desirable feature of the cabin windows closing from the outside (not good when it starts raining after you are in your sleeping bag). But Gander Mountain (Box 248, Wilmot, WI 53192) says they have "plenty" of Model 2510 for just $150. Jan Brown, MA, 1988 & 89 (previously published by Women Outdoors Magazine, v8n4,v9n1,v9n4. Address on page A.)

Simple Lean-To Comfortable During Fall Travels With Pickup

For just one night during fair weather, I dispense with shelter. But if camping in a spot for some time, I build an open-faced lean-to. This is basically a canvas tarp stretched sloping from overhead to ground. With a fire in front, I've been comfortable in weather lowering into the twenties at night. Gary Cropper, POB 864, Snoqualmie, WA 98065; December

A Friend Lives Outdoors the Year Around

He normally sleeps, under a polythene tarp and in two sleeping bags, about 5 miles outside town. At that distance he doesn't get hassled. He tried a camoflage net but found it too bulky. Water is the single most important thing to carry, he says. His biggest problems are money, boredom, and loneliness. Others living this way in U.K. are welcome to write him c/o Huskisson,13 the close,Babrakam,Cambridge. Ellis, UK, Dec.

I Spend Summers in a Tipi and Winters in a Sailboat

I've been living this way, summers in MI, winters in FL, full time for 4 years. Before that it was a pickup camper for 3 years. Maintaining cars and trucks was costly, thus the boat. Yet tools and supplies for the boat also add up.

In Florida I was given a bicycle, then a 40cc Honda. The motorcycle is costlier, but faster, more fun, and easier. (I'm disabled with Guillian Berre syndrome, contracted while with Peace Corps in W. Africa. Previous travels included 'Nam and all over the Pacific with the U.S. Navy.) Harv Henry, MI, Sept.

Inexpensive Living Along the Sea of Cortez

No papers are needed north of San Felipe and there's no time limit. Anything can be taken across the border into Mexico except lumber. ($20 bribe gets it across too. Or it can be carried in a house trailer which are seldom inspected.)

Land can be leased for $35 a month (payable yearly), for ten years with another ten year option. You can tow a trailer south to put on your lot, or build a shack.

Brakish water is usually available for a $150 set-up fee, and fresh water is 25¢ a gallon or $7 for a 50-100 gal. tank.

Disadvantages: In summer, 120° during neep tides (when no tide stirs the wind). Fairly frequent sand storms are bearable but will drive you inside. There's little theft except food, booze, money, and (I suspect) solar panels and batteries. Don't believe the bandito stories!

Once you are there, options show up. Many Mexican families can provide things you need economically. Lee, CA, Aug.

Photovoltaic Lighting System Utilizes Cheap Used Batteries

Replying to Anne: Flame appliances are _probably_ safe to use during summer as you'll be using them less (longer days) and with better ventilation (summer warmth).

For winter lighting I use a small (12x12") ARCO solar panel, a 7-watt compact flourescent bulb, and an old car battery. The solar panel has a diode built in and is self regulating so no other gizmos are needed. All can be carried on an old pack frame. (Keep battery upright to not spill acid.)

Pluses: Quality light without flicker. No fumes or flame and thus safe with kids. The panel and bulb are long lasting.

Minuses: High initial expense (panel $85, bulb $20; in 1987 from Backwoods Solar Electric, 8530 Rapid Lightning Ck Rd, Sandpoint,ID 83864). Battery must not freeze. Battery is heavy and bulky. You need a sunny day to have a "sunny" night.

I can get 3½-4 hours of light on a charge without drawing down the battery all the way. Such use eventually ruins a car battery. A deep-cycle battery would last longer. But, in fall I can buy a used car battery from a junkyard for $10 and, come spring, turn it in for $5 salvage. Why spend more for a longer life battery which I don't use and can't maintain in summer?

I supplement the flourescent with candles. They are cheap, easily available, and give off little fumes. I also use them when I snow camp in winter. Rob, ID & VT, June

Avoid Dust if Cleaning Out Old Buildings

Histoplasmosis is a strange disease spread by air-driven spores released from dried, dusty bird feces. It enters the lungs, causing flu-like or even tuberculosis-like symptoms. From the lungs it travels through the blood to other body parts. It damages eyes most, scaring surfaces, often causing blurred or double vision and, if untreated, eventually blindness.

Many a victim had recently converted an old chicken house or barn to living quarters, or renovated an attic previously occupied by pigeons or bats. Not much is known about the disease, but I suggest wearing protective clothing and a good dust mask, and keeping dust to a minimum. Al Blanche, NY (condensed from Nov'90 Rural Network Advocate; addr. page C).

Dairy Goats Are Not Very Portable, We've Found

To set up their pen and house and feeding was almost as much work as moving the whole rest of our camp. Also, last time we had to move right when they were due to kid. Though the milk tastes great and is probably healthier, powdered milk is much less hassle. Anne Callaway, California, August

Many Recently-Made Victor Mousetraps Have Poor Springs

They are weak even when new, and soon slacken until useless. Did the company fear that somebody might carelessly let their pet hurt its paw - and then sue them for a million dollars? Or did they figure that if they built flimsier mousetraps, the world would beat a path to their door to buy replacements?

We are buying replacements. But not Victor. Others we have tried, McGill and Enoz, have stronger springs and seem generally better built. McGill bait pans won't hold hard bait such as corn. Reshaping with long-nose pliers helps. H & B

Efforts to Stop Nature's Aerialists

I assumed most outdoor people knew about those cones or discs on the lines which tie ships to docks. They keep rodents from tightrope walking onto the ship. But a tip I saw (not in MP) to hang gear up, failed to mention a guard on the rope.

Actually I've never seen a mouse or rat walk on a rope; only evidence that they had - and on very narrow cords. They might not get to a newly suspended line the first night, but given days or months they probably will. And they chew not only food and nesting material; they also chew for sport - anyway so it seems. (Rodents' teeth grow continually and will become too long if they don't chew, I've read.) Julie Summers

(Comment:) We have a regular cotton clothesline strung across our tent. I placed our bread in a plastic grocery bag and hung it from a hook in the middle of the clothesline. The mice walked down the rope to get to the bread.

Next, I fashioned a guard by drilling a hole in a pie plate to receive the hook. The mice simply jumped onto the pie plate and slid off onto the sack of bread. When they were done they dropped to the floor. One evening I watched the whole performance by candle light - they had gotten bold!

Perhaps a rigidly fixed, larger guard would work: rigid to prevent sliding off and bigger to "shadow" the whole bag. But someone gave us a metal bread box which works great.

Mice also went for the styrofoam sheets we put in the ceiling for insulation. They were chewing it up and taking it away. So we threw it out and are back to just blankets. Anne

Message Post

Portable Dwelling Info-letter
POB 190, Philomath, OR 97370

March 1991   One issue $1   Six issues $5 cash; $5½ check

Bracken Fern is Edible and Delicious in Fiddlehead Stage

Pick them by snapping off the fiddleheads (like asparagus, it will break above the fibrous section of the stem). Place them in a pot and cover with hardwood ashes. (You can use baking soda but you may need to treat the ferns two times before the astringent quality is gone.) Pour boiling water to cover the ferns. Let the ferns sit until the water is cool. Drain (can you dye wool with this water?) and rinse off all the ashes. Now cook: simmer in water seasoned with soy sauce and honey until most of the liquid is gone. Or dry by spreading on baskets in a shady, breezy place. Reconstitute by soaking in warm water with a pinch of salt for 3 hours. Anne Schein, California, January

(Comments:) Bert likes fiddleheads of bracken raw (after rubbing off the fuzz), but not so much cooked (plain boiled - has not tried your recipe). He hasn't noticed any astringency. Difference of tastes? Or difference of ferns there and here? I (Holly) don't like the taste of bracken raw or cooked (at least not plain boiled).

An article in March'81 Coltsfoot and June'81 MP, mentioned reports that eating bracken (Pteridium aquilinum) was linked with stomach cancer, but did not say how mature or fresh was the bracken. Were fiddleheads defuzzed and eaten promptly as an occasional salad or pot herb? Or were mature fronds cut and dried as hay, and fed in large quantity to livestock? (Many edible greens become toxic as they wilt.) H & B, OR, March

"Edible" Mushrooms Can Cause Allergic Reactions

Quite often I eat wild mushrooms, including morels, puffballs, chantrelles, and corals. Recently I was given a large amount of chicken-of-the-woods, a mushroom I had never eaten before. I ate it with relish but, afterwards, suffered from stomach illness. This experience reinforces the warning to eat only small quantities of a new mushroom (or any new food), even though it is listed as, and positively identified as "edible". Gary Cropper, POB 86, Snoqualmie, WA 98065; December

The Trick to Cooking Rice Fast is to Soak It Like Beans

Lee Mauck, California, January

We Are Building a Solar Cooker as a Homeschool Project

We are using Joseph Radabaugh's design. It is made by nesting cardboard boxes, so it is not weatherproof. My guess is that careful covering with aluminum foil could prevent damage by rain and damp. Our cooker will have a plexiglass door. I bought the book, Heaven's Flame ($5 from Radabough, POB 1392, MtShasta, CA 96067) after reading a review in Home Power. Anne Schein, California, January

More About Nature's Aerialists

Mice have sometimes eaten food that I suspended overnight in a backpack 12 feet off the ground. I suspect they ran up the rope. The food had not been well sealed (zipper left undone, bags not tied, etc.). I've had no problem with bears though. Aarran Rainbow, British Columbia, December

I Have Lived in Vehicles and Tents Most of My Life

When I was 18, I left home and went to Europe with a large canvas rucksack on my back, a sleeping bag, a train pass, and very little money. I slept in vacant barns, fields, youth hostels, and trains or train stations. I've also backpacked a lot in the mountains of California and Oregon.

However, I prefer living and traveling in vehicles, because the freedom I enjoy most is the freedom of travel. I've had two VW vans (too Spartan), a pickup with camper (too tight), a house-truck - a house built on a 16' long flatbed truck (comfortable, but drew too much attention because of all the wood), and now a raised-roof school bus painted blue.

Unlike cars, buses are very simple to work on. And if you have a Chevy or GMC bus, most pickup and car engine parts are the same - and cheap! We carry a spare fuel pump, water pump, spark plugs, points, distributor and starter (all rebuilt, or gotten off an abandoned Chevy somewhere).

I converted my rigs to run on non-polluting propane. I got giant truck tanks for $10 and a carburator for $10,used.

The bus has two solar panels, two deep-cycle batteries, 12 volt lights and a propane light. I easily wired it for 110 volts and 12 volts with used, heavy extension cords.

The bus has a full kitchen with double sink, cabinets, stove/oven, propane RV refrigerator, and Paloma instant hot water heater. A plastic utility washtub/sink (30x30" by 14" deep) has above it a shower curtain on a track for a shower (total cost $20). The water tank is 80 gallons. Most came from yard sales, swap meets, or, used, at RV service centers.

I have (and sell) Multi-Pure water filters. This filter removes all bacteria, giardia, and chemicals. It has an inexpensive cartridge inside. We don't get sick down in Mexico any more. And when we fill our tank with city water, it takes out all the chlorine and bad taste. We also got a hand pump for it that goes backpacking with us, to pump water out of puddles, lakes or streams.

I got eight sliding RV windows with screens for $45. Scrap linoleum went on the floor and cheap, thin indoor-outdoor carpet went on the ceiling. Two bus seats and a piece of nice birch plywood scrap makes the dinette. (You can reupholster bus seats with a screw driver, a staple gun, and any scrap materials.) The bus has a propane furnace. I have a sign shop in the back for making money on the road.

I added up the time we (3 kids, 2 adults) have lived in the bus off and on over the last 6 years and it totals 2½ years. We don't register it; we just buy a $5 trip permit when we go traveling - usually to Mexico.

I'd like to communicate with other vehicle dwellers. Prem Dhanesh, 332 Otis St., Ashland, OR 97520; Jan. & Febr.

(Question:) With a trip permit, what do you do about insurance? I've heard that the cops require insurance. B & H

Cooperative Bus Would Tour Craft Fairs

I like the idea of confluences: communities without leaders. Specifically, I'm interested in a cooperative bus. Divide it into individual (or family) sleeping compartments, and into common kitchenette, dinette-lounge, and workshop areas. Make the rounds of craft fairs. (There are hundreds.) Each person has their own art/craft project, and also helps promote   recycling, bus living, confluences, etc.

I've seen retired school buses, still running, for sale cheap - some under $1000. (But better have at least one

person along who's a mechanic.) Write me if you are interested.
(But don't print my address.) Dale, North Carolina, February

(Comment:) Seems to me that a cooperative bus would need a
manager - making it a mobile community, not a confluence. (For
the difference, see Jan'91 MP p.5.) However, if the members
stay light (able to drop off easily), I think you could avoid
most of the problems of a settled community (where members who
grow disgruntled can't easily leave). B & H, OR, March

Comfortable Compact Car Camping.   Part III: The Furnishings
        I invested in a Thermarest mattress (full size, standard;
not 3/4 or Ultralite). When the mattress is deflated and
rolled up, secure it with a webbing strap with a fastec buckle.
American Camper's 26x72" folding cot was fine. (They also have
one that is padded, with which a separate mattress isn't needed.)
        In the summer you'll only need a light weight sleeping bag.
You may be able to pick up one in a salvage store for under $20,
and Campmor (Box 997,Paramus, NJ 07653) and other mail-order
stores have some good buys on new ones. If it gets really nippy,
wear a hat, socks, and polypro underwear to bed. (A wonderful
hat of angora/wool blend that packs into nothing and is incredibly soft and warm is made to order by Karen Sue Van Tine (Star
Rt Bx 14,Penobscot,ME 04476.) Recently I discovered that a hooded sweatshirt is even better than a hat for keeping warm on
chilly nights - it doesn't slip off! If traveling in style,
take your favorite pillow along. (Or use your life-jacket.)
        We've found the Gadabout folding chair from Sporty's
(Clermont Airport,Batavia,OH 45301), which is the same as the
Anywhere Chair from Thos. Oak (901 Main St.,Salem,VA 24156),
expensive but worth it because it is durable, light weight,
comfortable, and very compact when folded. A good, small folding table is even harder to find. We have used a dandy one
made by American Camper (available in many sporting goods stores,
they say). It folded down to 3x24x24", yet could be raised to
a comfortable 28" for cooking, with an area of 24x48". CO-OP
America (2100 M St.,NW,#310,DC 20063) has a folding table well-
built of oak. L.L.Bean (Freeport,ME 04033) has one with adjustable legs. Many companies carry roll-up tables.
        For lighting, there are a number of options, from "nothing"
in the high Arctic with its long hours of summer daylight, to a
fancy flourescent lantern powered by four 6-volt batteries if
you like to read a lot at night. In any case, you'll want a
couple of Tekna flashlights for your car and tent, preferably
with long-lasting lithium batteries and bulb, and at least a
Coleman Peak 1 lantern (with spare mantles and a durable plastic
lantern case) for the dirty dishes you've left too late.
Jan Brown, MA, 1988 & 89 (previously in Women Outdoors Magazine)

Cooking on the engine of a vehicle.
        For several years my main job has been driving a cab,
and I have become quite adept at cooking on the engine block.
I wrap food in aluminum foil and place on top of or around the
engine. While driving, a large stew usually cooks in a little
over an hour. (On long trips, my customers have been amused
when I told them I had to get dinner off the engine block
before it caught fire.) I have also tried the old trick that
hobos did with campfires: punch a small hole in canned food
and place on the engine block. Unfortunately, this is
difficult with a moving vehicle because one must find a place
to wedge the can without interfering with the engine.
        When placing and removing food, I wear industrial work
gloves. Be very careful: escaping steam can burn badly.
        There is a book on the subject: Manifold Destiny. I've
only read reviews, but it sounds pretty good. Kurt Wettstein,

Traveling By Train in Mexico

I always go regular first class. Around $25 gets me to Guadalajara. There is also a primera first, which has beds by reservation only and is nicer, and a third class which is more crowded (you may not get a seat) and pretty skungy after a couple of days. The train takes a day and two nights. Venders get on and off selling delicious food. It's never made me sick.

The train leaves Mexicali (near CA) or Nogales (near AZ) at 10 p.m., but people get in line before lunch. Your gear will hold your place while you wander around and nobody will steal it then, but watch it when you are on the train.

Getting from the border (called "la liñe" in Mexico) to the station is a project. The distance is about 5 miles. A taxi is $10; a bus only 5¢-15¢. But I've never found a bus that goes directly to the train station. Instead I keep asking "Donde 'sta auto bus central" to find a bus going to the bus center, and then ask "Donde 'sta estacion de tren" to find a bus that goes there. You can walk from the bus to the train station, but they are two very long blocks apart.

The train arrives in Guadalajara at 8 or 10 p.m. From there you can get a bus or train (second class) to Mexico City. (You are unlikely to get a place on a first-class train.)

Take the bus back home. Catching the train is not unlike a cattle stampede - after waiting hours for it to arrive. To get directed toward the border, ask "Donde 'sta la liñe."

Yes, solo females can do it (without Spanish). Just don't try to say "no" and be cute at the same time. Lee Mauck, CA

Senseless About Homeless

"Homeless in America" was the cover article in the Dec. 17 1990 issue of *Time* magazine. One photo shows a sleeping box, made by telescoping together several cardboard cartons, which looks snug and warm. On the same page a headline claims: "After a decade of despair, Americans are finding solutions that work - tailor-made, cost effective, time tested."

Yes, indeed! A sleeping box, built by the user out of scrap, is certainly tailor-made, cost effective, and time tested.

However, sleeping boxes are not the kind of solution that reporters and officials have in mind. The kind of solution they want, are programs that train the homeless to earn rent money (and help officials advance their careers).

What would happen to those who don't want or can't win steady jobs? One hint. According to *Time*, releasing people from mental institutions who had "no place to go", was a "stunning social blunder."

In San Francisco near city hall, some folks built "a second city of cardboard condos, clogged with traffic of shopping carts through makeshift living rooms, outfitted with easy chairs." They were evicted by the mayor.

But the mayor has a remedy for homelessness. "If you give me the money, we have a chance to end sleeping on the streets."

True. If you give the mayor the money, you can be sure the mayor won't be sleeping on the streets!

Politicians and officials cause homelessness when they interfere with people's efforts to build what they can afford.

Poor folks around many Latin American cities manage to shelter themselves (when the cops leave them alone). And dumpsters there aren't so rich with reuseable materials as are dumpsters in the U.S. Bert & Holly, Oregon, February (Thanks to Aarran for sending us the clipping.)

Message Post

Portable Dwelling Info-letter
POB 190, Philomath, OR 97370

May 1991   One issue $1   Six issues $5 cash; $5½ check

Years Ago, I Made a Tent Out of a Parachute

I bought the 19-foot (as I recall) diameter chute inexpensively from a surplus store. Most of the cords had been cut off, but enough length was left to form peg loops.

For the center pole, I bought a large 2-3" diameter bamboo pole from a supplier of commercial fishing boats and cut to 12'.

To waterproof the chute, I put it in a bucket with some Thompson Waterseal and then hung it out to dry.

A slit served as a door. (There wasn't Velcro then; I would use it now.) Inside, under the chute's air-spill hole, I rigged a collector and siphon for rain water. The hole still allowed hot air to escape. Even so, sunshine made the chute hot inside. (With another, I'd have peg loops one foot long, in addition to the short ones, so it could be rigged above the ground, like a circus tent, to let in the breezes.)

To erect it, I stuck a peg in the ground, tied another peg to it with about 10' of cord, and drew a circle. The edges of the chute were pegged to this circle. Then I inserted the center pole. Usually it had to be raised with rocks or lowered by digging a trench to get the proper tension. Perhaps a pole of plastic pipe sections would have been easier to adjust.

Slack in the fabric went wild in the wind, but uncoated ripstop is quiet and the tent never blew down. Henry, AZ, March

I Am Looking for Inexpensive Portable Housing for Summer

I would like something bigger and more stable than most tents, but yet capable of being taken down, folded up, and put in the back of a station wagon. Maybe a tipi, yurt, or portable geodesic. But except for one dome I saw in Real Good's catalog, I have no idea where to acquire one. After June 1, you can reach me c/o Oesterreich, Rt 1 Box 55, Harris, MN 55032.

I want something mosquito proofable (I will be in MN on a friend's land), big enough to stand up in, and without metal supports. (I can enjoy storms if not worried about being struck by lightening.) Donna Berry, Minnesota, April

We Lived in Tipis at 9000 Feet Elevation for Twelve Years

My four sons and I spent 3 to 6 months a year in them. The boys are all on their own now, and the tipis are old and leak like sieves. I'm working on a yurt - hope to move in this summer. Jerry, San Juan Mtn Bikes, POB 777, LakeCity, CO 81235; Feb.

Insulated Gravel Floor in Dome Lessens Humidity

To reduce living expenses and impact less on resources, I am using a Shelter Systems' 18' LightHouse dome.

I set up the dome between two live oaks near Santa Rosa. It gets afternoon sun but is protected from the wind. The last few days it experienced several inches of rain with high winds (50 mph in unprotected areas). I am pleased with its performance.

To reduce humidity, I created an insulated pea gravel floor system.

↑ dome

bender board

4 ml plastic

6 ml plastic

5" pea gravel

5" shredded redwood bark

After setting the dome on cleared ground, I put two yards of shredded redwood bark over a plastic vapor barrier on the ground. Inside I ran 3½" bender board up against the poles and used 50 pn nails where needed to keep the board in place. The bottom plastic was brought up over the bender board to prevent outside rain water from getting it wet. Then I put another layer of plastic over the bark, and spread four yards of pea gravel on it. This plastic, too, was brought up over the bender board to prevent outside water from getting into the rock. As I spread the rock, I made sure the bottom fabric of the dome was folded in so I could shovel rock over the bender board and fill up the space between board and dome. This also holds down the dome all the way around (except at the doors).

The gravel absorbs humidity slowly and then lets it off when the weather is dry. So far I've had no mold.

As a floor, the gravel is fine so long as care is taken when preparing and eating food and when entering with boots not cleaned. To cover the gravel, I am experimenting with $1.50 a sq yd carpet padding made from recycled acrylic sweaters.

For a clean sleeping and meditation space, I set up a 10' dome inside the big one, and put a carpet on its floor.

I have a MacCracken (Alturas,CA) solar distiller which gives drinking and cooking water. I am still plugged into the grid for washing water. I will convert to a solar-powered pump system if the year-around creek is not too polluted.

For hot water, a simple passive collector hung on the garden fence, works noon to five on sunny days. I am experimenting with radiant floor heating by running black pipe thru the pea gravel under the inner bedroom dome, but so far the heat exchange is not enough to make a difference. Maybe after I build the greenhouse, that will heat the rocks 10° or so.

For pee, I built a urinal pit which does not cause smell or pollution. My next two projects will be an underground grey water system that automatically waters the roots of a food growing bed, and, the most difficult, a compost toilet producing night soil for garden use.

For night light, I use a solar lantern (Real Goods, $110) which works great. My only other electrical device is a Walkman with rechargeable AA batteries. Randy Riis, CA, March

(Comments:) For a floor, did you first try just bare dirt with plastic covering? Did adding the bark and gravel to the floor noticably reduce humidity? For setups more portable or remote, I wonder what other materials would have a similar effect. (Bark and rock are plentiful some places but not others. Where we are now, the rocks are weak and soon crush into muddy sand.)

I believe we get a similar effect during cold weather when we bring in jugs of collected rain water (to keep them from freezing and bursting). Our dwelling, which is small and insulated, warms quickly when we come inside, and warms further when we cook or the sun shines. The jugs remain cool for a while, moisture condenses on them, runs down their sides, and forms little puddles beneath, which we occasionally sponge up and add to the kitchen waste water for disposal outside. (With some elaboration, we could set the jugs in a trough that would automatically drain outside.) But the jugs further crowd our 9' diameter dwelling, so, as soon as the weather moderates, they go back outside. Bert & Holly, Oregon, March

More About Simple Drainage Systems

To dispose of waste water and pee, we sometimes use a large funnel (actually a narrow-mouth plastic jug with the bottom cut off - which can be used as a bowl or plate) feeding into a hose

(or bike innertube, or several, depending on length wanted).
    Compared to a drain bucket (in Oct'90 MP, p.2), a funnel
seems easier to connect and less likely to leak - assuming I
find hose just a little larger than the mouth of the funnel/jug,
so that the funnel fits snuggly _inside_ the hose. Also, with
the funnel, there is no problem of a residual remaining in the
bottom and not draining. What advantages has the bucket?
Faster pouring? Bert, Oregon, October

(Reply:) We use a big bucket because the six of us use lots
of washing water. Also boy power doesn't have very good aim.
    We installed a piece of ¼" hardware cloth over the top of
the bucket to catch debris that could plug up the hose leading
away from the bucket. It also catches the silverware and jar
lids our 11-year-old leaves behind in the dishpan. Anne,CA,Dec.

The Simple Shower Was Helpful Recently When the Pipes Froze
    My mobile home had no running water for a few days, yet I
still had a hospital expecting me to be there and in the
hygenic condition of an emergency-room nurse.
    Two 2-liter pop bottles, filled with water from the tea
kettle to provide the desired warmth, served me nicely. One
provided enough water to soak and lather, and the second
provided a luxuriously thorough rinse. Standing in the tub
took care of the run-off. My kids also thought it fine.
    Regulating the flow with the caps was tricky the first
couple of times. If this was an ongoing situation, I would
secure duplicate caps, and perforate the duplicates with a
fine nail, to provide a shower head I could turn off by
setting the bottle down. Jon Seaver, Michigan, March

(Comment:) When showering, we simply remove the cap and tilt
the bottle to regulate the flow. (I tried it with the cap on
loose and didn't like it as well. I didn't try perforating
the cap.) The illustration in the June'87 MP (and 1987-88
Summary-Index) may be misleading because it shows the bottle
completely inverted. With the cap off, that would occur only
when the bottle was almost empty. Do other readers prefer
cap on? Or cap off? Holly & Bert, Oregon, April

Comfortable Compact Car Camping.   Part IV: The Water
    Some campgrounds have only one pump for all the sites, so
we've found a three-gallon water pail is very handy. Collapsible
plastic water containers are not as good as they are hard to
clean. Also handy, if there is a tree to hang it from, is a
bag that zips open at the top for filling and has a spout at
the bottom. What did not work? A collapsible bucket. Empty
or full, it collapsed!
    We assume that the water supplied in a campground is safe
to drink (if in doubt, boil) but nevertheless it may have
suspended dirt particles or an awful taste from chlorination.
A First Need filter will cure the first fault and a little lime
juice will take care of the second.
    Most campgrounds don't have showers; those that do often
have very little dry space, so a washbag that opens up and can
be hung from a hook or over a door is very useful. For non-
shower days, a pot of water is fine for a sponge bath. Or, if
we camp on a sunny day in good time, we use our Solar Shower;
first placing it in the sun to warm up, then attaching it to a
secluded tree with the handy webbing strap. This is often a
good time to string up the clothesline too, and catch up on the
underwear. Larger soiled clothes go into a big ditty bag for
a laundermat stop every few weeks. Jan Brown, MA, 1988 & 1989
(previously published in _Women Outdoors_ Magazine (addr. on p.A))

Message Post

August 1991   One issue $1

Portable Dwelling Info-letter
POB 190, Philomath, OR 97370
Six issues $5 cash; $5½ check

Home-Made Berry Comb

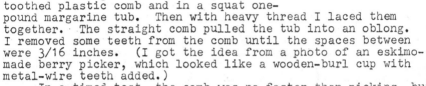

Red huckleberries (Vaccinium parvifolium) were prolific here last year. Tho fairly sour, they are pleasantly fruity (like pink lemonade).

However, picking them is tedious for me. So I made a berry comb with attached cup. Using a nail held with a vice grip and heated in a flame, I melted matching holes in a large coarse-toothed plastic comb and in a squat one-pound margarine tub. Then with heavy thread I laced them together. The straight comb pulled the tub into an oblong. I removed some teeth from the comb until the spaces between were 3/16 inches. (I got the idea from a photo of an eskimo-made berry picker, which looked like a wooden-burl cup with metal-wire teeth added.)

In a timed test, the comb was no faster than picking, but did provide variety. I wonder if speed would increase with practice, or if speed depends on the kind of bush. (I don't know what berries the eskimos were gathering.) Julie Summers, OR, June

Comfortable Compact Car Camping. Part V: The Kitchen

In the past we often took lots of freeze dry food - and found we returned with it. The U.S. and Canada are loaded with supermarkets and farm stands, so there's no reason not to "eat fresh". Some homemade granola and pancake mix, powdered milk and minute rice, a plastic lime or lemon, some dried apricots and Baker's semi-sweet chocolate (which doesn't melt) is about all we take now. In Canada, a delight is supermarkets with "bulk" produce sections. Probably they are meant for large quantity buyers, but no one seemed to object when we purchased minute quantities to refill our spice and drink containers. Recent additions to our larder were hearty Magic Pantry boil-in-a-bag dinners (in Canadian supermarkets), maple syrup crystals for pancakes (from Walnut Acres), and Uncle Ben's Rice in an Instant (better than the usual minute rice).

Almost all our kitchen and food gear goes into two milk crates. They are durable, easy to carry, and don't collapse in the rain as do cardboard cartons.

In one we put three small nesting pots (a larger serving as a lid for a smaller), a small frying pan, potholders, three metal plates, two plastic cups and two plastic drinking glasses, a two-cup plastic measuring cup which serves as a mixing bowl, a small plastic shaker for mixing milk, and the silverware and utensil bag. This is easy to make: just fold up a square of nylon, sew in some pockets, and secure it with velcro or a sewn-on shoelace. It contains forks, steak knives, tea and soup spoons, a sharp folding knife from Early Winters, sandwich spreader, vegetable peeler, slotted cooking spoon, metal spatula, can-opener, pot lifter, scissors, tongs, plastic scraper, small wisk, and a gadget that sparks when squeezed to light the stove. In addition, we take one larger pot for cooling wine, rinsing dishes, washing hair, and storing wet bathing suits, tarps and washclothes.

The other crate contains paper towels, plastic bags, toilet paper in a Ziplock bag, garbage bags, dish towel, empty plastic containers for left overs, three ditty bags with cord

locks, and our staples. The ditty bags can be open mesh so you
can see what is inside, or color coded. One is for washing up:
liquid soap, a sponge cloth and a scrubber; one is for drink
mixes in labelled plastic bottles (instant coffee, cocoa, tea,
etc.); one is for a selection of our favorite spices, also
preferably in small, labelled plastic bottles.

We also take a small cooler which keeps perishables like
butter, salad makings, and a small bottle of cooking oil, (no
ice; you can only buy it in too-large quantities); and a small
insulated bag (L.L.Bean or Early Winters) in which we pack
lunch after breakfast so that we needn't unpack the car at noon.

Unfortunately, the stove we have used for many years is
no longer available. (Its two burners ran on propane, available in any hardware store, and it has a griddle, all of which
packs into a lightweight double "roasting pan" which can be
used for baking and dishwashing.) A Coleman two-burner stove
is probably the best current bet because of its reliability.
L.L.Bean, Famous Cookware and Store 64 have griddles that fit
this stove, and you can probably find an inexpensive roasting
pan that will fit over the burners - recommended for an in-tent
bath or for washing dishes. Jan Brown, MA, 1988 & 1989
(previously published in Women Outdoors Magazine, addr. on p.A).

We Use Gallon Milk Jugs With NO CAPS for Our Simple Showers
We call it "jugging". Works fine.

Most of our plastic pails have come from health food
stores. We paid $1 or $2 each. Friends have given us some in
which bulk laundry detergent is sold - at Cost Co I think.
Many of our pails have labels indicating baking supplies -
e.g. artificial raspberry filling. Anne Callaway, CA, May

Sources for Hot Water When in City or Traveling
If washing clothes at a laundromat lacking a sink, the
washing machine can also furnish hot water for a simple shower.
When the machine starts filling, open the lid momentarily and
place a bowl under the inflow, close the lid to restart the
flow (which will stop while the lid is up), then open again
and empty the bowl into the jugs or bottles to be used for
showering. Repeat until the jugs are full. The water inflow
remains on until the washer fills to a certain level, so I
don't believe this affects the laundering.

Another source (if you don't mind free-loading — or are
a customer) are the rest rooms at a McDonald's. (Many public
rest rooms have only cold water.) To fill a jug, you may
need a cup or small bowl that will fit under the spigot.

B & H, OR, Nov.

How Large Were Indigenous Groups?
Indigenous peoples tribes (both nomadic and more rooted
communities), that lived in relative balance and survived
quite well, were usually made up of several dozen and upward
to a few hundred folks. Bands/clans of a dozen or less were
almost unheard of, other than short-term hunting and gathering parties. Usually when you found groups of less than a
dozen, unless they were going about the larger clan/tribe
business or going to visit other clans/tribes, they were the
outcast that simply couldn't get along with other folks for
long, or they were living in environments so desolate that the

local ecology simply could not support a larger group. In fact, when folks were living closer to nature you normally found nuclear families of a dozen or so - and those were parts of an extended family/clan/tribe of several dozen to a few hundred, with size largely depending upon what the ecological balance could support. Rainbow Hawk, New York, May

(Comment:) To clarify: a band is a group that lives and works together; a tribe is everyone who shares a heritage and who considers each other "my people".

Among nomadic foragers/hunters, the band might be as small as one nuclear family (mama, papa, and kids) or as large as two dozen. I don't recall reading of nomadic bands much larger (other than some pastoral peoples which are relatively recent). A larger band would need more territory for sustenance and would have to forage farther from camp or move camp oftener, and thus be less efficient. Also, a band of two dozen probably includes ±8 able-bodied adults and adolescents of each sex (the rest being small kids, the lame, and the very old) - the most efficient size for many kinds of work and group hunting. (That is why, today, ±8 is also the size of most sport teams, most military squads, and most task groups.)

A nomadic tribe may number from several hundred to many thousand. But they all congregate (if they do) only for special occasions. I have read that the Paiutes of the Great Basin usually roamed as nuclear families, but gathered into larger groups occasionally to round up rabbits and for social functions. (Some might call their environment "desolate", but I imagine most of them liked it.)

Settled communities were often much larger, primarily for military reasons. People who want exclusive use of much fertile land, must be able to defend that land against all comers, or become the subjects of some gang who can. To coordinate the larger number and to suppress disagreements, requires authoritarian organization. (Moving apart, an option for nomads, is not practical for settled folks.) That also seems to hold for those present-day intentional communities that last.
H & B

Avoiding Wrenching Experiences

Some frown upon grabbing trailside vegetation to assist a climb or prevent a fall. But I presume most hikers do it, at least in emergencies. For least trauma to both plants and people:

Try to select sturdy, non-brittle plants that will take your weight without breaking.

Apply force in line with a branch. Do not bend it far.

Keep aware of your arms' range of movement. (Try moving them now.) They cannot bend far back - without tearing something. Consequently you must keep facing (more or less) toward each handhold. E.g., when going downhill, your body must either keep facing uphill, or else must pivot as you pass each handhold. Julie Summers, Oregon, 1990

Hat Can Be Used as Pocket

If you need a pocket but are without one, or the ones you have are covered up, keep your hat in mind. Its shape, stretchiness, and how tightly it clings will limit its capacity, but most hats will accomodate at least note paper and a pencil.

The voyageurs used their long stocking caps for various odds and ends; and Thoreau used his crown-and-brim hat for what he considered an ideal vasculum (plant collecting container) - with just the right humidity. Julie Summers, OR, November

Message Post

Portable Dwelling Info-letter
POB 190, Philomath, OR 97370

November 1991 $1 per issue   Add 50¢ to check/mo under $10

Two Lean-Tos Together Provide More Shelter

During the fall, when temperatures are invigorating yet pleasant and I'm not yet ready to be completely enclosed, I find open-faced lean-tos sufficient for my needs.

I found I could make a comfortable camp out of canvas tarps by erecting two lean-tos, face to face about 6 feet apart, with a fireplace between. (See top diagram.) Then I close off the sides with visqueen, old blankets, or whatever is handy. This leaves sky overhead and plenty of walking space.

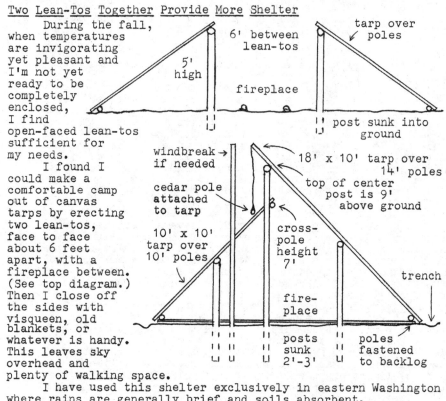

[Top diagram labels: 6' between lean-tos · tarp over poles · 5' high · fireplace · post sunk into ground]

[Bottom diagram labels: windbreak if needed · cedar pole attached to tarp · 10' x 10' tarp over 10' poles · 18' x 10' tarp over 14' poles · top of center post is 9' above ground · cross-pole height 7' · trench · fire-place · posts sunk 2'-3' · poles fastened to backlog]

I have used this shelter exclusively in eastern Washington where rains are generally brief and soils absorbent.

In a wetter climate I would overlap the leantos. (See bottom diagram.) This would give full rain protection yet allow the smoke to escape. Also this requires fewer supporting poles. When there is no fire, a moveable flap closes the smoke outlet to reduce heat loss. Total floor space is 16' by 10', and space at 5' height is 6' by 10'

Ideally, I would erect this shelter where there are natural windbreaks to the north, and face the smoke outlet that way. If not possible, a windbreak must be constructed (shown).

The top tarps and the sides would be doubled for protection. Various materials could be used. Light colored tarps are preferred, for increased light within and also because of the solar-oven qualities of olive drab. Some adjusting may be required to achieve proper draft for the smoke outlet. Not shown is crossbracing which I would add for extra support and to keep the visqueen from flapping and being destroyed by wind.

With the various lean-to arrangements, there are possibilities of being able to walk into the woods, axe in hand, and build them from available materials. The chief advantage I see over a tipi, is no exposure of poles to the rain.

I like a shelter that includes a suitable source of fire heat (preferably wood), especially in a wet climate. If using an open fire, I stick to non-sparking deciduous woods such as alder. Cross poles may be hung in the rafters for smoking fish

and meats. If using a wood stove, I carry a small piece of plywood thru which a round hole has been cut wider than the stove pipe, plus a metal collar that fits between pipe and plywood, and install this someplace on the upright side walls.
I am of the Metis people from Canada. Traditional shelters have been the tipi, the lean to, and the wigawam - a round dome-type shelter made from bent willow sapplings. These have stood the test of time. Each was designed for a different purpose: the tipi for nomadic plains travel, the wigawam for forest dwelling (the frames are left standing to be returned to from time to time), and the simple open-faced lean-to for lightweight travel. Gary Cropper,POB 864, Snoqu. WA 98065; Feb.

Comfortable Compact Car Camping. Part VI: The Other Equipment

A third milk crate (in addition to two kitchen crates) holds items we seldom need to take out of the car: the backup Peak 1 stove, lantern and mantles, directions, extra fuel and matches in a waterproof container; string; trowel; a pocket hammock; a 15' cord with clothes pins in a ditty bag; a Solar Shower; the First Need Filter; and a small pair of pruning shears - useful when a shrub stalk is in just the wrong place.

We each have a day pack with camera, film, binoculars (pocket ones fit nicely in a small ditty bag padded with foam rubber), pocket knife, Kleenex in a Ziplock bag, bandana, hat with visor, sun screen, bug dope in a small leakproof metal box, and Wash 'n Dris. Wallet, keys, etc., can also go in the day pack, or, as has proved handier, in a purse along with sun glasses. If you smoke, a metal bandaid box covered with contact paper, makes a fireproof ashtray to carry.

What clothing you take obviously depends on the weather. The Times World Weather Guide, Pearce and Smith, gives high and low temperatures, humidity and precipitation each month for various cities throughout the world. We have found that a large ditty bag or duffle for uncrushables and a small suitcase for crushables provides ample room for each person. Along with dress up clothes, the suitcase contains extra and exposed film, a sewing kit, address book, traveller's checks, first aid supplies and medicines. We got along fine with just boat mocs for driving and at campsites and sneakers for swimming in unknown waters.

Catalog stores: L.L.Bean (Freeport,ME 04033) is notable for quick service and a special women's sport catalog. REI (Box C-88125,Sea.,WA 98188) gives dividends to members. Wearguard (Hingham,MA 02043) features inexpensive, sturdy work clothes. SI (Box 3796,Gardena,CA 90247) has good buys on used military clothes. Bass Pro (1935 S.Campbell,Sprfld, MO 65898), Ramsey (Bx 1680, NJ 07653), and Campmor (Bx 997, Paramus,NJ 07653) have many standard items at lower prices than the fancier catalogs. Don Gleason's (Bx 87,Nhmtn,MA 01061) has many spare parts and accessories. James River Traders (Hampton,VA 23631) and Lands'End have some good buys on clothing. And worth getting just for its luscious layout is Patagonia (Bx 86,Ventura,CA 93002). Jan Brown, MA, 1988/89 (previously published in Women Outdoors magazine, addr.on p.A)

For Obtaining Hot Water from a Washing Machine

Most washers have a push-in switch at the bottom of the lid door. You can often reach it while the lid is up, allowing you to hold the jug while it is filling if the water isn't too hot. Ken Scharabok, August, Ohio

More Items Useful for "Out There" Repairs

I buy hot glue sticks in bulk packs. They store well for years. When heated with candle, etc., can seal holes in pails, bottles, boats; glue solid surfaces together; mend wood; etc.

Plastic zip/stop/lock ties, commonly used to bundle wires together or to an object, also serve to fasten wire frames together (such as a fish trap) or fasten poles together for a structural frame. They are a good substitute for wire in corrosive areas like salt-water boats. I buy assorted sizes.

Acrylic clear nail polish is useful not only for coating your finger nails to protect them when working dirt or cement, but also for waterproofing cord bindings, coating cracked wire insulation against short circuiting, coating soldered wire joints against corrosion, coating (dry) fingertips (twice) to obscure prints, and fixing pinhole leaks in plastic sheets.

I also take a Portasol butane-powered tool ($40-$60). With interchangeable heads, it provides a soldering iron, hot knife, hot air blower, and torch. I use it to solder wires, thaw frozen locks, start fires, cut plastic, and seal plastic. Burns 30-90 minutes. Refillable. Wildflower, CT, 1990

Bye Spy: Tips for Staying Free and Effective

As police agencies target more and more activities, many people feel their only choices are slavish conformity or paralyzing paranoia. However, my compatriots and I accomplish most of what we want, in relative safety, by apply three rules: (1) Seem small and unimportant. (2) Trust only those closely involved with you. (3) Minimize time in dangerous situations.

The police might like you to believe that they watch every move, listen to every conversation, and study every letter. But they can't. They can pay close attention to relatively few. They will choose you only if you are an easy target or if they consider you and your group especially important.

Keeping groups small and numerous, or thoroly decentralized, not only increases your safety, but by "cluttering the field" reduces risks for everyone.

Who are important in the eyes of inquisitors will vary from agency to agency and year to year.... Whether or not an activity is explicitly illegal does not matter very much because thousands of vague laws grant police broad powers. The announced reason for suppression may not be the chief reason - as with marijuana....

In the coming decade, the activities targeted will probably include low-cost ways of living. Requiring less income, they reduce tax collections and threaten all those who have grown dependant on Uncle Sapsucker. Back in the 70's, there was more redirection (or co-option) than prosecution: the mass media publicized a few fashionable "alternatives" (such as $100,000 "homesteads") and some self-reliance trivia (such as making your own handkerchiefs), while largely ignoring options offering big savings. But in the 90's, with fewer people affluent, redirection may not suffice. If it doesn't, expect overt attacks.... (Only relatively large groups) will probably be infiltrated. Lesser groups and individuals will be monitored if they can be easily; else ignored.

Distinguishing between infiltration and monitoring: An "infiltrator" is someone who devotes much time to penetrating one specific group or activity. A "monitor" is someone who attempts to track a number of groups or individuals without devoting much time to any one. A large part of monitoring is collecting and correlating information publicly available.

But making sense of the data and weeding out disinformation usually requires reports from persons on the scene....
The one trait all monitors possess (as long as they remain monitors rather than infiltrators) is an unwillingness to devote much time to one target.... This brings me to rule 2: Trust only those closely involved with you. Looked at another way: either be very close to someone, or else very distant. Try not to mess with mister or ms in-between. Looked at yet another way: a few steady companions are usually worth more than many occasional friends....
Without limiting myself to existing companions, I cannot avoid in-between relationships entirely. So I minimize them by developing new relationships rapidly and by ending unproductive ones promptly and completely. I.e., either come in or go out. Don't loiter in the doorway....
Unlike monitors, infiltrators may be impossible to spot. A top-notch one may be hired and trained to penetrate one specific group or activity, and may devote years to gaining trust.... Intelligence agencies expect losses and lapses. Against an important target, they may send several agents unaware of each other and cross-check reports. No way can a targeted group prevent infiltration and still function well. But, because deep-cover agents are costly, relatively few groups can be infiltrated. That brings me once again to rule 1: Seem small and unimportant. I say "seem" because, what matters is not how much impact your work actually has, but what your enemies believe....
A group's optimum size will depend on the activity, but seldom will exceed a dozen near-full-time members. If larger, advantages of scale and specialization may be lost in higher overhead, even if the group should escape infiltration.
Finally, rule 3: minimize time in dangerous situations.... You can best judge what is riskiest for you.
Advice to dress and act inconspicuously, is well and good. But no matter how careful you are - accidents happen! I've had very few encounters with police, which I attribute, not to great ability at blending in, but to my spending little time where police are common. Most places they frequent are dangerous in other ways as well. E.g., highways: one survivalist seriously injured himself in a wreck while driving hundreds of miles to attend a survival workshop.... (Reprinting welcome if this notice is included.) Frieda Linkbetter, 1991 (much condensed)

How Do You Avoid Annoying Marijuana Cultivators?
Those paragons of free enterprise are reputedly more willing to be violent than formerly. I learned to be streetsmart as a medic in Detroit. Backpacking infrequently, I suspect I've yet to become "trailsmart". Jon Seaver, MI, March

(Reply:) We steer clear of any cultivation or structure, unless there are clear signs of welcome or of long abandonment. Tramping through a garden or picking the plants will naturally infuriate the gardener, be the crop marijuana or marigolds.
We've seen only two small patches of marijuana (many years ago). Both were on low land near water. So, in hilly country, most cultivation can probably be missed by staying high.
Though a few cultivators may plant booby traps or stand armed guard, I suspect that attacks on innocent hikers are rare, and that the problem has been much exaggerated by big media in collaboration with drug hunters anxious to justify their jobs.
On the west coast, most serious cultivation seems to be indoors or farther south (in CA). (Most summers here are too cloudy to produce potent marijuana, we've heard.) Perhaps readers in northern CA will comment further. Bert & Holly, OR

MY CHILDREN AND I WERE IN OUR TENT DURING A THUNDER STORM

The lightning struck so close we saw light even with our eyes closed. I kept everyone away from the poles and we had no trouble. Once in a tipi with Native American friends during a night-long ceremony, lightning struck just outside. Everything went blue. The man next to me was leaning on one of the tipi poles and felt the current go down the pole.

The Plains Indians weathered the most violent storms in their tipis. I suspect they kept away from the poles.
Laura Martin-Buhler, The Gentle Survivalist, Utah, August

SEVERAL LAYERS OF OLD CARPET INSULATE THE ROOF OF OUR YURT

They make a big difference when the sun beats down. The yurt is now slightly cooler inside than is the air under the shadiest nearby trees. The yurt can support the extra weight.

My husband found the carpet in a dumpster behind a carpet store - the manager was glad for him to take it. To get the smell out, I had to bake it in the sun and spray it with a bleach solution. Anne Callaway, California, August

TEMPERATURE AND HUMIDITY AFFECT TENSION OF RIPSTOP NYLON

It stretches when cold and wet; contracts when hot and dry. During a cold rainstorm, a nylon tent slackens, and will flap and jerk until you tighten it. But don't forget to loosen it afterwards. I did one morning and went hiking. The afternoon sun drew it tighter than a drum. Henry, Arizona

SIMPLE DWELLING IS COMFORTABLE IN MOST WEATHER

The Hillodge is designed for portable living year around on steep slopes. A clear front wall, combined »»

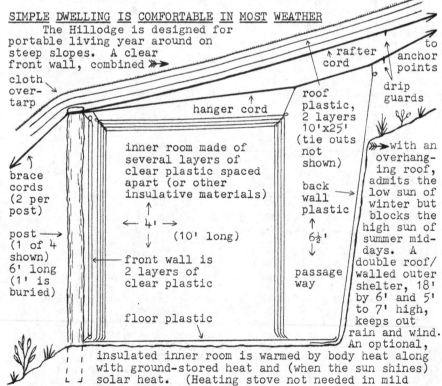

cloth over-tarp

hanger cord

rafter cord

to anchor points

drip guards

roof plastic, 2 layers 10'x25' (tie outs not shown)

inner room made of several layers of clear plastic spaced apart (or other insulative materials)

brace cords (2 per post)

post (1 of 4 shown) 6' long (1' is buried)

← 4' →

(10' long)

front wall is 2 layers of clear plastic

floor plastic

back wall plastic

6½'

passage way

with an overhanging roof, admits the low sun of winter but blocks the high sun of summer mid-days. A double roof/walled outer shelter, 18' by 6' and 5' to 7' high, keeps out rain and wind. An optional,

insulated inner room is warmed by body heat along with ground-stored heat and (when the sun shines) solar heat. (Heating stove not needed in mild

climates.) Materials cost $30 to $60 in 1991.
The frame consists of only four posts, each with 4 cords.
Each post sets up independently, minimizing readjustments.
The roof consists of two sheets of plastic 10 x 25' (the
commonest size) uncut, which are simply layed upon the frame
and tied out. An optional overtarp of cloth or light matting
will extend the life of the plastic and reduce visibility.
The front wall and one end are formed from one 10x25 sheet
of clear plastic, folded double. (Tips for erecting on page 3.)

I BOUGHT AN 8 x 10 x 6 DOME AND PUT IT UP ON MY LAND
I will use it this summer. It includes a tent, rain fly,
poles and stakes, which all fit in a small bag. It is easy for
one person to carry and to put up. I got it instead of a tipi
because it has a floor. I almost bought a "Mountainshelter"
but it was too expensive. After reading Henry's comments (p.4)
I am glad I didn't. I did buy their stove but found it cheaply
made and feel I wasted money. Gloria Orr, New York, June

OUR PARTTIME NEIGHBOR HAS AN 18-FOOT DOME FROM SHELTER SYSTEMS
She had trouble with rain coming in at the doors. (I don't
know if she followed the advice in the manual.) Left unoccupied
for a few weeks last November, the dome was flattened by 6 to 8
inches of wet snow. Most of the plastic pipes and connectors
were broken, but the fabric appeared undamaged. Moral: never
leave a lightweight dome unattended. Anne Schein, CA, Jan.1991
(Shelter Systems' catalog cautions that snow must be removed.)

I USE BLUE CLOSED-CELL FOAM ON TOP OF OPEN-CELL FOAM
It blocks the cold and keeps both foams from pancaking.
I haven't slept on closed-cell foam by itself. There are at
least two grades of blue closed-cell foam. I get the better
grade but, even so, it starts thinning after a month or two
(less quickly if used together with open-cell foam) losing
insulation and cushioning value. Lee Mauck, CA, Feb. 1991

COMPARTMENTED AIR MATTRESSES ARE NOT VERY DURABLE
I had one with tube inserts which developed pin-hole leaks
and went flat. Samples in the store did too. You can carry
spare tubes but that runs up weight and cost. Lee, CA

OUTER COVER PROTECTS AND NEATENS WORN BEDDING
Ragged blankets, quilts, and sleeping bags used as quilts,
provide good insulation. But I don't like their looks nor the
way my fingers and toes snag their holes - and enlarge them.
To cover, I make a simple envelope, joined at top and
sides, open at bottom. It's a foot longer than the bedding to
allow for creep-up at the bottom. For material I look at
garage sales and for discontinued styles in fabric stores.
Some sheets have pretty patterns; white ones can be dyed.
The bedding is held in place within the cover by ball ties
at corners and top center: bunch all layers over a wad of rag
and secure with a rubber band. Easily removed for washing.
Julie

EXTRA CLOTHES AND BLANKETS SERVE AS CUSHIONS
That way they remain useful, rather than taking up storage
space. And the frequent movement discourages moths. I sewed
cushion covers out of heavy cloth I found. Paul Doerr, CA

WE ARE MOVING INTO AN 18' DOME-TENT ON FIVE WILD ACRES
We first thought of a yurt but couldn't find any 18'+ ones
for less than $1300. Laurel & Charles, Texas, Jan.

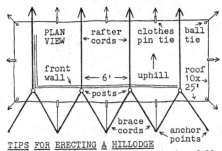

PLAN VIEW · rafter cords → · clothes pin tie · ball tie

front wall · ← 6' → · uphill · roof 10x 25'

← posts →

brace cords · anchor points

TIPS FOR ERECTING A HILLODGE

I prefer southerly slopes during fall and winter, and easterly slopes during spring and summer (for morning warmth).

For a site, choose a 10 by 25 foot area clear of high bushes or trees. Uphill must either be steep, or else have fair size trees to provide elevated anchor points for the rafter cords. (Avoid large trees dangerously close.) Downhill ideally has no trees or tall bushes close enough to block light. Level and smooth a 6' by 18' terrace.

Only shallow post holes are needed, because cords will brace the posts. I round and smooth the top of each post so that it won't puncture the roof plastic. Carving a groove close to the top helps to keep the rafter cords in place.

Seldom are anchor points for rafter cords ideally located. I use whatever are available and then reposition each rafter cord with an auxilliary cord pulling sideways. I run separate cords for hanging things on, rather than use the rafter cords and sag them.

If the rafter cords must fasten to trees (because uphill isn't steep), I tie to the bases of branches (rather than around trunks, to avoid bruising), and then brace to logs, roots, or bases of bushes (to avoid bending the trees).

For the roof, black plastic will out-last clear, especially if no cloth over-tarp. To tie out the plastic, I use 1½-2" diameter ball ties on the corners, but spring-clamp clothespins on the sides (where ball ties might form rain-collecting pockets). Where clothespin-ning, I roll the edge of the plastic a few times around a straight twig, ¼" diameter a few inches long; clamp to the roll; then tighten the grip by wrapping a narrow rubber strap around the clothes pin. I tie the tie-out cord through the clothespin's spring.

plastic — ball — cord

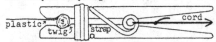

plastic · twig · strap · cord

I stretch the roof's upper layer tauter than the lower layer, to form ±1" air spaces between. For an overtarp, I use any old drab-colored cloth, pieced together. Because the plastic is water-proof, the cloth need not be.

On the uphill side, just inward from the edge of the plastic, I wrap a piece of string or strap around each cord, so that any water running along the cord will drip off there rather than inside.

I ball-tie the front wall plastic to the posts, bottom as well as top (rather than just set rocks/dirt on the bottom), for reliability and to save time moving.

I cover the back wall and floor with plastic, to block moisture and confine any loose dirt or leaves. Odd/holed/salvaged pieces may be used, overlapping as necessary. For comfort and appearance I add mats, rugs or drapes.

An insulated inner room can be built in various ways out of many different materials: anything that can be kept in position and will provide several inches of loft. We have used our Hillodge only during spring so far, and thus have not needed an inner room. When I build one I plan to use several layers of clear plastic for sides and top, suspending them ½" to 1" apart with a succession of ball-ties-with-tails. Such can be made by tying a bulky knot in a short length of cord. To erect, wrap the top layer of plastic over the bulky knot and tie the suspension cord around the base of the bundle, letting the tail hang through. Then tie the tail to the next layer of plastic in a similar manner. Etc. How I build the ends of the inner room will depend on the materials at hand.

If a 6 by 18' Hillodge is not roomy enough, rather than enlarging, I would build additional shelters near by. (Leveling a site for a Hillodge twice as big would disturb 8 times as much dirt.)

Limitations of the Hillodge: The roof is not steep enough to shed snow, nor strong enough to support an accumulation, and therefore should not be left up and untended when heavy snow is likely. The plastic roof and front wall may not take gales. The frame is not well suited for areas which are both flat and treeless. The outer shell includes seams that will admit insects unless carefully chinked. (A bug net can be hung in inner room.)

Tho the frame, roof, and most walls are simple, the end closures are irregular - and are left for the builder to work out. (Detailed instructions would not only fill many pages, but might take longer to read and understand than to invent for yourself.)

Comparing the Hillodge with Wanda's Tleanto (in Sept'85 and Sept'86 MP):

The Tleanto's roof is steeper and stronger, and thus can shed snow or support an accumulation. The frame is self supporting, not requiring high anchor points; thus is not restricted to steep hillsides or edges of groves. The front wall is higher, providing more solar heating and more light inside, especially high up. If south facing, a Tleanto does not need a cloth overtarp to prevent reflections of the sun.

The Hillodge's frame (only 4 posts) is much simpler and lighter. The rafters are cords instead of poles, and thus are not hazardous if they break. The roof slopes the same direction as the land, and thus is less intrusive and less buffeted by wind. The inner room can be placed at the front, with a full-height passageway behind it. For the same width of terrace, it has more floor space. B&H

REPORT ON THE "MOUNTAINSHELTER"

In the Jan. 1991 issue, I evaluated the 9x9' Chouinard "Megamid" and asked if there were similar tents twice as big. I found one: a Mountainsmith 8-man "Mountainshelter". It has an oval cone shape with floor diameters of 14 and 18'. Like the "Megamid", it has an adjustable center pole, coated ripstop nylon, and no floor. It weighs 9½ pounds, and the 8½' pole breaks down into four sections, easy to backpack. The zippers are heavy duty YKK coils and should hold up well as long as you don't try to stuff the tent into too small a bundle.

However, while living in it this past fall and winter in the mountains of AZ and NM, I discovered major problems.

For some reason the fabric's coated side is out, rather than in. So, unlike the Megamid where condensation droplets inside run harmlessly down the smooth walls to the eaves, in the Mountainshelter they adhere to the fabric's rough inside until a breeze shakes them loose and they rain on everything. Consequently, when breaking camp, you have to wait for your sleeping bag to dry.

The Mountainshelter has two windows. But they are less than a sq. foot each and are covered with a heavy duty mosquito netting, which not only reduces air flow, but being white clouds the view.

The stove-pipe vent near the apex is made of a Kevlar fabric that resembles plastic-coated fiberglass cloth. Being near the apex it experiences much stress and stitches in it pull out easily. I have glued and then sewn on a patch of coated nylon packcloth to prevent pulling away from the edges, but have left the hole open as an air vent.

The folding stainless-steel stove sold for the tent ($170), is so small you must fuel it with twigs every 20 min. They also sell for $85 a propane stove. But you can get one with nearly as many BTUs from Walmart for $15, which is also lighter and more compact.

The 6" pegs supplied with the tent are inadequate for anyplace but a lawn in fair weather. I've tried a number of commercially available pegs and presently prefer 10" Durapegs for most situations. These pegs alone will not hold with high winds and either water-saturated soil or the gravelly sand common in southwest mountains. To reinforce them, I tie a piece of 1/8" braided nylon cord around each peg, and tie the ends together to form a 4" loop. Another peg can then be put through the first peg's loop, bracing it; and then a third peg in its loop cord, etc. This may be over kill, but is better than having your tent blow down during a freezing rainstorm on a pitch black night. The loops also aid removal of pegs from hard or frozen ground. The tent's original loops are rather small, so to them I have tied 4" loops of cord.

The tent has some two dozen peg loops and you might think it would be a beast to erect. Not so. One person can do it in 15 minutes, even in high winds. Stretch out the tent along the long diameter and temporarily peg it at both ends. Then move each end in 2' toward the center and drive the pegs in. Next pull each end of the short diameter out

until taut, then in 1½' and peg firmly. You now have the base held at four points and can insert the center pole. Then, starting next to the short diameter and alternating sides, stretch the loops out and peg away. (A method such as this would also probably be a good way to erect a parachute tent like the one I described in the May 1991 issue.)

A final problem of the Mountainshelter is the price: $600 list. I bought mine through REI for $500 and will get a 10% member rebate on that. Henry, AZ, Mar'91

EARTH FLOORS WARM AND COOL NATURALLY

During hot weather, the ground takes heat from the air above; during cold weather, it gives heat back. Where we live is usually mild, with extreme cold and heat infrequent and brief. If we lived where subfreezing temperatures persisted many months, we would insulate not only our shelter, but also the earth around it for several feet (perhaps with mulch or extra snow) to keep the frost from creeping in under us.

Shelter Systems also likes earth floors. "Being on the ground is warmer than being on a deck (wooden platform) unless the deck is heavily insulated - because of cool air flowing under (the deck). Earth floors are incredibly inexpensive compared to decks, they save trees and are easier to construct. (On a sloping site) make a level area with a ditch around the uphill side for drainage. On a flat site, raise an area above the surrounding ground to insure that water will flow away." Add plastic as barrier to vapor and dirt. H & B, OR

PORTABLE DWELLINGS SAFER IN EARTHQUAKES

A best-selling prehistoric novel begins with an earthquake. The ground cracks open, a woman falls in, and the ground closes again - while her daughter watches in horror. A few people may have died that way, but many more are crushed by collapsing buildings or trapped in wreckage which then burns. As a geologist said after one major quake: "Earthquakes don't kill people. Buildings kill people."

Portable dwellings are generally much safer in quakes, both because they are flexible and bend instead of breaking, and because, if they do collapse, there is less weight to hurt anyone. "In the days following the 7.1 quake in Santa Cruz in Oct.'89, our neighbors find more security in a flexible 'LightHouse' (portable dome) than in their damaged home", writes Robert & Catherine Gillis in Shelter Systems' catalog (see p.C).

Places like California and Japan are lucky in a way, because the frequent quakes relieve the stresses before they become extremely large. According to geologic evidence, the northwest gets colossal earthquakes every 1000 years or so (not very regular) much more severe than the quake that wrecked San Francisco. These are often accompanied by waves hundreds of feet high smashing the coast. Other "earthquake free" areas may also. (No one knows yet.)

Animals acting oddly, strange odors, early tremors, sometimes give warning.
April 1992   H & B

FREE RV PARKING IN SOUTHEAST CALIFORNIA

"The Slabs" is the remains of a military base on the east side of the Salton Sea about 50 miles north of the Mexican border. During winter several thousand people live there in various rigs. You can camp without vehicle if you like but it's rough. Winters are mild: dates grow around there. Summers are often hot (120° sometimes), sometimes humid from irrigation and the Salton Sea, sometimes sand storms. Few people stay the entire summer. Lee Mauck, CA,Feb'91

MORE ABOUT CAMPING IN BAJA CALIFORNIA

There is abundant free camping once you know where to go. Be discrete and take your time. If no one is around, it is free. There are various little roads off the highway to the Sea of Cortez. At one spot camping may be $7 a night, while expensive motorhomes 100 yards away are parking free because they knew a road that led to government land.

Some people out in the country can advise you on what is free. I don't think you can get this info in town.

The main difficulty is getting fresh water. You can buy it for about 25¢ a gallon and then have to get it to your camp. Second-class buses are cheap, clean and safe, and stop anywhere.

Without papers you can go south as far as San Felipe on the Sea of Cortez and a few miles past Ensenada on the Pacific. The U.S. and Mex. governments are negotiating for an open border, but presently, bringing computers, TVs,VCRs, etc. into Mexico is a hassle. If you cross the border during commute hours and don't look like a tourist, you probably won't be stopped.

Just as you get street wise, you get Mexico wise. Cops are creeps but bribe-able - they just want their cut. Unless you are arrogant you can't get into much trouble. Working for money is a crime: if caught you get deposited on the U.S. side of the border and the cops keep what you had. Mexicans know poverty and have an eye for it but are not hostile toward it as in the U.S. Lee Mauck

GETTING DENTAL WORK IN MEXICO

During the past 20 years I've had 8 teeth crowned by four dentists in Mexican border cities; most in Tijuana. Three of them did work that lasted,and seemed honest; one did poor work,and lied. (On average, bit better than U.S.)

The dentists themselves seem to net about as much as north of the border (and seem about as well trained and equipped). But lab work such as crowns and bridges costs much less, and over-head is lower - legal liability especially. In 1989 for an alloy crown I paid $70 U.S. (a gold crown would have been $170). A U.S. dentist asked $350 for gold. (I now have four alloy crowns. They have given no trouble; however the oldest is only 8 years; whereas my oldest gold crown is 30 years.)

Get recommendations from people who have had the same kind of.work you need. If lacking recommendations, ask dentist (or any skill-person in any country) what they do most of, before saying what you need. Tho most dentists will do crowns, some do many more, and not only

get better at them, but also faster and may charge less. The average Mexican border dentist probably does crowns better than the average U.S. dentist simply because of doing more of them.

Unless fluent in Spanish, seek English speaking dentists (in border cities where available). A Spanish-only dentist is apt to quote higher, to allow extra time for the language barrier. Dentists expect a 50% deposit; U.S. currency seems welcome.

With dentists anywhere, do get a firm quote, making sure it includes everything. Before getting a root canal, obtain second and third opinions. (In my experience, if a tooth doesn't hurt, it doesn't need a root canal.) Chal, CA,Jan.

DENTAL SELF HELP AND MORE HELP

For a temporary filling (if an old one falls out) I keep myrhh handy. Heat it until it becomes a sticky sap, then apply it to the tooth where it hardens once more. It's also antiseptic. It won't work long, but will protect the tooth until you can get further treatment.

Dental prices are much lower in Mexico. If looking without personal recommendations, you are as apt to find a good dentist there as here. A U.S. consulate or embassy will provide a list of dentists they think competant, but who may charge more than the local norm.

In the U.S., universities with dental schools provide low/no-cost work done by students supervised by teachers who are some of the best in their field.
Rainbow Hawk, New York, August

FOR IMPROVISED FILLING OF CAVITY IN TOOTH

Tamp in a ball of wax or pine resin.
Wildflr.

CONIFER RESIN NATURAL BANDAID

Spread on small wounds, it keeps out dirt and bacteria. I've found it soothing and it may even promote healing. In Plants With A Purpose, Richard Mabey says resin (pitch) may be antibiotic to fungi and bacteria. Thin, somewhat runny pitch seems to sooth more than the thick, gummy kind. After applying pitch, I dust it with fern spores, ashes, or flour - whatever is handiest, to keep it from sticking to things. I've used pitch from hemlock (Tsuga) and doug-fir (Pseudotsuga). Young trees with thin bark often have small pitch-filled blisters. Julie

AMERICAN INDIAN MEDICINE

Virgil J. Vogel's book extracts from the vast literature on Indians. Altho ineffective against introduced diseases such as smallpox, "Indian treatment of externally caused injuries (such as bites and fractures) was usually rational and often effective." Vogel, a historian, "renders no judgement on efficacy...."

To poison ivy, various Indians applied Grindelia robusta (tarweed), Astragalus nitidus (milk vetch), Lactuca canadensis (wild lettuce) juice, Impatiens biflora (jewelweed) leaves, Lepidium virginicum (Virginia peppergrass), Fagus grandifolia (beech) bark tea, Rhus glabra (sumach) poultice of leaves or berries.

Vogel surveys only 200 plants (ones in USP/NF). The Cherokees alone used ±800.

1970, 584pp, $29 in'86, University of Oklahoma Press, POB 787,Norman,OK 73070.

TIPS FOR SEEING BETTER AT NIGHT

People can see surprisingly well in dim light after their eyes become accustomed: allow ten minutes or more. If using a light briefly, keep one eye closed (I was amazed how dark-adapted it remained). Look near, rather than directly at an object. If observing a large area, keep eyes moving.

To prepare, avoid carbon monoxide (cigarette smoke especially) which decreases oxygen to eyes; avoid alcohol; get good nutrition (particularly vitamin A) and adequate rest. Minimize time in bright light during the day, to conserve the eyes' chemicals for night use. (From Sept'91 Directions; see p.A)

EASY-TO-MAKE CANDLE LANTERN DOES NOT BLOW OUT

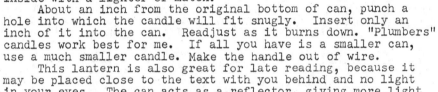

Furthermore, it directs the light away from you and thus does not blind you. And it keeps your hands warm. Any can with a shiny inside may be used, but a 3-pound coffee can is the best size. It does not get overly hot, and it is easy to light in a wind because you can put your whole hand inside with a lighter or match.

About an inch from the original bottom of can, punch a hole into which the candle will fit snugly. Insert only an inch of it into the can. Readjust as it burns down. "Plumbers" candles work best for me. If all you have is a smaller can, use a much smaller candle. Make the handle out of wire.

This lantern is also great for late reading, because it may be placed close to the text with you behind and no light in your eyes. The can acts as a reflector, giving more light than you might expect. Paul White, WA, April & May 1991

VENTILATION IS VITAL WHERE ANYTHING IS BURNING

Responding to Jan'91 issue: Just because "the fumes don't smell bad" does not mean they are safe to breathe. What do you suppose is the "black deposit" collecting on the mantles? It isn't CO_2, it isn't water, and it doesn't belong in your lungs.

Though an alcohol lamp might produce only CO_2 and water if perfectly adjusted, any imperfection causing incomplete combustion will produce carbon monoxide, which is not only poisonous but also explosive. (Ask any firefighter about flashover.)

I urge you to VENTILATE when using ANY flame OR catalytic appliance. Ideally, air for burning comes directly from outside and goes directly back to outside. Check frequently that intake duct and chimney are airtight. Jon Seaver, R.N., MI

KEEP EXHAUSTED LIGHTERS TO USE AS SPARK GENERATORS

After a disposable lighter runs out of fuel, remove the metal shield, and use to ignite tinder or propane appliances.

Dry sawdust mixed with dry lint (clothes driers are a source) provide good tinder. Store in an airtight container until needed. Wildflower, Connecticut, February 1991

DISPOSABLE LIGHTERS CAN CORRODE - AND MAY BE HAZARDOUS

Tho not as vulnerable to moisture as matches are, a lighter left a few days in a damp raincoat pocket became inoperable. The nozzle corroded shut, the flint corroded stuck, and much of the sparker wheel's purposely rough surface rusted away.

While repairing, the flint and spring shot out - with amazing force! Moral: don't point lighter at anything hurtable.

Lighters removed from wet within a few minutes and allowed to air dry did not corrode. When drying, don't subject a lighter to much heat: treat it like the bomb it is. Julie, OR

STICK WITH STUB BRANCH HELPS WASH CLOTHES BY HAND

I sit on a log (or covered pail with cushion) next to a 5-gallon pail of laundry, and agitate with one hand at a time. To minimize back bending and detergent contact, I use an L-shaped stick about 2 feet long (5/8" diameter is strong enough without excess weight) with a 4-inch-long branch-stub flush on the end that goes in the wash. For easier gripping, I enlarge the handle end by wrapping with a strap or rags. Julie Summers, Oregon, March 1991

BULKY CLOTHING CAN BE WASHED BY WALKING ON

Prepare a tub-size hole in the ground, removing any sharp projections. Line with plastic. Place in it a sleeping bag, etc., and soapy water. Let soak, then agitate by walking on. Add more water to rinse. Most cheap sleeping bags may be washed this way. Paul Doerr, California, February 1991

SOME MILK JUGS HAVE SCREW CAPS THAT SEAL WELL

One kind of cap has no gasket to wear out, but rather an inner lip molded out of the cap's plastic. These continue to seal well over time. I prefer them for portable faucets (LLL plans) on which leaky caps would be undesirable. (I collect strays I find, as spares for any missing or broken.) Julie

JUGS THAT DEVELOP LEAKS CAN BE MADE INTO SINKS AND TRAYS

The 2½ and 5 gallon rectangular narrow-mouth plastic jugs, discarded by restaurants and bakeries, are handy sizes. I use intact jugs for water hauling and storage. But in time, some spring leaks. Cut in two vertically, the leakless half can be used as a sink or dish drain; the leaky half as storage tray.

FUNNEL MADE FROM VINYL DRINK BOTTLE FITS MOST ONE-GALLON JUGS

The two-liter size with a long neck fits down in well, and is wide enough to pass grain. (Suggested by Kurt Saxon.) The cut-off bottom can be used as a cup or bowl. To fit into jugs with narrow mouths, I file off the threads. Julie, OR

DURING HOT WEATHER I USE PAPER BAGS FOR CARRYING BREAD

The paper (unlike plastic) lets the food dry out, thus preventing mold. If the bread gets rock hard, it can be softened with water before eating. Julie Summers, Oregon

POPCORN POPPED WITHOUT OIL KEEPS WELL

It does not mold, nor go rancid. Because of its bulk I tie it outside of my pack, or compact by grinding it. Plastic bags will keep it dry. If ground, I eat it like granola with raisins, nuts, sunflower seeds. Because popcorn stores well, I reserve it for last, and eat perishables first. Julie, OR

COVERING BERRIES WITH JUICE PRESERVES THEM FOR SEVERAL DAYS

Picking just before eating is best for taste and nutrition. But sometimes I have a surplus of blackberries, raspberries or huckleberries and no refrigeration. If nothing is done, some berries are moldy the next day. To prevent mold, immediately after picking I juice enough to cover the rest and store in the coolest place available. I use a 10x12" drawstring bag, made of fine-weave nylon curtain fabric, to hold back the seeds while squeezing out the juice. The pulp can be soaked in water and squeezed again to yield berry-ade, which I drink promptly (seems to sour faster than berries). Julie

Dwelling Portably

(formerly named Message Post)
POB 190, Philomath, OR 97370
Sept. 1992 $1 per issue   Add 50¢ to check/mo under $10

HOW IS A STOVE INSTALLED IN A TENT?

How far from the walls is it placed? Does the chimney go
out the sides or out the top? How is the outside part secured?
Where do you get a non-combustible collar, and how do you keep
the liner and tent from touching there? If you use a spacer
between liner and tent, what is it made out of?

I am making a tent that a hammock can be hung in. I will
let you know how it turns out. Bob Barker, WA, March

A FRIEND DID THIS:

Where tent would be, dug
pit for a small wood stove
plus a trench for the flue pipe.
The pipe was buried with 6" of
dirt between it and the tent's
wall. The outside chimney was
supported with 3/4" iron pipe.
The surplus canvas tent in
northern Canada was heated all
winter this way. Wildflower, July

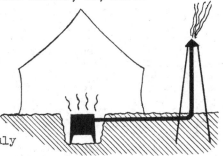

MORE INFO WANTED REGARDING COLD WEATHER LIVING

It seems most of you are living in moderate winter
climates. Here it is nearly zero every night for a month or
more. Scott Shaward, New Mexico, January

COMMENTS ON VENTILATION AND BURNING APPLIANCES

Whenever a stove or lantern is used inside, the oxygen
for combustion must come from somewhere and the end products
of combustion (chiefly CO_2, H_2O vapor and - if combustion is
incomplete - CO (the silent killer) and any of a host of
potentially carcinogenic substances) must go somewhere.

True enough, the solution is to provide ventilation in
excess of the needs of the appliance plus any occupants.
When faced with the necessity of using a stove inside a tent
in mountaineering situations when providing adequate ventilation is difficult because of weather - and this is a common
situation - and your life depends on getting snow melted, etc.,
then a stove which is least likely to generate deadly carbon
monoxide will be safest. Water vapor and CO_2 are normal
byproducts of human respiration and pose not the extraordinary
risks associated with CO which, without warning, can cause
unconsciousness and death.

Alcohol produces less heat per fuel weight than does
petroleum (including white gas, kerosene, butane). That means
that alcohol will be considered as a fuel in situations where
weight is critical only if the devices that burn it are, by
design, more efficient. Designs which rely on minimal moving
parts (operator adjustments) to obtain efficient combustion,
will tend to be safer in the situations described above.

Be aware of factors that can compromise the efficiency
and safety of alcohol-burning stoves such as Trangia, Optimus
or Westwind. One is burning a fuel other than ethanol or
methanol. Another is burning a fuel contaminated with other
chemicals. The color of the flame (it should be blue, not
yellow) and the absence of soot accumulation on bottoms of
pots are good indications of efficient combustion. Robert, VT

SUGGESTIONS FOR GATHERING AND SELLING ALUMINUM DRINK CANS

I find that a mop handle, with a right angle "hook" (with threads) screwed into the end, is perfect for retrieving drink cans from dumpsters. Barbeque tongs are good for retrieving cans from regular garbage containers. Any rest area is a great collecting place during hot weather when people drink a lot. When you go to sell them, the best prices are given by metal dealers rather than recycling centers which in turn resell them to a metal dealer. Tumbleweed, Desert SW, Oct.

IDEA FOR CONNECTING REMOTE LIVING WITH CITY JOB

To put together and mail the May'90 MP, I hiked and biked over the mountains to a close-to-city camp site (where I had left stashed a sleeping bag, tarp, etc.) I stayed several days and, from there, made two one-day trips into the city (picking up the printed MP, putting it together at my camp, then returning to the city to mail).

I wonder if a family who has a steady business or employment in a big city, but who would like to live far out in the backcountry, might do something similar. One family member drives to the city several times a month and, each trip, works several days straight while sleeping in the vehicle. Other family members remain at their base camp. (In our case, Holly did. I went to the city camp alone.)

Of course this assumes a vehicle is needed for work (else would not be economical), and that the work can be performed in spurts. Bert, Oregon, November 1990

WHERE CAN YOU CAMP WHILE GAINING EXPERIENCE?

Do you know of anyone selling a plot of land really cheap that would be exempt from taxes? I think that I would first have to start in a tipi or something that is on land of my own, before I could entertain the idea of nomadic living. Brenda, CA, Febr. 1991

(Reply:) If you want to camp (or park) in one place for a long time, I suggest renting or swapping services (such as caretaking) for land, at least at first. I recommend not buying land, at least until you gain experience with your new dwellingway (whatever it may be), because, until you have experience, you won't know what kind of land or what area is good for what you want to do, or even if you will want to own land at all. I believe you could find suitable swap arrangements in various areas of northern CA and the northwest; maybe in southern CA. You may have to do quite a lot of advertising or looking around to find a situation you like. Place ads in places (stores, rural shoppers, etc.) frequented by rural property owners. Bert, Oregon, April 1991

SLEEPING ON STYROFOAM SHEETS IN WINTER

That is the most comfortable I've ever been at 0° F. Reflects body heat. Paul White, Washington, April 1991

ANY PLASTIC BOTTLE CAN SERVE AS A HOT-WATER BOTTLE

All it needs is a tight-closing cap. If my feet are cold when I go to bed, it warms them fast. Otherwise they may remain cold for hours. Holly, Oregon, December

TOOL MAKES COLLECTING MATERIALS FROM DUMPSTERS EASIER

To a mop handle 4 to 6 feet long, tape to one end a magnet from a speaker - for picking up metal hardware, and tape to the other end a 10/0 fishhook (with sharp point cut off) for pulling materials to you. Saves climbing into bins that might be hazardous to be in. Wildflower, Connecticut, September

SQUARE PLASTIC JARS MAKE GREAT STORAGE

I have some that Japanese seasoned seaweed comes in. They are durable, light weight, and don't waste space as round containers do. They hold 3 to 4 cups. A disadvantage is they don't collapse as the contents are used, like a plastic bag would. The seasoned seaweed makes a great snack. Lee Mauck, June

HOW TO GET RID OF THINGS AND HAVE THEM TOO

As living and storage space become more expensive, a clutter of advice on reducing clutter has appeared: "If you haven't used it in two years, throw it away." "Destroy it before throwing in the waste basket so you won't be able to change your mind." "Throw out everything you don't really need." These kinds of suggestions can best be discarded because they ignore the crucial factor: comparative costs.

If holding on to something costs you little (in money, time, or emotions) there is no reason to throw it away. In fact, disposing of some things may cost more than keeping.

For written items, consider putting them on microfiche. That way they take up negligible space. For other items, consider getting some 5 gallon pails (free or cheap at many in-store bakeries). Fill them with what you don't really need but don't want to destroy, go for a ride, and cache them in the boonies. If you never go back, little is lost; if you do, they might still be there. Julie Summers, Oregon, April

MORE USES FOR OLD INNER TUBES

Float self or equipment over water.

Float basket, bucket or net inside to hold crabs, clams, or fish while catching more.

Tractor tire tubes roped under wood platform form a raft or support a small dometent (an expedient houseboat).

On shore, if lined with plastic sheet, bag or poncho, an inflated tube forms a basin for washing clothes, dishes or feet, or as a small bin for veggies and fruit. Wildflower, July

BIRD NETTING CAN BE USED TO COVER PLASTIC TENTS OR TARPS

Weave various natural materials into the netting to conceal the plastic or to protect it from the sun. A 14' by 14' section costs about $10 in New England garden/nursery outlets. Wildflower, Connecticut, November 1991

FORGET YOUR COOKING UTENSILS? DON'T WORRY!

Many foods can be cooked directly on coals. The coals keep the food above any dirt or gravel, and the ashes brush off surprisingly well. The secret is to wait until all flames are gone before cooking. Also, remember that the food will become more susceptible to burning toward the end of cooking, as water content is· reduced, so pay closer attention then. Drier foods, like toast, require closer supervision than do moister ones, like potatoes or steak. Julie Summers, Apr.'91

Dwelling Portably

(formerly named Message Post)
POB 190, Philomath, OR 97370

Dec. 1992 $1 per issue   Add 50¢ to check/mo under $7

I BUILT A WIGWAM

I use it for rendezvous, Renaissance
Faires, and Pirate get togethers. It is 8'
by 10', and 8' high - giving plenty of head
room so I don't have to hunch over. Eight
people have slept in it. It has stood up in
some strong winds.

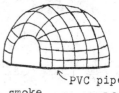

I use dome-tent poles and PVC pipe for
framing, and blankets and tablecloths for
cover. I put carpets on the floor. All
goods and bedding is stored in chests around
the sides. I have hung lamps on long hooks
from the frame. I even have a smoke flap,
so I can have a fire inside like in a tipi
if I want. I can partition the inside by
hanging blankets.

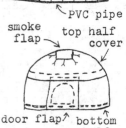

The whole thing lashes together in an
hour. 1. Put together PVC-pipe floor frame
(stake down). 2. Fit dome-tent pole arches
into holes drilled in pipe. 3. Weave dome-
tent side poles in and out of the arches
and lash in position. (Looks like a basket
upside down.) 4. Put on covering (any kind
you want). It comes apart in half an hour
and folds up into a small bundle that goes
in one chest.

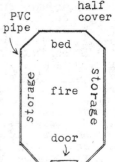

Instead of poles and pipes, you may
use bamboo or branches - dug into ground.

I am looking for additional information
on wickiup, wigwam and yurt construction.
Lani Tucker, California, April

IMPROVISED COVERING KEEPS FEET AND LEGS WARM AT NIGHT

If your sleeping bag is marginal for warmth, but you have
extra clothes, use a sweater to insert your legs into. If one
sleeve is roomy enough to accomodate both legs, you can fold
the garment in half and invert one sleeve into the other. This
doubles the insulation, and keeps both legs together, reducing
exposed surface area and hence heat loss. (Mittens are warmer
than gloves for the same reason.)

Keep the garment zipped or buttoned as it normally would
be, and enter from the waist end, with the sleeves extended
away from you. To keep feet from protruding, I close the
cuffs with multiple turns of rubber bands.

This idea comes from One Day in the Life of Ivan Deniso-
vich, by Alexander S. Izhenitsyn (Bantam, 1963). Ivan, a
Siberian work camp prisoner in Stalinist Russia, slept with
his blanket and coat spread on top, "and both his feet tucked
in the sleeve of his jacket." (It is an extraordinary book,
showing how extremely harsh conditions can become taken for
granted, and how people build a life around them.) I got to
try the idea the very same week I read about it, during some
unseasonably cold spring days. Worked nicely. Julie Summers,

Is there anything non-toxic that will repel biting flies?

I have tried every suggestion I've heard: oils of pennyroyal and lavender, citronella, garlic juice. The pennyroyal
seems to repel crawling creatures, but the flies still bite.
Lavender seemed best, but the flies still bite, maybe less
often. Any ideas will be immediately tested! L.N.Smith, WI

Dwelling Portably (formerly Message Post) #29
POB 190, Philomath OR 97370
May 1993 $1 per issue   Add 50¢ to check/mo under $7

How to Simple Shower in winter more comfortably.
Here's how we now bathe during cold weather. (1) Start
water heating. (2) Inside our inner (insulated) tent where
warm, soap up one part at a time. Rub each part until dry
before soaping the next part. (3) When water is the hottest
that will be comfortable, partially fill several plastic jugs.
(4) Wearing only thongs, carry jugs outside, along with
towels. (5) Rinse from the top down. (6) Dry off.
Advantages: less time outside; less time wet all over; no
fumbling with soap outside (and sometimes dropping in dirt).
(The soap-and-rub-dry technique was discovered by Mar at
age 7 as a magic trick. Soap on skin becomes invisible when
dry. Add water and get suds "from nowhere".) Wanda, CA, Jan.

Simple Shower saved energy and time - even in house.
Two years ago, Holly and I care-took a big old country
house for a month during the winter holidays. The electric
water heater was close to the kitchen sink, but far from the
bathroom. So, instead of running the shower faucet until warm
water finally came through, I simply filled a jug at the
kitchen sink, carried it to the bathroom, and Simple Showered.
This not only saved electricity, but saved me time. Also,
with a jug, easy to get the temperature you want before
undressing and wetting. (Holly opted for long hot soaks in the
tub: something we don't have at our camps.) Bert, OR, Dec.

Three-sided reflector solar heats water faster.
I made mine from polished aluminum sheet,
but a cut-down cardboard box covered with
aluminum foil works fine. It can warm jugs for
Simple Showers. Brother Bat, AZ, August

Jugs tested for solar heating water.
The four one-gallon plastic jugs were:
clear (milk/juice); white (bleach) painted
"dull" black (but somewhat shiny) on one side
(which faced sun); dark brown (syrup?); dark
brown, set in front of used, crinkly aluminum foil 18x18"(like
reflector shown except no bottom), and both covered by one
clear, used plastic bag. All were full; outsides dried off.
The jugs were set tilted (for best sun angle) on pieces
of bark in hazy sunlight at 11:20 AM daylight time, April 19.
Air 55°, light breeze. All water 46°. (We were still at a
winter camp-site on a south slope where the sun did not rise
completely clear of trees to the east until 11 AM. The jugs
had been outside beneath a tarp overnight. If not testing,
we would have taken water from inside: water 61°; air 69°.)
At 1:50 PM (after 2½ hours), sky half covered with thin
clouds. Air 63° in shade, breezy. Water (after shaking each
jug to equalize): clear 74°; black & white 76°; brown 80°;
brown in bag 84°. The jugs were repositioned for best angle.
At 4:20 (after 5 hrs total), sky bright overcast. Air 59°
calm. Water: clear 84°; b&w 86°; brown 88°; brown in bag 101°.
Comments: This was a mediocre day for solar heating -
but therefore good for testing. On a clear day with an early
start (or with water from inside), water just in a brown jug
(without bag or reflector) gets too hot for comfort (over 110°)
and needs cold water added. On this spring day with the sun
high in the sky, the bag probably helped more than did the

vertical reflector (which is best suited for mid winter when the sun is low). A bowl-shaped reflector set under the jug might have helped more. Holly & Bert, Oregon, April

I use flat-bottomed steel bowls for boiling water or food.
They don't tip and spill like a regular bowl. I also use to dig in sand or dirt. Pet shops sell: pt & qt sizes. Wildflwr

I cook and eat from the same pot. Saves dishwashing.
I use coat-hanger wire to make a handle around pot or metal cup. I like 8-oz metal spice shakers (from restaurants): a screw-on top keeps bugs and ashes out. Eugene Gonzales, Jan

A nylon stocking can be used as a large tea bag.
Place bulk tea or ground coffee in the end, tie off, and boil all. Keeps the grounds out of the pot or cup. After use, discard grounds, wash stocking, and reuse. Wildflower, March

Experience with various camping equipment.
While working and living for a year in a south Miami warehouse, and for 6 months in a van in northern Georgia, I used:
Coleman multi-fuel stove, new. Excellent, no problems. I used it twice a day for 6 months on Coleman fuel and 6 months on kerosene. Coleman fuel easier but too expensive.
Thermarest Camprest mattress, new. Excellent but costly.
Solar AA battery charger. About size of cigarette pack, holds four cells. First one was stolen at warehouse. Second one I've used for 6 months. Adequate.
Solar/battery/dynamo-powered AM-FM radio, bought through Emergency Essentials Co., Utah. 120 cranks of dynamo gives an hour of listening. Reliable, but cranking is noisy.
Igloo 36-qt Koolmate thermo-electric cooler, new. It can plug into a cigarette lighter. After 4 months continuous use at warehouse, I had to replace motor. Since then I've learned to do without a frig. I now use it for storage and to sit on.
Sunshower, 5 gallons, new. Direct sun heats cold water in 2-3 hours. I've had two. The first one, $15, was slashed while heating water on the back of the warehouse. The second one, a $10 imitation, I keep on the roof of my van when heating water. Eugene Gonzales, Georgia, August

Various combination tools tested.
The Leatherman(TM) combo plier tool had better knife blades, screw drivers and file; and cut "10" fence wire easiest.
The SOG(TM) had poor file and screwdriver, knives hard to resharpen, poor grip as pliers, and pinched hands cutting wire.
Both SOG and Gerber are expensive, yet not worth having. Also beware of poorly-made Leatherman look-alikes. Wildflower

I use a plastic fresnel lens for reading small print.
Sold for telephone books, it is cheap, light, flexible, and nearly unbreakable. And, being big (8½x11), it will start a fire any day unless thick overcast. L. Smith, WI, October

I carry at least three sealed containers holding lighters.
Or matches. That way I always have one that is dry when needed. I also recommend learning alternative methods using fresnel lens, flint, etc. Wildflower, Connecticut, January

Underground fire could heat a winter camp.
    Wildflower's stove set-up (in Sept
'92 DP) reminded me of a drawing I
once saw. It showed how dwellings
were heated in northern Korea
during the bitter winters.
    From an underground fire pit
at one end, tunnels fanned out
under the floor and came together
in a chimney at the other end.
The tunnels were made by digging
trenches and covering with rocks and earth.
    Advantages: Because the earth floor stores heat, a fire
is needed only occasionally (rather than continually as it is
if heating air). Also, the fire can be outside of and away
from the dwelling: less fire hazard and fumes, and no inside
space taken up and soiled by ashes. David French, SD, Nov.

I lived in the wilderness for $4\frac{1}{2}$ years.
    I had three different campsites in Tennessee. I built
shelters mostly out of materials at hand, stretching plastic
over bent saplings. I ate game I snared or shot with a 22
rifle. I grew "spot gardens". The wildlife got about half,
but that was okay because I harvested them too.
    I've stored beans, rice, noodles, yellow cornmeal, wheat
flour, brown sugar, and coffee in five-gallon plastic buckets
that have garbage-can liners placed in them and then tied off
twice. After putting the lid on, I place the whole bucket in
a garbage bag, then bury about two feet below ground level.
I've had no problems yet.
    I did all my cooking over a Dakota hole - below ground
level so the fire did not show, and burned only dead, dry
hardwood giving almost no smoke. One hole lasted two years.
    I've tried many sleeping bags. My Warmlite Stephenson
bag is the best. Tim Leathers, Florida, January

(Comment:) I read somewhere that colored garbage bags are not
recommended for food because they are made from recycled
plastic that might be contaminated. Bulk food stores often
give/throw away clear food-grade bags that foods came in. H&B

The easiest way to cook over a fire: BOIL EVERYTHING!
    Forget about broiling, baking, or frying. With boiling,
food is less likely to stick or burn, coals aren't needed,
and less time is spent over the fire. The pot can be hung
above the fire with a wire to a tripod or tri-rig (lines to 3
trees): the most stable way I've found to hold a pot. Heat
can be varied simply by raising or lowering the pot.
    Suppose I have rice, roots (eg, carrots), greens (eg,
nettles or lambsquarters), and meat. I put rice, roots
coarsely cut, and water in pot. (If measuring, I use $1\frac{3}{4}$ cups
of water per cup of rice. Or I may just put in ample water
and be content with soupy rice.) When the water comes to a
boil, I add chunks of meat (as big as chicken thighs). After
the water comes back to a boil, I reduce heat to a simmer -
by raising the pot. In a few minutes I turn over the meat.
After about 15 minutes I add the greens and increase the heat.
The greens need steam only a few minutes. Then I remove the
pot from the fire, put it in a paper bag (to confine soot),
cover it with sleeping bags, and let residual heat finish the
cooking (in about an hour). Now I can relax or do other
things until dinner is ready. Julie Summers, Oregon, January

Keep supplies in more than one place.

If living or moving about in one area, I suggest caching excess goods, extra food, and emergency kits in your local area but away from your home or usual camping spots - in case of sudden eviction for any reason. Even people with legal title to a house or land, or with permission to camp, are being forced to leave suddenly for various reasons; or, if away, are not able to return. Wildflower, Connecticut, January

After something unusual happens, be more cautious.

An accident analysis by the National Speleological Society discovered a pattern: deaths during scuba dives happened, not because of one mistake, but as the result of three or four.

I suppose the first goof disturbed and distracted the victim, leading to FURTHER errors.

After one blunder I try to be extra cautious, perhaps by slowing down or taking time out. To counter guilt I remind myself: "Life IS dangerous." "These things DO happen." Also, "No gain without goofs." Someone who NEVER makes a mistake, is either kidding self, or else being TOO cautious - thereby missing opportunities and learning experiences.

A triumph or stroke of luck is also a time for extra caution, because of distraction, albeit by GOOD feelings. Julie

A small squeeze bottle can be used for personal defense.

Filled with household ammonia, it will stop most four and two legged predators. One should not kill, but one should be able to stop another from killing. Wildflower, CT, April 1992

Succession of rinses removes skunk odor.

I reached back in memory 20 years to help a friend whose puppy got "skunked". First a wash with tomato juice, then a shampoo and water wash, then a rinse with a gallon of water containing a shot glass (1 oz) of ammonia, and finally a rinse with plain water. Very good results. Brother Bat, AZ, Dec.

Further technique for tick removal.

After grasping close to its head with tweezers, I twist and pull SLOWLY, so the tick knows it's in trouble and will let go. (If jerked out, the head is left.) Tumbleweed, Oct.

The most effective and least-toxic control of head lice.

Sheila Daar, at BIRC, recommends use of hot water, shampoo (preferably coconut or olive-oil based), and a specially-designed metal-toothed comb that removes both nits (eggs) and adult lice. Only if the infestation persists should an insecticide be considered. Not only can an insecticide applied to the scalp be absorbed into the bloodstream, but lice have become resistant to many, such as lindane.

Launder headgear or bedding in hot soapy water and place in a dryer where the high temperatures will kill any lice stages that survive the washing. Plastic sleeping pads where children nap can be wiped down with a solution of household bleach or ammonia. In schoolrooms, store hats, hooded clothes and pillows in separate cubbies. (A 24-page booklet on topic, $6¼ from BIRC, POB 7414, Berkeley, CA 94707; (510)524-2567)

Always wipe from front to back, especially if you are a woman.

So that bacteria from anus is not transferred to genitals. This is especially important in places where water may be scarce and washing of clothes and body infrequent. Julie

Tleantos, too, need tending during snows.
In your comparison of Hillodge and Tleanto (Apr'92 DP p.3) you said, "The Tleanto roof is steeper and stronger, and thus can shed snow or support an accumulation."
Correction: The Tleanto will support a few inches of snow - or shed it. (To shed wet, sticky snow,we have to shake fly.) However, as the snow sheds, it accumulates between the roof and uphill and, if not removed, would eventually sag the coverings or break the ceiling poles.

(fly is black plastic or cloth - use ball ties to hold out sides)
ground (covering not shown)

Removal is not easy. You must squat uphill (and try not to slide down onto the roof) while throwing the snow OVER the tleanto and downhill, or else out beyond the ends. (Throw snow uphill and it will slide back down.) We use a pot to throw it. (A shovel might cut the roof.) This has been tolerable because heavy snows are not frequent where we have been living.
Your Hillodge might actually be better for snow removal because, with some massaging, I think the snow would slide off on the DOWNHILL side. If we ever live where poles are hard to get, we may try a Hillodge. However, I like the Tleanto's tall window-wall which lets in plenty of light. A Hillodge might be bright enough while the plastic is new, if there is no growth downhill. But how is it when the plastic gets grungy or bushes grow up? Wanda, California, January

Experimenting with tarp/tent structures in Appalachians.
At present I am house-sitting a rural barn/house so I can work on my van. For privacy, I have a camp-site a few miles away. There, I made an A-tent by tying a cord between two trees and hanging over it a 9x11' tarp. I closed off both ends with plastic and duct tape.
Inside I pitched a pup tent (found in the trash). I lined it with a "space blanket" attached with duct tape to the pup tent. Two plastic tarps cover the ground. I sleep in a 10° hollofill sleeping bag ($50 new) on a Thermarest Camprest. I had cold feet until I discovered putting the sleeping bag foot end inside my jacket (M-65 army, with liner) and zipping jacket up. With the combination of layers, I'm comfortable at 35°. I expect to test in colder weather soon.
For cooking or heat, I use left-over sterno from the restaurant's garbage bin - about one can a day. (Unbelievable waste at those ritzy places.) Also left-over candles for light.
My job as cook is winding down and will end Nov 1. Camping has enabled me to save lots of money, so I may not work again for a while (even tho I have a part-time job offer in town). I want more time for experimenting and having fun in the woods. Eugene Gonzales, Georgia, October

Which materials best for shelter: natural or synthetic?
Some portable dwellers use plastic. Others criticize. Considering esthetics, utility, and environment:
I don't like the feel of plastic sheeting - the way it clings to my skin if I contact. However, I like the way plastic sheds rain yet passes light. So I use it for portions of a shelter I seldom have to touch.
An enclosure made ENTIRELY of natural materials, such as thatch or leaves, is dark inside. That may be tolerable during summer when one wall can be open or we can work outside. But not during the cold, wet days of winter. Therefore, we make at least one wall of an all-weather shelter from plastic.

What natural materials pass light? Oiled animal skins do - poorly. Some Eskimos use sheets of ice: ice soon melts here. I've not tried to make glass out of native materials. (BOUGHT glass seems as artificial as bought plastic, besides being heavier, more breakable, and more hazardous if it breaks.)

Polyethylene (most plastic sheeting) has been used for several decades to hold fruit juice, milk and distilled water - without bad health effects we've heard of. Anyway, we don't eat off our plastic walls. Plastic can burn, but so can most natural materials. Rocks can't, but are dangerous in earth-quakes. Plastic is not very durable, especially in sunlight. It breaks up into flakes - no uglier to me than bones or hair.

As for environmental impact, quantity counts. ANY house that costs $100,000 uses MUCH resources - whether the walls are logs or plastic. (Logs may be natural, but power saws and logging trucks aren't.)

Most plastic presently comes from petroleum, but could be made from such materials as saw dust or fallen leaves (we've heard), and probably will be when the oil wells run dry. Any-how, a plastic tent uses less than a motorist burns in one week.

Environmentally, cotton cloth may be worse: grown with insecticides, and soaked in fungicide and waterproofing for outdoor use. Even so, I'd choose cotton in dry climates because it withstands sunlight longer. But where wet much, even with fungicide, cotton eventually rots.

Many people still living in houses/apartments can no longer afford them and need quick and easy alternatives. Natural materials may require too much time or skill.

By the way, folks who prefer houses should be grateful to portable dwellers: WE aren't pushing up prices of building sites or existing units by bidding against them! Holly & Bert

I have been living in my tipi for a year.
But I've had difficulty keeping rain out. Nomadics, the maker, says: DON'T waterproof. Also, the natural-fiber ropes rot in the rain we get here. (I'm in the wet western part of the Columbia Gorge; not in the dryer east.) Sherilyn, March

I have added a canopy to my pyramid tent.
The sides are held by poles. During good weather, it provides shade. During inclement weather, poles are lowered and it becomes a storm shield. It could be easily adapted to other structures. Brother Bat, Arizona, January

For shelter, I prefer tarps.
They are lightweight, cheap, waterproof, versatile, easy to replace, and come in many colors. I've used them in all kinds of weather and places - while climbing, bicycling, canoeing, camping, etc. Also, they can cover other gear while packing or biking. And, if bright colored, they can signal an airplane in an emergency. David French, South Dakota, Nov.

A small shelter is easy to make from thatch.
Thatch can be formed from many kinds of vegetation (grass, boughs, fronds, some leaves). It can be supported and held together by various means. It provides insulation. And, if steep enough and properly overlapped, it will shed rain. I use it when manufactured materials are not at hand. Some tips:
For support, take advantage of any natural formations that are safe. A small tree partially fallen and sturdily

hung up, can be the ridge pole of an A-frame. A large tree-trunk lying on the ground can hold up and form one wall of a lean-to. A big bush with branches bent over can provide the ribs of an arc hut.

Build a simple shape. A lean-to or A-frame is best for shedding rain. An arc hut is warmest. Also consider what materials are available: straight, stiff sticks are good for an A-frame; curved limber branches for an arc hut's ribs.

Make your shelter tiny at first: just large enough to crawl into. (You may add on later as you have time.)

Angle roof steep to shed rain. The more irregular or porous the thatch, the steeper the roof needs to be.

Thatch from the bottom up if working from outside (or top down if working inside), overlapping so that each row of thatch will drain onto the OUTSIDE of the row beneath.

If you have some waterproof material but only a small amount (plastic bags, large leaves), put it over the peak - the place where any leaks will be the most serious.

Bushcraft, Richard Graves, Schocken Books, 1973, shows some simple ways to thatch. (In print? Try libraries.)

On a spring trip, when a ride failed to show, I hiked to where I had cached a sleeping bag and tarps several years before, but could not find them by the half-moon light in a shady forest. I built my shelter at the base of a tree that had large low branches still alive, using one branch (left attached to tree) as a ridge pole. A recent heavy snow had broken off many doug-fir boughs which I used for thatch. I hooked a branchlet of each bough over the ridge pole; tip end down. Snuggling in, I slept quite warm (except for cold feet) in just the clothes I was wearing. (No rain fell to test my nightime thatch work - just as well.) Bert, OR, Apr.

A rain poncho is easy to make from a large plastic bag.
Just cut a slit near one corner for your face.
Or, with a sheet of plastic, fold it in half and ball-tie the edges together in a few places, leaving an opening for your face.
If you have a rain jacket but lack a rain hat, a triangular piece of plastic (or a square piece folded in half diagonally) can be used as a kerchief. Tie under your chin. In my tests, it got clammy but kept the rain off. Julie Summers, OR, 1991

Experience with various Gortex garments.
I have camped, climbed, packed and bicycled for years.
A pair of mittens were fine: kept rain and snow off hands.
An overparka was okay: big enough to allow air to circulate; but moisture did build up now and then.
A bivouac sack worked ONCE in a snow blizzard while climbing the Tetons. Every other time, even with vent open, moisture collected inside and "rained" - wetting my sleeping bag. David French, South Dakota, November

Hammock helpful. Suggestions for using.
I slept in a hammock in Florida to avoid ant bites and wet cold ground. A tarp over it gave rain protection.
A net hammock is difficult to get in or out of. To make easier, I line with a strip of rug or a foam pad. With that I can get in even when wearing a sleeping bag. Wildflower, CT

My watch cap stays in place better if I fold cuff to INside.
I fold in front only, to keep cap out of my eyes. I let back and sides hang down to warm ears and neck. Julie

Ball ties keep socks up.

When hiking, some socks work their way down my ankles until they disappear into my shoes and become uncomfortable wads. My quick and easy solution does not cut off circulation nor require wearing garter belts or long pants, and saves otherwise sound socks from the rag bag. The result looks much like the little pom-poms at the back of low-cut tennis/golf socks.

At the back of my ankle, I insert a ball between skin and sock - a little above the shoe top to allow slack. Then I gather the fabric around the ball and hold it with multiple windings of a rubber band. For a ball, I trim a 3/4" diameter piece of styrofoam from discarded packaging materials. Styrofoam is light, firm, and easily shaped. Lacking it, I use acorn, small tree cone, or wad of leaves.

During wet weather, I often wear plastic bags inside my shoes but over my socks to keep them dry (for a while). I ball-tie the bags along with the socks. Julie Summers, OR

Hints for easier hand sewing:

Use a piece of thread no longer than your reach, so that you can pull it taut after each stitch with just one motion.

To lubricate the thread so it goes thru easier and twists/tangles less, pull it over some wax such as a candle stub.

If thread still twists, hold the garment up every few stitches and let needle and thread dangle so it unwinds.

When mending clothes, a glass jar can be used as a darning egg. The smooth curved surface deflects the needle, helping to direct it out of the fabric where desired. Julie

Detergent and fasteners found in laundromats.

If I run out of detergent or am traveling light, rather than buy overpriced little boxes from a laundromat's vending machine, I check the trash both inside and out back. I often find containers with considerable residue. After pouring out what I can, I rinse to get out the rest.

I also find many discarded garments. Even clothes not worth mending often have good zippers and buttons which I salvage for replacing broken/lost ones or making new garments.
                                                              Julie

Motor oil containers often found alongside roads.

Those with caps on usually still contain a tablespoon or more of clean oil. I transfer oil to a small plastic bottle (attached to my bike's basket by a rubber strap) for cleaning and lubricating the drive chain and other parts. Julie Summers

Packframe with added support holds bucket easily.

I bought an external frame at a flea market for $3. At the bottom, using the same hardware that attaches the straps, I mounted a U-shaped support piece cut from an aluminum chair. I braced it using ¼" nylon rope with metal rings on each end. They slip over the frame's tips. A bucket can be set on the support. The bucket protects its contents better than a bag does, and is also useful at camp. Eugene Gonzales, Georgia, January

I carry two compasses - so I have a spare.

One, fairly large, I use with maps. The other, pinned on, I use for general navigation. Wildflower

Dwelling Portably

(formerly named Message Post)
POB 190, Philomath OR 97370
Oct. 1993 $1 per issue   To check/mo under $7, add 50¢

Candle formed in jar provides wind-proof light.
I use a one-pint jar with lid. I place a
stick across the mouth of the jar, and from it
suspend a wick so it barely touches the bottom.
Then I half-fill the jar with melted wax.
After the wax cools, I trim wick to 3/4" high
and put on the lid. I carry matches in jar.
    To melt wax safely, I use a double boiler.
The wax goes in a 64 oz juice can with wire
bail, which sets on 2" of small rocks placed
in the bottom of a #10 (3 lb) coffee can
partially filled with water. A small fire
beneath the coffee can heats the wax without
scorching or igniting it.

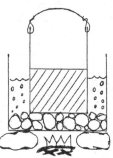

    A double boiler can also be used to melt
and refine fat for making soap, or to melt
resin for use as glue, etc. After melting,
pour and filter into a clean container.
I make a filter by removing both ends from an
empty can and wrapping and tying wire screen
over the bottom end. Wildflower, CT, Oct.90

With flames or candles, always have a fire extinguisher handy.
    I found out the hard way that a WD-40 can is a happy
camper's nightmare if punctured near flame. Eugene, Jan 1993

(Comment:) I recommend thinking in advance about simple AND
RELIABLE ways to cope with a fire in various situations.
    I recall once (in a bus at a gathering, not in a tent)
seeing a frying pan catch fire. On the wall near the stove
was an impressive-looking fire extinguisher. It was applied -
and didn't work! Quickwittedly, someone grabbed the pan and
carried it outside. Nothing got burnt except some bacon.
    Most small fires can be smothered with a towel (prefer-
ably damp) or rug or any heavy garment. If outside, a few
shovelfuls of dirt may suffice. On an oil/grease fire, soil
or garments is better than water. Water may splatter it.
    With any flammable fluid (many lubricants, solvents,
paints), best not use it in any enclosed space, even if no
flame. Static electricity could ignite it. Holly & Bert

If your car burns oil, use synthetic oil.
    It doesn't smoke, which will save you hassles by the
'clean air police'. Mobil One is now down to about $2.
    If I need a vehicle and come across a good-running older
vehicle, I buy it. It has been running good to last this
long and thusly may keep running. My last vehicle was a '71
Toyota Corona Delux. I paid $200 for it and drove it 26
months. One day it just quit running while going down the
road. I sold it for $50 (and had 30 callers!). I got a $575
'74 Ford pickup. It runs good, and hauls my trailer too.
Insurance is only $107 for 6 months. It has a 302 and is
easy on the gas. David French, South Dakota, December

Don't go to jail for old traffic violations.
    Judges jail people who have priors on the books. With a
little effort, priors can be erased. Write to your state
motor vehicle department for a listing of traffic-violation
courts that still have charges against you. Al Fry, ID, Febr.

drawing
is by
Amanda
Lewis,
Minx
Comix

March 1994

Dwelling Portably
P.O. BOX 190-FFF, Philomath, OR. 97370

$1 per issue

Trailer useful for storage - and living in.

For $400 I bought a 25 ft trailer. I gutted it except
for the bathroom. Originally I got it for storage, it being
much cheaper than a rental storage. However, the first year
I used it for 5 months during summer as a base to come home
to while camping around the area. Savings in rent and utilities more than paid for the trailer.

Now I live in my trailer full time. I have propane for
heat, a solar panel for electricity, and a large queen-size
bed for comfort. The bed is built 25" above the floor so I
can store almost 40 12x12x12" boxes underneath.

Used construction-office trailers can be had for $500-
$700. They are not filled in like a regular travel trailer,
letting you build inside what you want.

A 5 gal tank of propane lasts about a week. I use it
mostly for heating.   David French, South Dakota, December

Suggestions for washing.

I bathe about once every 3 days. I put 3 gals of water
in a 5 gal bucket. I heat up 2 gals of water on my propane
stove and add it to the 5 gal bucket. I use a cup to pour
the water slowly over my head. I wash my head and use the
suds to wash my body. I use biodegradable soap - Dr. Bonners.
This system has worked well for me for 1½ years.

About once every two weeks I go to a truck stop to use
their shower. For only $1 I get a hot shower one hour long.
Most truck stops I've seen have showers. I've used them when
bicycle touring too.

Instead of WASHING my clothes every time, often I just
rinse them. This extends the time between washings by two or
three times, and saves on soap too. To rinse, I put them in
a 5 gal bucket, fill with water, mix them up with a broom
handle. I then let them sit over night and ring out the next
day. I've been doing this since 1984.

If you can find old silver spoons, buy them. The silver
kills germs. So, to clean, I just wipe off thoroughly.
I have one I've been using for 2 years.   David French, SD, Dec.

Gatherings: experience and recommendations.

I got back from trip south 3 hours ahead of the recent snowstorm - lucky! I was to two regional Rainbow gatherings, one in Florida, and other in Georgia. At both, I encountered "the law"; a lot of nice people; some bozos; and some good memories. Recommendations:

Do come with proper gear, including flashlight and/or lantern, toilet paper, and extra food. Do remember this is held in "primitive camping" areas. Use a light at night on dark trails. Otherwise you might end up lost like some "nightwalkers" did (and they were local people). No matter how dead a plant looks, toilet paper is safer.

Nights get cold. The warmer your sleeping bags, the happier you will be in the morning.

Tools and supplies to bring: water; bulk food for kitchens; extra cookpots; tarps (12x20' and larger); cord and rope; GI folding shovel; bow saw and extra blade; machete (or ax) with file; 5 gallon pails with lids (numerous uses); kero lanterns and extra fuel. "Extra" is better than "not enough".

Leave the pills, drugs, alcohol, and hostile ego at home. Nobody is perfect. Don't expect it.

Do try to help set up, run errands, cleanup! If you pack it in, pack your trash out.

Expect "courtesy checks" by local law as you enter or leave, for valid ID, sobriety, etc. Wildflower, CT, March'93

(Comments:) We generally recommend bringing and preparing your OWN food. Large field kitchens can have problems with diseases - and egos. However, if you will be eating at a kitchen, do bring food or money for them, and help out.

Scrutiny by people who will fine you, jail you or shoot you if you don't do what they tell you to: that I would NOT call a "courtesy check". (Next we'll be hearing about "courtesy robberies" and "courtesy rapes".)

Why should gatherers travel hundreds or thousands of miles, and spend thousands of dollars for fuel and food, enriching local businesses - only to be hassled - or worse? Let's stay away from such areas, and do our gathering where we are welcome, or where no one else is around.

Rainbows are not the only gatherings being harassed. We have heard of arrests at primitive rendezvous for wearing feathers that were FOUND (discarded by the birds). We have heard of fines at sci-fi conventions, completely enclosed in hotel suites, for "indecent exposure" though no one had complained. We have heard of road blocks in resort areas.

Perhaps this is a time to forgo national gatherings (or to hold them in exile), and only gather locally, with people we trust, in areas where we will be alone (and maybe have ham radio link-ups between gatherings).

We have long been supporters of gatherings including big Rainbows (and have gone to quite a few). But we will not go to or encourage gatherings where we must kowtow to the police (or to anyone else). We can find better things to do. H & B

Suggestions for low-impact backpacking.

Avoid popular areas. Avoid holidays and weekends. Travel and camp in small groups. Buy gear in subdued, earth-toned colors. On a short excursion, bring foods that require no cooking. When traveling cross-country, use rocky or timbered terrain as much as possible. Allow right-of-way to horses. Look at and photograph, rather than pick or collect.

Seek ridge-top or timbered campsites (but not near trees big enough to injure if they or their branches fall). Choose well-drained and needle-strewn or sandy campsites; avoid leveling or digging hip holes or tent ditches. Use existing fire rings (or, better, don't use fire). Gather downed, small firewood from timbered areas outside camp; never cut standing trees, living or dead. Stir ashes with water, hand test, then sprinkle aside or bury. Camp, wash, brush teeth and dispose of waste water at least 200 feet from water sources. Wear soft shoes around camp and avoid trampling vegetation. Bury human waste and fish entrails 6" deep and at least 200 feet from drainage areas. Bury toilet tissue with human waste or burn in pit. Camp as quietly as possible so others can also savor the solitude. Leave radios at home. Save bright colors and loud noises for emergencies. Pick up all litter. Pack out non-burnables. (Adapted from "Without a Trace", Pacific Northwest Region USFS, 1985)

Suggestions for more enjoyable trips.

Don't choose it as a time to give up caffeine. Tufts U. Diet and Nutrition Letter, Feb'91, says going off "cold turkey" can result in a severe headache and other symptoms. They advise cutting back one cup every few days. This applies to caffeine soft drinks as well as coffee.

To avoid constipation: drink plenty of water, and eat high-fiber foods such as carrots. Coarsely ground whole wheat is even better. On long drives, take a 10 minute break every two hours and walk around. That will stimulate peristalsis.

Writing "after-action" reports can make future trips more enjoyable. Make it a family or group affair. To stimulate thought, ask questions such as: What went right? What went wrong? What did I take that I didn't use (and will omit next time)? What didn't I take that I wished I'd had? What do I wish I had done differently? Julie Summers, Oregon, 1992

Springing snare needs dry wood.

Many outdoor people are familiar with the springing snare. However, a word of advice. The trigger should be made of hard "dry" wood. Green wood has resin "sap" that can become sticky, making the trigger hard to spring once the animal has been snared. Tim Leathers, FL, May

snare

sapling

ground

I'm experimenting growing vegetables.

Mostly in very poor, gravelly soils. So far I have been successful with various varieties of kale, as well as peas, greenbeans, potatoes, and husk tomatoes. I've also tried many varieties that haven't grown. However, by composting small spots at a time with leaves I gather (and with everything at all compostable), and growing in raised hills, I've found some recent success. The raised hills concentrate more soil in one spot, and also make watering much easier during the severe dry spells we have been having of late. I simply poke a hole in the center of each hill, and pour a jar of water into each hole. I use wood ashes to adjust the PH balance of acidic soils. Last season I got some squash for the first time. This year my hopes abound. Gary R. Cropper, Washington, March

The Dakota hole.

This burns hotter and is more easily regulated than an open fire, due to the air shaft which feeds air from the bottom. If dry hardwood is burned, there is little smoke; and, being underground, the fire is less visible at night.

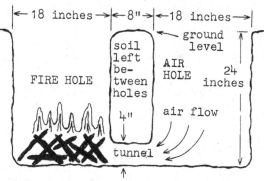

Dig two holes 18" diameter by 24" deep, leaving 8" of dirt between them. Then burrow a 4" diameter tunnel between them.

Build your fire in the bottom of one hole. Regulate the air flow by partly covering other hole. CAUTION: this fire can burn hot enough to ruin a pot. Tim Leathers, TN, May & Dec.

(Comment:) This seems much better than an open fire, yet is simple and without the problems of a wood stove (which is nasty to carry and, if thin metal, soon rusts through). B & H

Some ways to suspend a pot.

Setting a pot on rocks isn't too satisfactory. The pot can slide off and spill, its height can't be changed easily, and refueling the fire under the pot (which is where you want the fire) will be difficult if the pot is in a hole.

With the Dakota hole, I might make slots in the ground on each side of the hole, then place a stick across the hole and in the slots. The slots keep the stick in place. The stick should be stout enough not to burn if the fire momentarily blazes high (and preferably damp or green) and clean of dirt or loose bark (which could fall into the pot if the cover is removed). I would suspend the pot with wire that goes over the stick and attaches to a cord. I tie several loops in the cord. One loop goes over a small stump, a low stub-branch, or a stake. I change the pot's height by placing a different loop over.

Or, I would rig 3 cords to form a Y (if seen from above), tying them out to trees. The cords join in a ring above the pot. The wire/cord from the pot goes up thru the ring and then outward, and one of several loops hooks over a stub branch. This allows pot to be raised completely out of hole.

For suspending a pot above an open fire, Julie Summers suggested (in June'84 MP) a tripod and hanger stick, which allows the pot to be moved sideways (by moving the tripod) as well as up or down (by placing a different crotch over the joint of the tripod - see pic on next page). However, with some solar cookers and maybe with the Dakota hole, the tripod would be in the way unless very large.

With any system, rig the pot before lighting the fire. Bert & Holly Davis, Oregon, April

Some alternatives to campfires.

In the media, an open fire is supposed to indicate outdoor know-how. But in reality, an open fire may indicate a LACK of know-how. An open fire wastes time, wastes fuel, produces smoke, and may be dangerous. Smoke is bad to breathe - and alarming. Even smoke from a safe woodstove can invite hassles, because it can't be distinguished from a beginning forest fire.

We usually live in well-insulated shelters or mild weather. Only once during the past ten years did we need a fire for warming ourselves. Therefore this article will concern cooking. Alternatives:

Don't cook. While light camping during summer, we often go for days, sometimes weeks without cooking. Instead we eat: raw berries we forage; dry foods we cooked previously, such as popcorn, biscuits/crackers/hardtack, pinole; ready-to-eat foods such as bread or tortillas we buy if camped near cities.

Use barbeque pit in a park. An option when in a city.

Solar cook. Though not possible year-around here, we now often do so in summer - the very time when fires are most risky and alarming. Some proven solar-cookers are cheap and fairly simple to build, and semi portable - light but bulky. (We will soon test another that is very portable.)

Cook on a portable propane stove. We now do so when at a base camp - about 8 months a year. By using insulative cooking techniques (see Sept'84 MP p.5; now part of Feb'85m) we burn less than two 5-gallon tanks per year. Refills cost us $6-$7½ per tank. Be sure to get a stove and fittings that connect to 5-gal tanks (not the little canisters). Some people favor kerosene or gasoline stoves. But propane seems less smelly and may be safer. Principal disadvantage: propane tanks are heavier. But we use too little to fret.

Cook with charcoal. We would if we lived too remote for backpacking propane. We may anyway some day. Charcoal can be made, we've read, by heating wood in a closed but vented container. (By condensing the fumes, wood alcohol and other chemicals can be collected.) We would make charcoal in quantity during the wet season (when no fire hazard) at a site away from our base camp (so no odors there) and near plentiful down wood which we would gather in advance during the dry season and tarp. IMPORTANT: have adequate ventilation with ANY combustion, especially with charcoal because its fumes are odorless (we've heard).

Make a lightweight woodstove out of a 3-or-5-gal metal can (see Jim Burnap's design in Sept'84 MP p.1; now part of June'84m). Or buy a portable stove. Or form a stove or equivalent (eg, Dakota hole) out of earth. Compared to an open fire, a stove is easier to ignite, needs less tending, burns hotter, can burn damper wood, produces less smoke, uses less wood, and is safer. The smoke outlet should include a metal screen to stop sparks.

If necessary to build an open fire when the woods are dryish, the safest place is probably close by a creek in the bottom of a narrow canyon, where the ground is wet and the air calm. Clear surface debris from several yards, pre-soak the soil, dig a pit for the fire, and keep the fire small. The safest time is usually just before dawn when things are cool and damp from dew. Afterwards drench whole area. B & H

A wild salad green that is widely available.

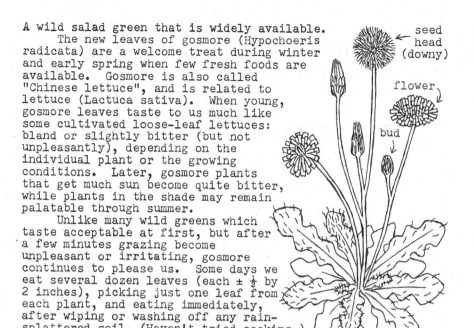

The new leaves of gosmore (Hypochoeris radicata) are a welcome treat during winter and early spring when few fresh foods are available. Gosmore is also called "Chinese lettuce", and is related to lettuce (Lactuca sativa). When young, gosmore leaves taste to us much like some cultivated loose-leaf lettuces: bland or slightly bitter (but not unpleasantly), depending on the individual plant or the growing conditions. Later, gosmore plants that get much sun become quite bitter, while plants in the shade may remain palatable through summer.

Unlike many wild greens which taste acceptable at first, but after a few minutes grazing become unpleasant or irritating, gosmore continues to please us. Some days we eat several dozen leaves (each ± ½ by 2 inches), picking just one leaf from each plant, and eating immediately, after wiping or washing off any rain-splattered soil. (Haven't tried cooking.)

Gosmore is also called "false dandelion", and is related to dandelion (Taraxacum officinale). Like a dandelion, gosmore starts as a rosette (flat, circular cluster) close to the ground of pinnately-lobed-or-toothed leaves with milky juice that are basal only (none on the flower stalk); then produces yellow blossoms which mature into downy seeds spread by wind. But gosmore leaves may be hairier ("cats-ear" is yet another name) and the flower stalks are tougher, often branched, and can grow taller (up to 2 feet).

One more look-alike relative of gosmore is hawkbit (Leontodon nudicaulis). It often grows with gosmore and we may have foraged them together without distinguishing them.

All the plants mentioned above, and several others with dandelion-like leaves, belong to the chicory tribe (a botanical subdivision of the daisy family (compositae)). I know of no members that are poisonous. However, at least one more-distant relative is: tansy ragwort (Senecio jacobaea) which also bears yellow daisy-like flowers. But compared to gosmore, dandelion and hawkbit; ragwort's leaves are more divided and raggedy, and some leaves are on the flower stalks which often grow taller (to 4') and more branched.

Plants can be most easily identified while blooming. Patches could be marked then for harvesting later. With an unfamiliar GREEN plant, sample just a tiny piece at first, chew and spit out. If irritating to mouth, reject. If not irritating, wait a few hours before trying more. (Don't do this with mushrooms. Some deadly mushrooms taste fine.)

Gosmore "is especially abundant west of the Cascade Range, from Canada to California; perhaps the most conspicuous pasture and roadside weed during summer" writes Ronald Taylor in Northwest Weeds. Fortunately for us, gosmore is also common on some forested hills in open/semi-open spots, especially on north slopes where the ground was disturbed by logging. Several species also grow in the east, and in Europe to which it is native. Gosmore is perennial, but some species are annual. Holly, Oregon

We eat raw greens AS WE PICK.

We don't collect them to later make a salad, because, unlike some cultivated salad plants such as head lettuce and head cabbage which were bred partly for keeping qualities, most wild greens start wilting as soon as they are picked and produce toxins not found in the fresh plants.

Also, eating one leaf at a time, we immediately taste any unpleasant and possibly poisonous look-alike, which we might not notice if mixed up in a salad.

Very few mammals collect greens to eat later. One that does is the sewella (Aplodontia rufa), a rodent that actually makes hay. But apes and monkeys graze as they go, we've read.
                                                          H & B

Foraging wild edibles saves us much money and time.

We are not purists. When one of us gets to a store (not often), if (eg) cabbage is on sale at 19¢ a pound, we usually buy some - provided we don't have to carry it far before eating it (it's mostly water). But when cabbage is 69¢ a pound and other vegies even higher, or when we are far from stores, we eat only wild greens.

"But you can't survive on just greens - you aren't cows" we hear. "What do you eat instead of potatos?"

We eat rice, popcorn, wheat, corn, oatmeal, flour - all of which we buy. But, if bought in bulk, grains are cheap; and being dry, are light and keep well. Fruits, vegetables and meat are what are expensive to buy and troublesome to keep. So foraging those foods can pay off big. Holly & Bert

Rotting vegetation produces some heat.

Under tent floors or stacked alongside mini-shelters, straw or similar 'rottables' can be more effective than is passive insulation. That is a little-known secret for keeping pipes and water containers unfrozen during cold weather. A few inches of compressed straw above and below the water line will provide just enough heat to do the trick.

If I needed a cheap warm shelter, I'd build a tiny straw or hay-bale shack. Better than a tent any winter day. Al Fry,
                                                          ID, Feb.

Considerations when chosing insulative materials.

In farming areas, hay sometimes gets damp and moldy (not good as animal feed) and can be purchased cheaply. In some cities during fall, huge quantities of leaves can be easily collected from lawns and sidewalks, etc. (Property owners even pay for removal.) But in most woods, leaves are difficult to gather in quantity. Where most trees are conifers, leaves are scarce. But even where plentiful, fallen leaves may be intermixed with bushes, vines and fallen branches.

So, if a material is heavy or bulky, I would use it only if it is easily obtained AND CLOSE to a good camp-site. (Hay bales or leaves are no bargain if you need a pickup to haul them to the mountains, or a rented site to camp near them.)

If leaves ARE abundant and close, I might build a sturdy framework out of interwoven branches, cover that with something to keep fine particles from sifting in (old drapes, often discarded, may be good; plastic is fair but will puncture), pile the leaves over and around (at least a foot thick, preferably thicker - they will compact), and lean more branches to hold the leaves in place. (I haven't done this much.) If rain or snow-melt is likely, suspend a tarp a few inches above (so that moisture in the leaves can escape).

If I plan to live in it long, I would make one side (the side with least foliage) out of many layers of clear plastic to let in light. Bert & Holly, Oregon

Report on Shelter Systems' dome-tent.
　　Ours has been in continuous use for two years, set up in
a shady spot. The cover is still good. The insect net ripped
long ago. The wall seams tend to open up and have to be often
fooled with: we have to readjust the clips before a rain.
　　On the whole, this tent has been worth the cost for us.
The 3 boys use it as a separate bedroom, so that our main tent
is less crowded at night. Gives the parents some privacy.
　　　　　　　　　　　　　　　　　　　　　　　　　　Anne, CA
Our tipi lasted only five years of summer-only use.
　　It was waterproofed (cotton canvas?). Now sticks poke
right through it. Jai Loon, Washington, July

Durable fabric salvaged from no-longer-inflatable building.
　　It was a military-surplus blow-up hospital, which can be
purchased cheaply if the bladders get leaky, but may be
difficult to find. The rubberized nylon usually lasts 15 or
20 years. With a treadle sewing machine, I made a 15-foot
tipi which I use for socializing during summers. Al Fry, ID

Strong fabric can be salvaged from discarded sails.
　　If you happen to be near a sailboat storage area, check
the dumpbins now and then, especially at the beginning and
end of the sailing season. Many boaters replace their sails
every year or two, and the cloth may still be good enough for
resewing into tents or tipis. (Many sails are polyester.)
Discarded tarps and ropes are also found. Wildflower, CT,

Legality of salvaging from dumpsters.
　　Amy Dacyczyn, who phoned several police officials, said
(in The Tightwad Gazette, July 1993), "dumpster diving is
generally considered to be legal with the following exceptions: -- If the container is on CLEARLY MARKED private land,
behind a fence or locked up. However, most dumpsters in
'semi-public' areas such as parking lots are fair game. --
If the discarded items are outside the dumpster they should
not be taken. -- If you make a mess. Leave a dumpster site
cleaner than you found it." A deputy district attorney in
Santa Clara, CA, where many people rummage for high-tech
discards, told Amy: "By putting items in a dumpster, the
companies have abandoned ownership.... The idea that people
are stealing is not a prosecutable case." (sent by Julie)

How to prevent unraveling of synthetic fabric.
　　I pass the edges through a candle flame, which melts the
ends of the threads and sticks them together. When I do this
I wear sunglasses. They prevent the temporary vision loss I
otherwise get from looking into the flame, and might guard
against long-term eye damage. Julie Summers, Oregon, January

How to render canvas tents and bags water-resistant.
　　One method: Measure 3 cups soybean oil and 1½ cups
turpentine. Mix well, then paint on outer surface. Allow to
dry fully before use. Only for articles used only outdoors.
　　Another method: Rub soft wax onto surface of cloth.
What waterproofing do you recommend? Wildflower, CT

(Reply:) In June'87 MP p.11, Dennis reported on "RainCheck",
which worked fairly well on some materials, not others.
　　We often use NON-waterproof cloth as a top tarp, with a
plastic under tarp. (Most waterproofers smelly (and toxic?)).
　　If waterproofing doubtful, pitching a tarp STEEP helps.

Golf cart converted to trail cart.

I found a second-hand golf-bag cart at a yard sale. By removing the bag and adding a surplus military pack-frame, I now have a rugged "all terrain" handcart for bulky items. Wflr

Choosing portable dwellings easy to find places for.

The smaller, lighter and more backpackable your dwelling is, the more places it will fit. On the other hand, the better equipped (and presumably larger) your dwelling is, the further you can live from settlements and the more territory you have in which to find places. What will be optimum?

For a remote over-winter camp, Holly and I may carry in 10 to 20 backloads, which includes much of the food we will eat. For a summer camp, which may be near a city or a good foraging area, we may carry in only two backloads initially (one trip by the two of us), but may add to it gradually.

Width of a structure is more crucial than length, at least around here where forests and brushlands are usually on slopes, often steep. A long, narrow structure (eg, 6x25') can be sited easier than a round or square structure (eg, 12x 12') with the same floor area, because long, narrow terraces are easier to find or to prepare than are short, wide ones. A long, narrow structure will also be brighter, assuming most light comes from the downhill side, and warmer when sunny.

Height is also important, especially if much wind. A low structure need not be as strong and thus can be built lighter. It will also be warmer, at least at night or on a cloudy or windy day. It will also be less visible and therefore less likely to provoke complaints or hassles.

For year-around living in the maritime northwest, our favorite user-built shelter is presently the Hillodge (long description in April'92 DP). In flatish interior desert areas, we might like a Twipi (described in LLL packet), though we have not had much experience with Twipis nor deserts.

For summer-only use, a much simpler and lighter shelter will suffice. If little wind, just bug net and plastic tarp.

Unfortunately, quite a few novices see a big, spectacular tipi, yurt or dome at a gathering or trade show, fall in love with it, and buy it - WITHOUT having a good place to put it. They wind up in a friend's backyard or some farmer's pasture, which usually leads to problems. A big tipi (etc) can be nice at a gathering for a council or concert on a rainy day. But for living in, we much prefer smaller shelters.

If we need more room, we cluster several small shelters. For winter warmth, we live mostly in just one of them which we insulate, and use the others mainly for storage. For a project requiring much space, we erect a temporary tarp - or wait until summer.

Any backpackable structure is easier to site than is any vehicle, except perhaps in some dense cities and intensively-farmed areas which might allow temporary parking on streets but have no unused lands. We don't have experience with vehicles since a little car-camping while traveling, 15 to 20 years ago. But our impression is: the smaller and more ordinary-looking a vehicle is, the more easily it can be parked. Hank and Barb Schultz, MP/DP founders, wrote (in Sept'82 MP p.2) about living out of and sometimes in a pickup with canopy which they insulated (not a big camper).

(In the early 1980s, they also wrote several articles about chosing shelters, which are in the Light Living Packet (or, if you prefer bigger print, set #W). Any later info?)

B&H

Tips for making a comfortable bed without a mattress.
I dig a hip hole that is actually a TRENCH - the whole
width of the bed, so that I can turn over freely. If I have
only a little padding, I place most of it under my hips
because that is where I bear heaviest. Julie Summers, Oregon

Bed and storage in van made from footlockers and plywood.
Living in a van can be a pain for lack of storage space.
I purchased four military-surplus footlockers, covered all
with a piece of 3/4" plywood, topped with a foam mattress.
I now have a comfortable bed with storage space under it.
And, I can easily remove all and temporarily store outside,
if I need to haul bulky items in the van.
Another footlocker I made into a standing storage-locker
with door by adding a few shelves. Wildflower, CT, July

Connecting remote living with city jobs.
My husband goes to the Bay area (a 2½ hour drive) for
two days every other week, to do his gardening jobs there.
He sleeps in his truck, parked at a friend's house.
One acquaintance lives in Oregon and spends every other
week washing windows in San Francisco. Another lives in
northern California and works two weeks per month as a lawyer
in Los Angeles. Anne Callaway, California, June

Cellular phone useful though not reliable.
There is much static and service often cuts off in the
middle of a call, even though we have an auxilliary antenna.
We tried recharging by plugging into a vehicle at night,
but that was inadequate. Now we have a 12-volt deep-cycle
battery that we get charged in town. (Someone goes often.)
The phone is EXPENSIVE to use, but worth it since both
my husband and oldest boy use it to schedule yard work and
odd jobs. Many people won't bother to hire someone they
cannot reach by phone. Anne Callaway, California, June

Gasoline Coleman lanterns are cheaper to fuel but break easily.
The old Coleman-fuel type was more reliable.
By calling the 800#, we get replacement generators fast,
but we would rather they not break. We cope by always having
an extra gasoline lantern. Anne Callaway, California, June

Our James washer works great but is too fragile.
It has broken many times, requiring welding or replacement of parts. We may be partly to blame: our muscleman teen
does the laundry and he overloads the machine. Anne, CA, June

Some rural landfills do not discourage scavenging.
They are like free hardware stores. Al Fry, Idaho, Febr.

Tips for avoiding trouble with rural settlers.
Someone in the southeast wrote that people there tend to
be inquisitive, hostile to unconventional dwellingways, and
likely to call the police. The same is true of some people
in the northwest - and probably everywhere.
Most house-dwellers are too busy working to earn money
to pay their rent or taxes (and to pay for the vehicle they
need to commute to work - etc.), to give much mind to what
goes on beyond their immediate neighborhood. However, SOME
people ARE nosy and, like the dog who didn't want a bone but
didn't want anyone else to have it either, would be hostile to
us if they could, even though we are no threat to them nor do

they covet our lifestyle. We avoid trouble by avoiding them.

We try to look conventional when traveling. Often we
bicycle. Bicycling is common here, else we wouldn't stay here.

We generally avoid any short, dead-end road that has
houses along it. Some people in those houses may be
acquainted with everyone who lives on that road, and will be
curious about anyone else they see repeatedly.

When leaving any road to go into the woods, we do so
where and when we are out of view of houses and motorists.

For long-period camping (more than a few nights), we
choose areas that are not near any road and not easy to hike
through. Generally our areas are steep, tangly or both.
(Western Oregon has many such areas to choose from.) We avoid
areas due for logging or thinning.

At our long-period campsites, we don't build open fires,
keep noisy animals (or any animals), cut down trees, or do
anything else that might attract attention. H & B, OR, April

Various comments on places and dwellingways.

Many people in the east seem to believe that the west is
mostly empty. True, there are large areas with almost no
people. But these are mostly deserts. There are such areas
in EASTERN Oregon (far from where we are), in much of Nevada,
and in parts of CA, AZ, NM, UT, WY, ID and other states.
But to find large WOODED areas that are unpopulated, I
I believe you must go to Alaska or northern Canada.

WESTERN Oregon is not trackless wilderness. On the
average it is as heavily populated as are most eastern states.
Though it has many unsettled areas, these are relatively
small (none much larger than 10x10 miles), are traversed by
logging roads, and are surrounded by farms, villages and
some big cities. However, we have portably dwelled here for
15 years without any serious problems. A few times we have
been hassled on roads and in cities (probably less than are
most people because we spend little time there). We have
never been hassled in the woods.

Sometimes we hear from people who would like to live
conventionally (in a house, or at least a large house trailer)
but to do so cheap. Western Oregon does not seem good for
that (at least not where we have been). (For more about western Oregon, including the weather, see April'92 DP p.5.)

We don't know of any place in the U.S. that is good for
conventional dwelling. There are some semi-ghost-towns out
on the plains where houses can be PURCHASED cheaply, sometimes for no more than back taxes. But TAXES there are as
high as anywhere (we've heard) - which may be one reason the
houses were abandoned. (Someone who wants a high-taxed dwelling, had better move somewhere they can make lots of money.)

We have heard of parts of Mexico where land can be rented
or leased inexpensively for trailers ($35/month, Lee reported
in Jan'91 MP p.10). I don't believe a U.S. citizen can BUY
land in Mexico unless married to a Mexican citizen.

Last winter was exceptionally cold and nasty in the east,
someone wrote. The northwest was somewhat milder than usual,
with no heavy snow. No prolonged cold where we were (in the
hills), but the cities (in the valleys) were often colder.
Some days, even in January, were sunny and warm enough by noon
on our south slope to sun bathe (70º?),while the weather radio
reported Eugene still foggy and 28º. Bert & Holly, OR, April

We welcome more reports, especially on shelters and equipment.
Payment: subscription/extension (or ?). What are you
using? In what conditions? How is it performing? May 1994

Dwelling Portably

(formerly named Message Post)
POB 190, Philomath OR 97370

July 1994 $1 per issue   To check/mo under $7, add 50¢

Panniers fit on bicycle along with crate.
The rack on my new bicycle has a metal hold-down spring. Therefore, in the cloth band that joins the two panniers, I recessed the rear for fitting under the spring, and made a hole for the lip of the spring to go through. The tabs attach to the bottom of the plastic milk crate. Some racks are different, so measure and modify accordingly.
Bob Barker, Washington, May

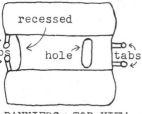

PANNIERS, TOP VIEW
← aft   forward →

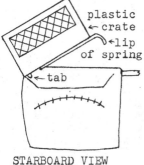

STARBOARD VIEW

I am leaving for the Amazon in two months.
Do you have any advice on rubber boots, mosquitos, etc? A water distiller would be neat. Any suggestions?
I think Stephenson builds the best tents and sleeping bags, and Fabiano the best mountain shoe. For stoves, I think propane is best. Who builds the best backpack and survival suit? George Malben
NV, June

Al Fry's Tipis.
Tipis are fun and tend to draw nice 'real' people to you. But most tipis are temporary playthings: the light-weight cloth turns to sun-rotted rags in a few years.
I use heavy rubber-coated nylon canvas, which is said to have a 20+ year life. I salvage it from surplus military blow-up hospitals. Buying new cloth to make a tipi, would cost much more than what I charge for a completed tipi. 14' diameter is $395 plus $20 shipping. Color grey. I use heavy industrial sewing thread and heavy straps for tie down.
I feel that the 14-foot size is best. Larger sizes are more difficult to set up, heat, carry, and find poles for.
To find your poles, you can go into an area where over-crowding and shade cause trees to grow long and slender. If that isn't practical, use a section of conduit pipe as a joint for shorter pole sections. Measure the pole length to match the tipi height and allow plenty of extra. Using a nail or notch to insure your rope won't slip down the pole, will save a hassle later. 12 poles are recommended for spiritual reasons. The front draft flaps are adjusted through the use of a couple of extra skinny poles - in the traditional manner.
Stake the tipi down or sooner or later you will probably find the wind moved your tipi elsewhere.
If you are going to winter in a tipi, you should insulate the interior with old carpet foam, etc. Running a stovepipe up through the draft hole is a lot smarter than breathing the nasty smoke all winter. Use fiberglass curtains and tin to make a fireproof exit hole for the pipe. For the floor, you can use a layer of plastic topped with rug padding and rugs.
For leaks, use silicon rubber glue and patches to re-sew. If you can't do it with a needle and thread, get a tent-and-awning outfit or upholsterer to. Decorating tipis can be fun and most libraries have books with Indian symbols and tipis. My tipis may have a few designs to cover up glue blemish areas in the re-used canvas. Al Fry, Box 2207, Garden Valley, ID 83622

I sold my boat and moved into an older log-cabin.
   The main reason was insufficient living space on the boat
for me and my 4-year-old son. Also, I have garden space behind
the cabin. Living on the boat was best during summer and fall;
winter was not very comfortable. But I would consider living
on a larger boat. Aarran Rainbow, British Columbia, May

City lacks low-cost housing that is legal.
   When the Centennial Car Camp for Homeless People closes
at the end of May, where are the campers going to go? All
alternatives are either expensive, distant, or illegal.
   Several people plan to move their trailer into a private,
commercial campground 20+ miles south of Eugene. The cost,
$230 per month, is quite low compared to most housing, but not
for someone trying to live on $270 per month disability.
   Others intend to use recreational campgrounds. Most have
stay limits of 14 days and are at least 50 miles from Eugene.
The Homeless Action Coalition and the Forest Service have
prepared a brochure for "homeless and financially distressed"
people, which lists various rules, regulations, helpful hints,
and nearest resources: available at social service agencies.
   The most viable choices are, unfortunately, illegal.
These include: living in a vehicle and parking on the street,
usually in a residential neighborhood; living in a vehicle that
is parked on private property (in a friend's driveway or back
yard, or on rural land); or living in a friend's garage or
storage shed. What makes these choices reasonable for many
people is that the laws are rarely enforced.
   The Eugene Police have a comparatively benign policy:
they don't bother someone who is sleeping in a vehicle, unless
they have been in the area more than 24 hours; and then they
issue warnings, requiring people to move, before issuing
citations. Even less often enforced are the zoning laws,
which regulate how many unrelated adults can live in a building
or prohibit people from living in vehicles on private property.
Literally thousands of people are living in these kinds of
situations. If these laws were fully enforced, the numbers of
"visible" homeless would probably quadruple.
   The local waiting time for subsidized low-cost housing,
is about 2 years for someone disabled; even longer for others.
What can we, as a community do? (1) Support proposals for a
permanent year-around car camp. Although no one likes to see
homeless people "forced" to camp; building, maintaining and
staffing indoor shelters costs 15 times as much per resident.
(2) End discrimination by adding homelessness to Eugene's
anti-discrimination ordinance. Wayne Ford (from Other Paper,
                                                 Spring1994)
Low-cost hay house hassled by city officials.
   Jim Simon and his son live in a house made of hay bales.
The squat one-room building measures 8x15 feet. It sits in
the backyard at 1038 Mason Street in Victoria, BC, surrounded
by poultry and gardens. Simon, 50, has lived here since the
courier company he was managing went out of business in 1991.
   At first he camped out in a tent. But after spending a
"summer in Eden" as he put it, he was not keen on wintering
in the dim and dismal room he could afford to rent on UI.
   So - why not a bale house, similar to what pioneers built
on the praries? $40 worth of hay and two weeks later, Simon
had a home. It was small but it was warm. Best of all, it
was cheap: less than $400 total including the two-by-fours
and plastic sheeting for the roof. And since then, $325 a
month rent for the space.

For shower and toilet Simon visits the main house, but otherwise lives quite independently, cooking on a small propane stove that doubles as a source of heat. A garden hose is coiled beside the camper-size stainless steel sink in corner.

Were he allowed to stay here, Simon had planned to stucco the place and put on a permanent roof. According to a report by the Canada Mortgage and Housing Corporation, hay bale houses are surprisingly resistant to fire if the walls are mortared properly. Some built in NE 90 years ago, still stand strong.

1038 Mason is also the address of Brett Black, known to many as Victoria's urban farmer. In the damp days of spring, his garden is a profusion of green, broken by a purplish splash of flowering rosemary. To many folks, it is a needed reminder of what is real and pungent amidst the asphalt and upward growth. But others find it a little too pungent. City bylaw officer Dan Scoone says he had several complaints from people upset about extra buildings (including a camper and chicken coop) on the property. He told Black to get rid of the straw house. Black says, the city will have to deal with Simon directly. "It's specious, really - when you look at all the illegal suites in town." In 1991, Black had to battle city hall to keep his 100 chickens. He won. But two years later he was battling again, this time fending off a proposal to rezone the property and put up 27 condominiums selling for $109,000 each. Linda Cassels (from Monday Magazine, May 1994, thanks to Aarran)

Hostility of local people prompts camper to leave.
For nearly four years, I lived by myself in a wall tent with a wood stove, and an abandoned VW Minibus on blocks, in the woods on 40 acres owned by a friend in western New York. It was beautiful from May through September, but got pretty cold in winter with -20° wind chills and tons of snow.

For a while I was not bothered much and I did pretty well. Last summer, however, I started to have problems. In August, loggers who were cutting my friend's land, deliberately crushed some of my firewood storage piles. I sued and won $60 in small-claims court. In Sept., another logger who was cutting up the crowns, bent a retaining bolt for the road chain so badly that I had to hammer it to straighten it out and refile the threads to reinstall it.

On December 5th, I came under a hail of gunfire from across a brook ravine about 400' away, from the property of an absentee landlord. Bullets were striking into trees 20 feet from me and I later found some bullet holes in my tent. I got into my car and drove to the nearest pay phone and called the sheriff's dept. Two cars arrived quickly and they flushed out two gunmen who had assault rifles. They claimed they were just target shooting. Though this is considered reckless endangerment under NY law, they were not charged nor were their weapons confiscated. That prompted me to move away, though I may go back. I did win a small claims judgement of $304 against one of the gunmen, and a hearing against the other is scheduled.

Also, whenever I left my campsite, someone would enter the rear of my tent. The front is locked and the sides are staked down, but the rear sod cloth is held down by a 10-foot 2x4 weighted with several heavy rocks. Someone kept removing this though nothing was ever taken. I suspect nosy neighbors and/or police. I interpret all of this as a concerted effort by the locals to drive me out of the area. Lather, NY, May

(Comments:) (1) I would move out of an area before logging. The faller has plenty on his mind (how to drop the trees so they don't smash on each other, and are easy to skid) without also worrying about not hitting my camp. (2) I would not sue for something so minor. If the faller was to blame (he may not have been in this case), I would ask him to fix my wood piles or to pay me to do so. If he refused, the most I might do is circulate a report to woodlot owners in the area, suggesting the faller was incompetent or careless.

Being hauled into court may have infuriated the logger - far more than the $60 damages. The faller probably had local friends. The tent break-ins may have been a search for illegal substances for which they could prosecute Lather. Presumably nothing was found, whereupon they resorted to guns.

General advice: When moving into an area, don't start or escalate a feud with long-time residents. They are probably more numerous and better organized. If someone damages property, don't quickly assume they did it deliberately, and do try to settle directly, without involving police or lawyers.

If, even so, a feud develops, do move. Bert & Holly

Supplies worth storing for barter or personal use.

As money becomes worth less each day, one wonders what to buy now for use or swap later. Some "survival experts" suggest gold or silver. But such metals are useful only if traded for any currency still afloat. Worth stashing for later trade: salt (especially in areas far from ocean); butane lighters (store 10+ years; longer than paper matches); tools (metal files, saw blades, taps, dies, drill bits - in oilcloth in air/water-tight containers); plastic bags and sheets; hot glue sticks; quality duct tape; aluminum foil; candles; soap bars; pens and pencils; paper goods (in vac-sealed plastic); iodine crystals (for disinfecting or water sterilizing).

Items to cache but NOT trade: ammo, powder and primers (buyers might use them on you); food (buyers may raid you later for more); books (even if not used now, future generations may need them; store in vac-sealed plastic); vitamins and pain relievers (if gone bad, may harm customer, resulting in deadly revenge!); spare parts for your equipment; solar electric panels (costly now but later worth more for power-on-tap).

Some guidelines for other items: Is it difficult to obtain even now? Is it difficult or impossible to make yourself now if not later? I know I will be able to salvage metals, plastics and wood from the ruins and abandoned automobiles about the area. But intact equipment or critical parts may be difficult to find. Wildflower, Connecticut, April

(Comments:) We've had vitamin C tablets turn brown (bad?). We now buy pure ascorbic acid powder (Bronson) which seems to have kept well a few years so far. (No experience with other vitamins.) We've had stickem on plastic tape either harden or come off after a few years. (Haven't used duct tape much.) I also wonder about pens. (I'd bet on pencils.) Supposedly most paper contains acid and self destructs before many generations. Better to borrow books and copy onto acid-free paper?
                                                                H&B

A woman walked across the U.S. eating (drinking) only grass.

Her method was to juice wild grasses. (She didn't say which ones. Perhaps any.) The machine is heavy (2 or 3 lbs) but grass juice is very nutritious. You just can't digest the cellulose as can a cow or goat. Also the silica will wear your teeth down. I tried garlic juicers and hammers on grass and found them useless for extracting juice.

I loved the article on gosmore. Tumbleweed, CA, May

Dwelling Portably
(formerly named Message Post)
POB 190, Philomath OR 97370
October 1994 $1 per issue   To check/mo under $7, add 50¢

To join two lines.

This hitch is much faster than splicing, and does not weaken the ropes or cords as much as does an ordinary joining knot.

Testing, I joined two thin monofilaments with this hitch and three times I pulled until one broke. It did not break at the hitch. Whereas a sheet bend reduces the strength to 60%.

This hitch holds even slippery plastic cords, provided they are about the same diameter and stiffness, and reasonably flexible. I do not recommend for stiff, large-diameter monofilament or wire. Another limitation: the big lump formed may jam if the rope feeds thru a block and tackle.

To form, wrap each line around the other five times or so. Then feed each end thru the middle. Work snug.

Some books call this a blood knot. I think of it as a double-ended pipe hitch. Hank Schultz, 1986?

Out of the rent race and into the woods.

When I told my mother about my plan to move out of my Flaggstaff apartment and into a tent, she wept. Her son, the college graduate, was soon to be homeless. "You have no idea what hardships you will face," she said. She was right. Until then, my only camping experience was a few weekends as a young Boy Scout. Nonetheless, I was determined. At 27, I was an aspiring writer whose biggest problem was simply finding time to write. I figured that if I didn't have to pay rent, I could spend less time working at a "real job" and more time working on my not-too-profitable writing.

Environment was another concern. My tent, unlike conventional dwellings, would be constructed and put in place without the need to cut down any trees. Also, living in a tent would force me to use less water, gas and electricity.

In August 1992, I sold most of my possessions, put a few things in storage, bought a tent, a sleeping bag and some other gear, and put my theory to the test. I pitched my flimsy little tent in the woods near Northern Arizona University.

Every morning, I packed up my tent and stuffed it, along with all my other camping gear, into the four large saddlebags on my mountain bike, trusting the tiny locks to deter thieves.

I spent most of my days at the library, where I could plug in my portable typewriter instead of relying on costly batteries. Later, when I found out about the university's computer lab, I sneaked in and did my writing on a computer.

In September, I began driving a school bus part time. To shorten my commute to the bus barn, I moved my campsite to a spot in the woods just east of town along a quiet stretch of Route 66. At this secluded spot, I left my tent set up even when I was gone all day, as I often was. I spent many of my off-duty hours typing or reading in the warm employee lounge at the bus barn. My evenings were often spent on a bench in the mall, my typewriter on my lap.

As winter approached, I invested in a slightly larger and much sturdier tent. I also bought a warmer sleeping bag, which when wrapped around my summer bag, helped keep me warm on sub-zero winter nights. When I was not in my sleeping bag, my propane lantern, hanging in the center of my tent, kept me surprisingly warm. Of course, the use of any gas (or other combustion) appliance within an enclosed space is extremely dangerous. I kept my lantern at least a foot from anything that might burn, and left the roof vent open to avoid asphyxiation. * I also kept a fire extinguisher in my tent.

The cold was just one of the challenges. Winter storms, some with winds gusting to over 40 mph, might have blown my tent away but for its wind-shedding shape and the many pounds of gear inside. Heavy snows were also a threat. When falling copiously, every few hours I went out and brushed the tent off to avoid being crushed. Later, I strengthened the tent by attaching guy lines to several surrounding trees.

Riding a bike in the snow was another challenge. However, I found that as long as the snow was not too deep for automobiles, it was not too deep for a healthy man on a bicycle. Fortunately, I was near a road that usually was among the first to be plowed. But getting my heavy bike from my tent to the road when the snow was knee-deep, was a struggle. Often, I simply stashed my bike behind some trees near the road.

One benefit of the snow was that I could always tell whether anyone had visited my campsite while I was away. Only once did I find the telltale tracks of a stranger, who got to within 50 feet, where my tent was clearly visible, before turning around and retracing steps. The only theft, of a shovel and small propane tank, happened weeks later, after the snows had melted and heavy rains had washed away any tracks.

Although my friends knew about my homeless lifestyle, I was careful not to tell my co-workers. They might not understand. I might even lose my job. What would parents think if they learned that homeless men were driving school buses.

To keep clean, I often used showers in university locker rooms. Sometimes, I paid for a shower at an RV camp or youth hostel. Occasionally, I would shower at a friend's place. To keep in touch, I rented a post-office box and a pager.

I made it through the entire school year without losing my job to paranoia. Over the summer, I found a new job across town, and have moved my campsite closer to it.

Though I have not achieved much success as a writer, I am having too much fun to pack up my tent. The only thing that might prompt me to, is the realization that few women take a homeless man seriously. But then, few women took me seriously even when I lived in an apartment. In any case, I'm hoping there is a woman out there somewhere with Helen Keller's outlook on life: "Life is either a daring adventure, or nothing."
Dan Frazier (shortened from The Arizona Republic, 9 Dec 1993).
　　　　　　　　　　* I never slept while lantern on.
I am looking for people who want to live along a river.
　　Preferably somewhere with a hot springs. I have a tipi.
Lisa Armstrong, Arizona, June

I need an inexpensive temporary shelter for a few years.
　　About 400 sq ft. What tents or domes do you offer? Alan,
　　　　　　　　　　　　　　　　　　　　　　CA, August
I have completed my first year in a yurt.
　　I am very interested in what works and what doesn't.
　　　　　　　　　　　　　　　　Robert Sanders, NM, Aug.
Where to go and what to do.
　　After high school I took a year off to figure that out.
I discovered that I do not want to conform to the "get a job, pay the bills, and die" mold. I am looking for contacts with other young people who have been able to resist the brainwash.
Tanya Vincent, Nova Scotia, June

I made a strong, light-weight tent pole for bike touring.
I have been using it for five years. It consists of three
sections which join together. Each section is 16" long, of ½"
schedule-40 PVC pipe. I plugged the bottom end of the bottom
section so it doesn't sink into the ground. I put union fittings on the other two sections for joining the sections.
I drilled a hole in a cap and installed a bolt 1½" long
¼" diameter with threads sticking out. Then I glued the cap
onto the top end of the top section. The bolt fits grommets on
tarps and tents. When disassembled, I keep the sections
together with a velcro strap. David French, SD, July

Mr Tuffy tire liners nearly eliminated bicycle flats.
I have gotten only 3 flats in 5 years. One was from a
thorn in the side of the tire, another from the inside due to
an old tube, and the third from a staplegun staple. D. French

Many states now have less money for game wardens.
Also for park rangers and other state officials, according to friends who camp. The result: less chance of harassment and more peace of mind for people living or walking in
these mountains, including the Ozarks in n. Arkansas and s.
Missouri, the whole state of Tennessee, and North Carolina,
Kentucky and West Virginia. Also, no reports of gun-happy pot
growers shooting at campers. (They are learning!) Tim Leathers
TN, Sept.

Are second-hand yurts available?
Or has anyone built their own from sapling wood or
scraps? In an old DP I read that Anne Callaway in CA built a
yurt. I would like to correspond with her, or with anyone
with info on yurts. While in OR this winter, we visited the
yurt builders near Eugene. New yurts seem expensive to us.
We have lived in various tents and vehicles in cities and
wilderness areas; a couple of summers in canoes in Alaska (we
will do more of that), and a couple of winters in Mexico.
Now we are living in ne Washington part of the year. We
bought some land because I am an avid gardener, and the
community garden seemed befret with politics and petty bicker-
ing. But we have refrained from building a permanent dwelling.
We live in an old Airstream trailer when necessary. Pat Evans,
WA, July
I have been looking for yurt plans for years.
I notice that Anne Callaway built a yurt using Chuck and
Laurel Cox's plans. Where can I obtain these? Frank Stephenson
VA, June

More van living, travel and working in the east.
At the resort in Georgia where I had worked, the owner
got greedy, wanting too much for rent. So in April I left.
Driving northward, I slept overnight in a truck stop, and
showered outside in a secluded campground, using my sunshower.
I drove the 100-mile-long Skyline Drive thru Shenandoah
National Park. Entry $5, speed limit 35 mph, and campsites
$10 a night. But beautiful scenery, especially in VA, despite
the rain and cold. I saw many deer and groundhogs, all tame.
Then came Murphy's Law: a flat tire, a clogged carburator
and a shorted condenser. Not expecting trouble with my new
engine, I had left all my spare parts in GA, so had to buy some.
Toll booths, at least in PA, now check that seat belts
fastened, ask for ID, and check tires for wear, etc.
Upon arrival in NY state, I became extremely ill, either
from apple seeds I had chewed (I usually swallow whole) or from
water out of a brand new garden hose (which tasted awful but I
swallowed some before noticing). I needed 4 days to recover.

Some old friends said they could not find work. Nonetheless, I was offered my old job back, with a raise, starting immediately. Typically, I do great in a new place until I get a negative attitude, usually from other people.

I am working on the landscape and also do a little of everything: pressure clean, recycle beer bottles, wash dishes, clean up, carpentry, etc. I think the owners prefer someone who will do all kinds of work. I usually work 8 AM to 6 PM.

The owners gave me permission to park my van behind the restaurant. It was a great spot, off the main road and complete with a spring. However, cops came around 9 PM and told me camping was illegal. Rushing to move in the darkness, I got stuck. The same cops returned at 10 PM and helped me get unstuck. They only checked my tag, which was current. They must have known my GA drivers license had been suspended because they did not ask for ID. They searched my van and found a pipe containing half a joint of pot which they dumped out. They implied they knew all about me, but said I was a "nice enough guy". I said I would not be any trouble. The cops said they had hassled me only because a neighbor, 100 feet away, had complained - twice.

In retrospect, I had felt too secure at my site and had shown obvious signs of camping, such as hanging my laundry out to dry. If I had been as clandestine as I usually am, I think I would have been okay. Also possibly, I could have met the neighbor immediately and maybe made friends.

Now I park in the parking lot, shower upstairs from the restaurant, and hang my laundry INSIDE my van even though drying takes longer. I have been laundering in a 5 gallon bucket. For an agitator I use a ski pole that has a plastic thing on the end. I tie 18" pieces of strong line to my buckets for more easily drawing water or tying onto branches.

I get to eat free at the restaurant. The only expenses I expect are batteries for my radio and postage stamps. I will use my bicycle for local transport.

I ran an extension cord to my van to operate a light, heater and radio. Most evenings I write letters and listen to shortwave. (One night I heard someone named "Wildflower" call a talk show. I wondered if the same "Wildflower" in DP.) Though only 50 miles from New York City, the moon and stars here are beautiful. Eugene Gonzalez, NY, October

We have been living in our home-made pickup-shell.
Also, house sitting when phriends are away, and just winging it. Stevyn & Kelly Prothero, Iron Feather, CO, June

My wife and I were almost ready to start living in our van.
And possibly land squat in Oregon or n. California. But a legal problem took much of our money. Also, we are expecting our first child in Feb. We are not giving up; we will just have to wait until we save a little money.

We are vegetarian and non-authoritarian. Do you know any families we might hook up with? Tree Frog, California, August

I am thinking of moving into a 26' travel trailer.
Instead of paying apartment rent, I would be putting the money toward owning something, plus have the mobility.

Although my little Toyota pickup won't tow the 4200 lb Airstream I am considering, I figure I can locate a tow vehicle when I desire to move it. Jim Wirth, California, September

Trailer living, travel and working in the west.

In Sept. 1992, my partner and I sold almost everything we had accumulated (a HUMONGOUS moving sale!) and bought a 32-ft travel trailer and an older (1976) truck with guts enough to tow it. Since then we have traveled in OR, NV, ID, AZ and UT. Sometimes we have made enough bucks to allow us the luxury of a small, cheap RV park; sometimes we've gotten by on ingenuity.

We lived on the east slope of Donner Pass (10 miles west of Reno) at 6900' altitude, during the worst winter the place had seen in 20 years (and trailers ain't insulated worth a damn). Some mornings were 28° INSIDE. We refused to waste propane heating the trailer while we slept.

Next we went to eastern Oregon at Malheur National Forest where I got a caretaker position at a summer conservation and scout camp for the season. It meant free rent and electricity and free meals (we are vegetarians).

From there, to Idaho. McCall is very pretty but it is a tourist spot. Deb got a fine job as Director of Nursing at a nursing home, but the administrator made the job too stressful.

Off we went again, this time with no job prospects. We stayed in Kingman AZ for awhile and really liked the high desert. But employment didn't materialize. Prescott AZ is very nice, but becoming overpopulated since a major magazine named it THE most desirable place to retire IN THE U.S. The cost of living wasn't too bad, but Deb found herself in another intolerable working situation.

Our next stop was Panquitch/Bryce Utah: very pretty country there close to Bryce Canyon. Great hiking and photography. We lived a month in a small RV park until it became obvious we would not get hired in that area unless we became Mormons. Running low on funds, we moved to a free campground while learning of job opportunities elsewhere. I hooked up a single solar panel (bought in Prescott) to light the trailer inside. We lived there April and May. Because of the 8000' elevation the Forest Service would not turn on water until mid June, but we found a wonderful spring. We showered every other day using our solar shower bag. Showering outside was fairly comfortable SOME TIMES. But many mornings were under 30°, and many afternoons the wind would pick up or clouds would accumulate. Often we had thunderstorms. There was no sewer hookup, and to avoid using our toilet and holding tank (odors inside even the newer units can be annoying), we would dash for the pit toilets not far from our site. Astonishingly often no other campers were there, even on May weekends, when many days reached the mid 70's. Utahns must be awful wimpy. But that allowed us to sunbathe nude without offending.

Now we are almost full circle from where we started near Donner Pass, except we are 44 miles farther east and 2000 feet lower. We are at an RV site at Pyramid Lake, on the Paiute Native American Reservation, and we are hooked to the grid. All utilities (except the small amount of propane we use) are included for $150 a month. And we have the view of a 21 x 9 mile lake surrounded by some pretty high peaks. The lake temperature is about 70°, great for swimming. Deb has a $40,000 per year position with a non-profit home health care corporation. I am caring for all else in our lives. I write environmental and human interest stories for publication, and am still seeking employment. We expect to stay here until we get some old debts/obligations paid off. Then we will once again be seeking a place in the woods where we can live with the land in a more native-like style. Wayne Packwood, NV, July

I once believed I would lead a "van revolution".
     With the restrictive housing and building codes, it may
be that portable housing is the only answer for those who do
not wish to devote their lifetimes to their housing needs
                                        Charles Wilson, VA, Aug
I seek tips for living cheaply in a small roomette.
                                        Dave, Quebec, Aug.
Much land is vacant and suitable for microhouses.
     Many churches own land surrounding their structures which
could hold small temporary buildings called "microhouses".
The church would provide basic utilities while the microhouses
provide shelter. Any unused space could be gardened.
     With shelter, food and basic sanitation needs met, people
could then seek productive work as well as help the church with
everything from cleanup to fund raising. A win-win action.
     To build microhouses, materials can be donated or recycled
from construction leftovers, and labor volunteered by seniors,
unions and other groups. Young people as apprentices could
learn useful trades. Examples of other places and uses:
     An older couple builds a microhouse in their backyard as
a hobby shop. Later, crippled by arthritis, they are cared for
by a young mother with 2-year-old who lives in the microhouse.
     In a small town, the owners of a big lot put a microhouse
on it for an elderly former farmer who tends their garden.
     A father laid off from his middle management job, does
appliance repair in his backyard microhouse. As business grows
he builds another microhouse for a part-time helper.
     My vision of the future: Instead of millions of people
homeless, I see many microhouses in backyards, woods and
forests - and everywhere there is a small space and some love.
What would bring this about? Just the willingness of good
people to build a simple shelter and make it available to those
in need. Bill Kaysing, Holy Terra Church, PO 832, Soquel CA
                                        95073;(408)4624176
(Comments:) Microhouses will be more acceptable if they are
portable - easy to move if an arrangement does not work out.
Also, portable microhouses can be taken into forests without
constructing driveways (which disrupt soil and trees).
     If the whole microhouse is too big to carry easily, I
would assemble it by bolting or lashing together sections that
ARE small enough to hand carry over steep or rough ground.
     I assume microhouses would have many different designs
using whatever materials are abundant locally: eg, straw huts
in hay-growing areas; adobe or cob where there is good clay;
wickiups along willow banks; pole frames in those woods where
there are many skinny trees. However, one general point:
     Most small cottages, trailers, and large tents we have
seen, tend to be imitations of big houses, with little windows
on every side. All these windows not only complicate construction, but most of them usually face trees or other buildings,
making them almost worthless for illumination. And the one or
two windows that do face sky are too small to admit much light.
     Instead, make ONE wall mostly window, at least from knee-
height up, and face it toward the most open sky. Build all
other walls solid. Big houses need many windows because they
have many separate rooms. Little houses don't.
     For economy, light-weight, insulation, and no breakage,
the window could be formed from several layers of clear
plastic. For UV resistance, use plastic sold for greenhouses.
Such a window can also serve as door and vent. Use rubber
straps to hold the lower corners down and to sides. Open simply
by raising the plastic. Easier and safer than doors. B&H, OR

Candle lantern easily made from plastic jug.
Cut off the upper portion of a one-gallon
milk/juice/water jug, leaving handle intact.
Place short candle (2" to 4" long) in
jug, centering it beneath the opening. Add
gravel, sand or dirt one inch deep around
candle to hold it upright. Tilt and gently
shake the jug to make sure the candle will
stay upright. (If it doesn't, add more gravel,
pack dirt firmer, or use a shorter candle.)
This lantern can be set on the ground or
carried about. Usable even in light wind,
because the jug shields the flame, and the
gravel weights the jug. The gravel also protects the plastic
bottom when the candle burns down. Wildflower, CT, 1993

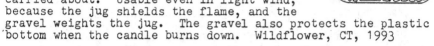

(Comment:) We wondered, if the jug was tilted would the flame
melt or ignite the plastic? But we used it several times with
no problem. (Compared with a different lantern on page 5) H&B

For storage of long items, consider PVC pipe.
It is widely available in diameters up to 4", and with
some hunting (at irrigation or building supplies) as large as
6", maybe even 8". (Common length is ten feet?) Put a glued
waterproof fitting on one end and a screw cap on the other.
PVC pipes cannot be sensed by metal detectors, provided
you don't store metal items in them. (If you do, consider
planting diversionary stashes of scrap metals.) Jon Seaver, MI

Desirable features if buying a travel trailer.
Two axles provide better load distribution; and a flat
tire won't dump the trailer sideways. Common-size car tires,
14 or 15 inch, are cheaper and easier to replace than special
trailer tires. 18 to 25 feet long: the smaller the trailer,
the easier it maneuvers, and the less wear on the tow vehicle.
If you gut the interior, you can build in a very efficient
use of space. (For that, I'd look for a trailer that is extra
cheap because damaged or shabby inside.) Otherwise you are
stuck with the tight fit of the original floor plan.
Add a photovoltaic solar panel for electrical freedom.
I have a pickup and a 25-foot travel trailer in which I
have been living since 1989. David French, South Dakota, Dec.

More about the Baja California border area.
A few miles north of San Felipe, 75 x 100' lots can still
be leased for $35 per month; for parking a trailer or building
a cabin or house. Though you can sell your structure, the land
still belongs to owner. Lease renewable every 10 to 30 years.
There are great buys on big old trailers and houses along
that coast: $3000 plus lease. Water can be bought from trucks.
Summers are very hot and humid with sand storms, salt, no
shade. If you go away, robbers break in and take booze, money
and food, but not items needing electricity (which they lack).
Beware of El Dorado where everyone "wins" a piece of land
with a country club on the beach. You will be miles from the
country club on crummy land where they want you to build house.
Many people buy prescription medicines in Mexico at great
savings, without border hassles. The California Pharmacy in

Algondonas, just across from Yuma AZ, can provide prescription.
  I now go to Mexico only during days: for dental work, $5
blankets, and great street tacos. I've never gotten sick eating
Mexican-style food, but have from American-style food in Mexico
(eg, cake with whipped cream) even in snazzy restaurants.
  You cannot legally work in Mexico doing anything that any
Mexican is capable of doing. The reality is: on a job you get
promised, but may never receive, a work permit. You get paid
and everybody is happy, but no job security. Teaching English
privately is possible. (Only Mexicans teach in public schools.)
                                                   Double Dorje

Vehicular camping near Yuma Arizona/California

  If you have a remote source of income such as retirement
or disability benefits, I recommend the BLM's Long Term Visitor
Areas (LTVA). LTVA includes many thousands of acres from Yuma
to Quartzite - even a hot springs (soaking only; no soap).
You can stay in LTVA with only a tent, car and ten-gallon water
tank (fill up free at RV store). Or buy a camper without truck
for $500 and pay someone $25 or $50 to move it. The "Green
Meanies" (rangers) may make you live in specific areas, and are
often arrogant and hostile if they suspect you are poor and,
though camping legally, not there on vacation. $50 per winter.
  Or, the Indians will rent you space on the bank of the
American Canal for the price of a fishing license ($60/year).
Places get broken into if left for the summer, but Christian
Center, about 18 miles north of Yuma on S24, will store
anything on wheels for $10 per month. They generally have 5 to
15 rigs for sale. For more information, ask campers you see;
especially ones with funky rigs.
  A few guys live along the river in the tules.
  Thousands of people are here during winter (7 or 8 months:
Sept - April). Most are old, honest but rigid, and tsk their
tongues at longhairs. Bible belters abound.
  Winter temperatures are typically 65° days; rarely as low
as freezing nights. (Clue to mild winters: date and orange
groves.) Sand storms may last hours or days but are survivable.
Double Dorje, California, December

I recently developed a bikeshelter.
  It consists of an 8 by 10 foot heavy nylon tarp over a
parked and secured bicycle. It can be set up in less than five
minutes with a bike specifically equipped for this: front wheel
brace, kickstand, parking brake, flippable rear basket (my own
design). It withstood a 35 mph wind.
  I plan to use it on long bike tours. The only disadvantage
- it looks 'dorky' and I may be snubbed by some cyclists with
high-fashion high-dollar stuff, who sleep in $200 one-person
tents while leaving expensive superbikes out in the rain.
  Another improvisation is a face shield for nasty weather
made from a 2-liter vinyl bottle which attaches to my helmet
visor. I have spent 9 years learning how to use non-bike gear
with bikes, including military surplus, ag items, and household
stuff; and found that I don't need expensive equipment to enjoy
bicycling. Randy Wyatt, Backroads Bicycling, Kansas, December

General rules for easier and safer trekking.
  The path of least resistance is usually safest and fastest.
Follow a path instead of breaking trail. Go around instead of
over. But also know when to go the hard way.
  Cliffs are too dangerous. Usually there are ways around.
  If you must cross a river, do so where the water is wide
and shallow. When I have to wade, I probe each step with a

stick. Even in slow-moving clear water, depth can be deceptive.

A raft can be improvised from two or more inner tubes lashed together with poles and covered with blankets or tarps. When not in use, deflate the innertubes by removing valves from the valve stems; then put valves back in and cap.

Crossing frozen water is best avoided. On running water, ice is thinnest and most risky in the middle of the river.

I prefer to travel from daybreak until noon or two p.m. People notice me less then, because either they are not up and about or else are busy. Also, this allows me ample time to set up a comfortable camp, forage, do chores, and play.

To travel and not be seen is almost impossible. However, to be visible but not noticed is quite easy. In populated areas, I wear the customary clothing, am clean and neatly groomed, and maintain a happy face with a bright smile and kind word. If a busybody confronts me or questions me about my presence, I keep walking while maintaining an ongoing chatter about anything. That soon discourages them. Guy Hengst, Ind.

Bivying in snow country.

A snug shelter can often be made at the base of an evergreen tree that has broad low limbs. Under the tree the ground may be bare, while beyond the tree snow accumulates. A snow bank a foot or two deep will normally turn the wind and blowing snow. Such spots may be 20° warmer than are exposed areas. Guy

A naturally warm-and-cool shelter that needs no poles.

The Snugiup is a small enclosed dugout formed entirely of earth and plastic. Thus it can be built even in areas that lack timber such as deserts and brushlands.

The roof and front wall are insulated by air spaces between the layers. The other three walls and the floor are mostly soil, and act as natural, automatic heaters-coolers; absorbing heat on warm days and giving it back during cold spells. In western Oregon winters: when occupied, inside is typically 65°; seldom below 50° even when 15°F outside. (We've not had any weather colder than that to test it.)

The roof is flush with the ground, which minimizes wind forces and facilitates concealment.

The roof will not support much snow, but may allow snow to slide off, depending on steepness of roof and the type of snow.

Materials cost $10 to $20. Erection requires an hour or so, NOT counting site preparation which may take several days (but can be done in advance of use).

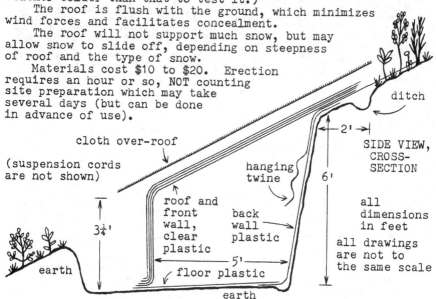

ditch

cloth over-roof

(suspension cords are not shown)

2'

SIDE VIEW, CROSS-SECTION

hanging twine

6'

all dimensions in feet

all drawings are not to the same scale

roof and front wall, clear plastic

back wall plastic

3¼'

5'

earth

floor plastic

earth

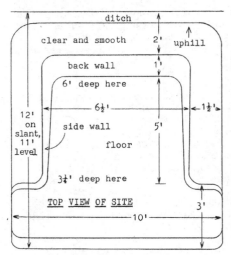

```
              ditch
       clear and smooth    2'  uphill
      ┌─────────────────────┐
      │   back wall      1' │
      │ ┌─────────────────┐ │
      │ │  6' deep here   │ │
12'   │ │ ◄──6½'──►  ◄─1½'►│ │
on    │ │side wall     5' │ │
slant,│ │  floor          │ │
11'   │ │                 │ │
level │ │ 3¼' deep here   │ │
      │ └─────────────────┘ │
      │  TOP VIEW OF SITE   │ 3'
      └─────────────────────┘
          ◄──────10'──────►
```

Suggestions for building a Snugiup.
  Construction is easiest on a steep
slope. For winter, a south-facing slope
will be brightest and warmest. For
summer, an east-facing slope will warm
during mornings and cool during afternoons. An ideal site has much foliage
overhead, but little foliage downhill.
  The Snugiup's walls require firm soil
that will not collapse. Avoid soils with
much sand or gravel. Roots are desirable
for reinforcement though they will slow
digging. Digging is usually easiest
when the soil is somewhat moist. Early
spring may be a good time to prepare a
site for use the following winter; and
allows time for soil instability to
maybe show up. CAUTION: build and live
in a Snugiup (or anything) at your own
risk! We make no guarantees and assume
no responsibilities or liabilities.
  For a site also consider: can the dirt
be disposed of easily and inconspicuously
  The illustrations assume a uniform
slope that rises one foot for every two
feet level distance. Most slopes don't.
Furthermore, less digging is needed where
a depression or irregularity exists.
Therefore, modify to suit your site.
  To prepare site, clear an area 10 by
12 feet. If much rain expected or if the
soil does not drain well, shallowly ditch
along the back (uphill) side of clearing.
  Dig out the portion shown. Slant the
walls, especially the back wall, to
reduce risk of slumping. (Don't make the
walls straight up and down.) Round all
corners. Remove any rocks protruding
from walls and tightly pack their holes
with moist dirt. Cut off roots flush
with wall. (Don't try to pull them out.)
  Slope the floor slightly downhill.
If ground water expected, ditch around.
  If the site is left vacant for long,
the walls will be eroded less by frost
or dryness if covered with plastic.

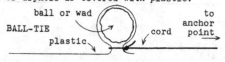

```
            ball or wad
                       ╭────╮
BALL-TIE             ↗        to
                            anchor
plastic         cord     point →
```

  To erect, hang pieces of white or
clear plastic over the walls, holding in
place with ball-ties going to bushes/
logs/rocks beyond the cleared area.
  Hang lengths of twine on the back
wall (for suspending light-weight items
when the Snugiup is occupied).
  Form the roof and front wall from a
piece of clear plastic 10 by 12½ feet.
(If the plastic comes in rolls 10 by 25
feet, simply cut in half.) Anchor with
ball-ties along sides and back. (Do not
put ball-ties along front of roof,
because they would form puddles.) Let
excess length lay on the floor.
  Suspend a second 10x12½ piece of
clear plastic ½" to 1" outward of the
first. If possible, tie its anchor
cords to different bushes than hold the
first layer, so that tension on one
layer does not slacken the other layer.
  Add additional layers as desired for
insulation. (For summer use only, two
layers are probably enough; for winter,
four or more layers may be desirable.)
  Cover floor with plastic. Add rugs,
drapes as desired for comfort or decor.
Entry is by raising the front wall
plastic and ducking under.
  Where not much foliage is overhead,
if shade during summer or concealment
from air are desired, form an over-roof
from appropriately-colored cloth 10½x10½
(need not be waterproof). Suspend it
about 6" above the roof plastic. Put
its front (downhill) edge so as to block
direct sunshine during summer when the
sun is high, but to admit sun during
winter when the sun is low in the sky.
  If extremely hot and sunny, add a
second over-roof of white or reflective
material, suspending it 6" above the
plastic and 6" below first over-roof.
  The Snugiup is small inside: floor 5
by 6 ft; height 3 to 6 ft. Therefore
most belongings must be kept outside in
stashes or under tarps when not in use.

Hints for building a longer dugout.
  If you want the inside bright while
the roof is shaded, the dugout must be
narrow up-down the slope. Make it long
only across the slope.
  Rafters will be needed every few feet
to hold up the roof. Poles supported by
posts may be used. The rafters must go
up-down the slope. (If put crosswise
they would form puddles.) Also will need
strips of carpet, moss or other insulative material to space roof layers apart.
  For more ideas and explanations, see
Hillodge in Apr'92 DP, which is similar
in shape though not as sunken.   Bert

Two candle lanterns compared.
  A lantern made from a 3# coffee can
was described by Paul White in Apr'92 DP.
Advantages: If inside shiny, more light
goes to front. Less light in eyes.
Metal won't melt or burn. Easier carry
(weight directly below hand). Lighter
(no gravel). Shelters flame from rain.
  Advantages of jug lantern on page 1:
Easier to make (plastic softer to cut
and precision not needed). Candle may
be any diameter (whereas can-lantern
needs candle that fits snugly in hole).
Easier to set down (candle not protruding below). Jug includes handle.
  Overall preference: when hiking, can
lantern; at camps, jug lantern.   H & B

Living aboard a boat.

Live on a boat? Don't be ridiculous. Might as well live in a camping trailer - there would be more room. Of course, going fishing in a camping trailer is difficult, but you wouldn't have to put up with the wind whistling through your neighbors' shrouds, the waves rocking your boat, the sea lions barking, and the herons caterwauling after dark.

I have been living on boats since April 1992. This has long been a dream of mine. Fulfilling it hasn't been easy.

Living on a boat is not for everyone. Actually, it's for hardly anyone. For instance, you've got to get used to the thought of being afloat all the time - even when sleeping. Think it would be great to enjoy those cool summer breezes each night? Well it is, except when they become cold, chilly winds in fall and winter - often accompanied by a downpour and occasional gale.

Speaking of winter: ever try to heat a boat sitting in near-freezing water? Very few boats have central heating systems or thick layers of insulation. Most marina slips have inadequate electricity, and few if any have natural gas piped from shore. Many boats are equipped with diesel heaters however, and some even have bottled-gas catalytic furnaces which do a fine job of heating.

Living aboard requires special skills like finding a nook and cranny for all the things you really want and need to have around. Few boats of any size have much free storage, especially hanging lockers (closets to you landlubbers). Don't expect me to wear a different outfit every day: I just don't have the space. Summers I wear nothing but a T-shirt, slacks, and dock-siders.

Enjoy large-screen television? Forget it if you want to live on a boat. Many of the permanent residents of this marina don't even own televisions, but if they do it's usually a small one. Besides, there's no cable service. And many video stores won't rent to someone who doesn't have a street address.

Which brings up check-cashing and identification. My checks are imprinted with my mailing address and telephone number, but cashiers always want to know my street address. When they learn I live on a dock in the bay I start getting those quizzical glances. And the Department of Licensing won't issue a license to a post office box - they want to know where to come and get you.

Live cheaply on a boat? The purchase price of a livable boat starts at around a thousand dollars a foot, and goes up from there. Every year it has to come out of the water to repaint the bottom (at $100 or more per gallon of paint), replace anti-corrosion zincs, and clean barnacles off of the propulsion system. Any wood above the water line must be stripped, cleaned and revarnished - not just for appearance, but to prevent corrosion from the sun and rain. Mooring lines, halyards, sheets and sails must be replaced due to wear and the effect of ultraviolet rays. BOAT is an acronym which means: Break Out Another Thousand.

Last year I noticed an older cabin cruiser in the shipyard undergoing a major refit. It was large, probably 45 foot overall. All the surfaces were stripped down to the bare wood and some planks and ports were being replaced. After many months in drydock it was launched last fall and suddenly appeared at the head of my dock. I watched as a young man and his obviously pregnant wife moved aboard. They were soon joined by a tiny black kitten and a furry Husky puppy - then a brand new baby. They were fulfilling their dream.

Within a few weeks however, a small tragedy struck: the wiring on the boat, inadequate for the demand placed upon it by several electrical heaters, caught fire. The inexperienced skipper, in violation of Coast Guard regulations, didn't have any fire extinguishers on board. Luckily, several Fire Department engines arrived and quickly extinguished the fire. The family moved off of the boat temporarily, and a large pile of singed and smoke-damaged clothing and other possessions appeared on the dock.

The puppy soon grew so large that it could no longer safely lounge on the aft deck without falling overboard, and had to be confined, alone most of each day, inside the enclosed bridge.

One sunny day the young skipper slipped the lines and ventured out into Port Gardner and points beyond, only to return from the expedition with obvious signs of a hostile encounter with a creosote-coated piling. A few days later a "for sale" sign appeared. Apparently living aboard had lost its appeal.

Myself, I live on a boat for many reasons. For one thing, how many people are surrounded by a moat? To get to my boat, one must have a key to the barbed-wire reinforced gate or be willing to swim in the chilling waters. A security guard walks past my boat several times daily, on the lookout for suspicious activity. The parking lot is well lighted and patrolled. The handful of other people who live on my dock watch out for my boat as I do for theirs. When an inexperienced skipper ties his boat up too loosely, someone will step forward to fix it, seeking neither recognition nor compensation.

We are a neighborhood and have interests in common beyond simply a love of boating. We are concerned with the water quality in the marina - after all we live there. Many of us are bird-lovers and environmentalists concerned with preserving the natural habitat of the harbors and wetlands, and especially with enhancing the fish and shellfish population in the bays because we enjoy viewing, gathering and eating them.

My best friends live on other boats nearby. They come over for chili; I go over for coffee. We share meals, boating tips, stories of successes and failures.

Last summer I took a sabbatical to restore my old wooden boat, arising each morning to row my dingy out into the bay to gather crabs or clams, and trolling for trout on the way in. Fresh trout or smelt for breakfast, crab salad for lunch; clam chowder for dinner on stormy days - that's heaven. Each day the sunset seems to out-do itself.

Doug Lewis, © March 1994; Washington

Piñon nuts are nutritious; but robbing pack rats hazardous.

All pines have edible seeds, but nuts large enough to be worth gathering are produced mainly by: Pinus edulis (needles in twos); P.quadrifolia (fours); and P.monophylla (needles singly). They grow in many areas of the southwest.

The nuts are in hard dark-brown shells found within the cone, with one shell under each cone scale. Some shells contain no seeds, and professional pickers have ways to tell.

The seeds are collected in late August or Sept by picking the almost-ripe cones and roasting them to release the seeds. An easier method, if there are not many squirrels, is to simply wait until the seeds fall and gather them from the ground. Not every year does an area have a large crop.

Some people collect pinon nuts from pack-rat dens. However an old Indian legend is confirmed by recent evidence: most people who died from Hanta virus had collected nuts from pack-rat dens. Pack rats commonly get Hanta virus (as do many other rats and mice) and their storage areas are filled with infected feces. Transmission is thought to be by breathing dust from feces. (from Christopher Nyerges, Coltsfoot, Nov'94; and Donald Kirk, Edible Wild Plants, Naturegraph, 1970)

Crawfish are abundant in streams of many areas.

After gathering, I purge them by placing in a bucket with extremely salty water. After a few minutes the crawfish will shit. I then take them out, rinse off, and cook. Tim Leathers

Marigolds are natural bug repellants.

I have found that rubbing marigold blossoms on exposed skin repells most insects very well, and seems to slow down even ticks. A potted marigold of a short variety can be transported easily. Guy R. Hengst, Indiana, September

Selecting clothes and equipment to be inconspicuous.

Choose clothes in styles you can wear daily and equipment you can use daily. And wear and use them daily. You will learn which are useful and which are junk. You will become handy with them. You will replace them when they show heavy wear. And you will always be ready, even on a date.

Camo clothes look very macho, but earth-color clothes in combination blend well, cost less, are less conspicuous when worn on streets, and don't set in closets when you need them miles away. Don't wear white clothes; not even underclothes which are conspicuous when hung to dry. Stores carry jock shorts and T-shirts (etc) in black and dark green.

Carry three sets of clothes: one to wear; one clean; and one to wash, or washed and drying. Sort clothes and gear into bags with different colors and textures, for easy finding in light (by color) or in dark (by feel).

Instead of a bunch of pouches or packs, I wear a fisherman's vest which has about 20 pockets. The weight is better distributed and the bulk isn't as obvious.

Two cheap rectangular sleeping bags, one light, the other medium or heavy, provide three temperature ranges. For cold conditions, put one inside the other. For additional warmth, wear a cap to bed: balaclava is best, and is also a mask - hiding light skin at night. Also wear socks and long jons.

Do not get synthetic sleeping bags. Turning over in them can be heard for half a mile, especially if the enemy has a sound magnifier. Paul Doerr, California, June

(Comments:) Dark clothes also dry faster than white if hung in the sun, because they absorb more heat.

In this climate, cotton sleeping-bag covers and liners soon rot and rip. We prefer synthetics. At a distance their rustle sounds much like foliage, wind and water noises. For military patrols bivying, the noise might be a concern. But for everyday living in the woods, the noise seems trivial compared to other sounds. The most unnatural, distinctively-human noise is metal striking metal: a pot against a stove; a lid or spoon against a pot; a fastener against a pack frame. For stealth, minimize metal (also glass). Carve a wooden pot lid. Use wood or plastic spoons. Put metal tools in separate cloth bags, etc.

Also conspicuous is the human voice. Better to whisper. Very conspicuous is music. Listen only with earphones. H & B

Spotting people from the air is difficult, even with infra-red.
As the National Guard OH-58 helicopter swept over sugar cane fields cloaked in darkness, searching for five escapees who had tunneled out of a Glades prison; the pilot said, that without good tips, spotting someone who doesn't want to be found "is like finding a needle in a haystack."

From 500 feet above the ground, the surreal images the pilots see through their goggles and on two small monitors cover an area half the size of a football field. At that distance, a herd of cattle shows up as white dots on the screens. A person could squat among them and be easily mistaken for a cow. And "a hubcap laying all day in the sun might look suspicious." Flying the chopper costs $140 an hour.

Equipment on the chopper's underside picks up slight temperature differences and converts them into a black and white image. Though it can't show what is inside a house, it can tell if one room is even 3 degrees warmer than another. Monika Gonzalez, Jan (from <u>Directions</u>; and <u>Palm</u> <u>Beach</u> <u>Post</u>)

Defenses against large animals.
The most dangerous animal is man. Next, in my experience, moose (but I've not dealt with grizzlies or boars). If threatened by a moose, keep a sturdy tree between you and it.

If using a stick, staff or spear for defense, keep hold of it and jab, stab or swat - never throw. If alone, I prefer a 6-foot whip in one hand and a 3-foot inch-diameter stick in the other. If with another person, one wields the whip and the other a 4½-to-6-foot staff or spear. Remember to give the creature a way to escape. It almost always will.

At night, the biggest danger may be your own fears. Most sounds are made by creatures you could hold in one hand. To avoid large intruders, camp or bed down in a spot requiring an effort to reach. Be clean and odorless (no garbage), be quiet, and do not allow a light to show. Guy Hengst, Indiana

Preparing sites and simple shelters for winter use.
I lived nomadically for three years in Kentucky around two lakes and one year in northwestern Minnesota. For me, winter was the best season: generally quiet and tranquil, with no flies or mosquitos and with few recreational people about.

The key to easy wintering is preparation. From late spring (after the rains) through early fall (until deer season), while exploring and foraging I also scout and prepare many camp sites and caches to use later.

I find excellent sites along abandoned fence lines, hedgerows, briar patches, and rose thickets. To prepare, I crawl into the thicket and, working from the center outward, cut canes at ground level and push them out until I have a big enough clearing.

Usually I want three chambers: a main chamber with length 1½ times my length, width equal to my length, and tall enough to kneel upright with several inches of clearance overhead; a sleeping chamber slightly larger than the most people that will use it;   an entryway between main chamber and outside.

I set a cache near each site or in the entryway. It typically includes: a complete change of clothes or a thin blanket; matches, tinder and kindling; candles; fish hooks and line; dental floss; ten pounds of unground wheat and two of rice; bouillion; salt; baking powder or soda; sharp knife; fork; a 3-pound coffee can to cook in; at least one tarp. Most of this stuff I get free or for pennies. I store in a 5-gallon (or larger) plastic jug or bucket-with-lid. (Most metal containers disintegrate in one or two seasons if buried here.) I bury with 8" of dirt over the container.

I usually also have two or three large caches somewhere in the area from which I draw most of the year. These are as out of the way and as difficult to find as I can make them. (Yes, once I hid one so well that I never found it.) These hold most of my food, equipment, and seasonal clothing.

When I move to a site, I erect within each chamber a clear plastic tarp, held up by a few saplings which I bend to form arches. Then I lay ground tarps in the main and sleeping chambers, fastening their edges up a few inches to provide fairly waterproof floors.

The only insulation is the thicket itself, and the only heat sources are bodies and candles. A candle or two quickly warms the main chamber, and can heat water to a boil for cooking if not in a rush. I have never built a fire in a shelter. Too dangerous. To reduce condensation and heat loss, I leave boots, outer clothing, and firewood in the entryway and do not heat it. When entering, I close off the outside before opening the interior. I have a second exit.

Frequent moves reduce problems with mice, rats, lice and other vermin; and with becoming noticed by busybodies. Rarely did I stay in one place longer than a week or two. Exceptions: during the fall gun season for deer (the most dangerous time), I stayed down and well hidden for two months; and during the spring rains I stayed put about one month.

During winter, when not raining or snowing I spent most time outdoors: exploring, fishing and hiking about with other people. The exercise generates heat; therefore I wear several layers of lightweight clothing which I remove as necessary to prevent sweating. I take with me: extra clothing; some food; a tarp; and fire makings. (Only once was I cold or worried - 7 miles from shelter in a blizzard that lasted two days.)

Evenings and rainy or snowy days, I spend in a shelter reading, talking, playing, and making stuff. Guy Hengst, Dec.

Tips for increasing privacy and security in the wilderness.
Before choosing a camp site, walk around it from different angles and at different distances. The harder your camp is to approach, the less likely someone will find it. Climb hills, climb trees, scan the area. Consider visibility from the air.
Don't camp in favorable hunting and fishing areas.
Never create paths or leave trails near your camp. Approach your camp from various directions; not the same way each time. Don't let your wandering become routine: stay aware of where you are and what way you are heading.
Be careful not to break limbs, turn over stones, or drop anything. When approaching your camp, move slowly and stop every 20 paces or so to look and listen for anything unnatural.

Think about how you can blend your camp into the surrounding terrain. Camo netting can be bought or made. Cover shiny objects or put them where the sun will never reach them.

Avoid or minimize fires at camp. Large fires are easily seen at night. Smoky fires are easily seen during the day.

Noise such as gunfire, barking dogs or chopping wood draws attention. Do any hunting away from camp and try for one-shot kills. (I prefer to snare or fish.) Rig equipment so it can't make noise. Eg, tie down anything that could blow around.

Having a dog around just for company isn't smart. You have all of the outdoors and the wild creatures to entertain you.

Keep anything valuable or incriminating well hidden. Try burying plastic buckets with tight-fitting lids. Tim Leathers
TN, Febr.

Additional security tips, especially for newcomers.

If new to the wilds, or in a kind of terrain new to you, expect mistakes at first. To minimize the consequences:

Best stay elsewhere during hunting seasons. (Sporting-good stores have schedules.) Chances of encounters then are much greater than at other times, and may be with people armed and trigger-happy. Autumn is also when many people enter the woods to gather mushrooms, firewood, and holiday decorations.

Keep important ID and most valuables well hidden (eg, in a buried jar). But have a little money and ID on you. (Otherwise robbers might assume you have a cache and threaten further.)

If living in a vehicle, move frequently - at least weekly. If not, use it briefly to bring in supplies, then QUICKLY get it AWAY (sell or store). Do light trips by bus/bike/hike.

If digging or brush-cutting much at a site, the best time is late winter, so spring growth soon helps cover disturbance.

Generally, foresters don't want unnecessary enemies (who could do much damage) and won't hassle unless something seems to threaten their property. You greatly improve your odds, both of not being discovered, and of not being hassled even if discovered, if you: don't smoke; don't make fires; don't cut trees; don't have power tools, pack animals, or a dog. B & H

What dangers seem likeliest in woods where we have been.

Poke eye with branch. (Wear safety glasses with top and side shields, or helmet with face plate - little kids espec.)

Step into unseen hole and break leg. (Where you can't see the ground, move slow and probe ahead with foot or staff.)

On wet slope, slip, slide, and possibly impale on a sharp stump. (Lean close to slope and keep hold or dig hands in.)

Chilling, because of change of weather or activity. (Take enough warm clothes. Also learn how to make an insulated "cocoon" out of leaves, moss, grass, ferns, boughs, etc.)

Carbon monoxide in tight enclosure. Sneaky and deadly! (Ventilate well if ANY combustion, even candle or catalytic.)

Collisions on back roads where vehicles are not expected.

The back country is probably the safest place to be.

We publish the foregoing to help DP readers take sensible precautions. But we don't feel threatened. The media gives a false impression by featuring the few assaults and accidents in the bush while largely ignoring many calamities elsewhere.

Bert and I have backpack camped almost continuously for 15 years without any hassles or serious injuries. (We had one minor theft - from a temporary stash near a road.) Most mishaps we hear of, occur to people traveling on roads, living in or with vehicles, or camping in city parks.

May your times be interesting - but not TOO interesting.
Holly & Bert

Dwelling Portably
formerly named Message Post
POB 190, Philomath OR 97370
October 1995 $1 per issue   Add 50¢ to check/mo under $7

Controlling water flow when showering with jugs.

On a spare cap that fits my bleach jugs, I installed a small shower head. That seems to give better control and coverage than just loosening the cap. I also drilled a 3/16" vent hole in each jug handle to allow the jugs to "breath" as the water drains. When a jug is empty, I transfer the shower head/cap to another jug. Two half-gallon jugs are adequate for a good shower. If extra water is required for extra people, I heat it in a solar shower bag and refill the jugs from that.   Brother Bat, Arizona, May

(Comments:) Did you try simply removing the cap? That is what we do and we have no difficulty controlling flow. (Did we at first? We don't remember. But any learning came quickly, requiring at most a few showers.)

Does the solar shower bag heat water faster than does a dark-colored or black-painted jug? Holly & Bert, OR, Oct.

More about the "Silly Shower".

I fill a yoghurt container with warm water and put it on my head upside down. Unless you are a skinhead, your hair will allow air to enter and water to trickle out all around the rim. Jai Loon, Washington, January

Portable shower enclosures.

REI sells one with inflatable frame, 30x30x65", 8¼ lbs, for $24 plus shipping. That is less expensive and lighter than Bivouac Buddy, which was $159 and 13 lbs (reviewed in March'89 MP/DP). But REI's lacks a holding tank (the water drains directly onto the ground) and thus can't be used in a room where you don't want to wet the floor.

For use outside to block wind or view, a piece of black plastic will do as well as REI's enclosure, and is lighter and much cheaper though not quite as easy to rig.   Holly

Technique for comfier showers also improves hand washing.

A first-grade-teacher friend complained that her kids used far too much water and soap when they washed up before lunch. I told her about Wanda's suggestion (in May'93 DP). Now she walks around the room and gives each kid a squirt of soap. They rub vigorously to make the soap disappear, then go rinse. Not only does that save water, but my friend thinks they also get their hands cleaner. Laura LaBree, WA

Orchard sprayers are portable and have many uses.

I love mine for showering; with a sink; and for better flushing a portable toilet. It is easily pressurized with its hand pump. The spray is adjustable. For frequent use, industrial models are far superior to garden-store varieties.

If used on food, I'd get a stainless steel model, remove lube, and replace with mineral oil. NEVER use on person or food a sprayer previously used with chemicals. L. Smith, WI

I have been catching a dozen crawfish a week.

I catch them in the lake at the resort where I work, near NYC. I made a trap out of chicken wire and baited it with kitchen left-overs. The crawfish go around the trap trying to get the bait, enter a funnel-shaped end, and get stuck inside. Or maybe they get lazy with all that food to eat and decide to stay. The door is for removing them.

This week, though, I found the door open and no crawfish inside. Maybe a fisherman took them. Or maybe the muskrat I see swimming around in the mornings.

I am catching muskies on topwater plug (rapala 11S(?)) and spinner/minnow combinations. I bought a fishing license ($35 if out of state) due to warnings from friends about enforcement. Eugene Gonzalez, New York, May

Keeping qualities of edible oils.
The cooking oil I've found most durable is Cannola. To me, it has no taste. It seems to handle high heat well. I've had corn oil go bad. Brother Bat, Arizona, May

(Comment:) A pint of cannola oil we bought in bulk at a large-volume co-op, went bad soon after purchase, developing an increasingly strong fishy smell and taste. Several previous batches had kept okay. We have never had corn oil go bad, neither refined nor unrefined. The latter is the oil we buy most often. Holly, Oregon, October

The three rock wok stove.
I developed this at my own personal cooking fire. It keeps a rounded cooking vessel squarely seated - no rocking, no spills. A small, economic, controllable fire underneath works best.

Regulate heat by pulling out or pushing in 3" diameter or smaller fuelwood. No more than 6" clearance between wok bottom and ground is fine. Scooping a bunch of large glowing embers under, works nicely also. Peter Bridge, Utah

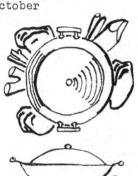

Portable heat pack does not work.
The "ReHeater" brand, re-usable, 3x6" that I spent money on is totally worthless. What's more, ReHeater Inc of Gardena CA seems to be out of business, so I can't even complain. Brother Bat

I live outside six months or more a year.
I am on some property I have. I live in a tent, haul water in buckets, and have no electricity. I prefer to live this way.

When cold, I burn small votive candles in my tent and am impressed how warm it can get. The candle is in a small glass container, which I feel is safer.

This year I put up a small strawbale shed for fun and storage, and plan to build another for living in. I know this option isn't practical for many of your readers, but strawbale structures are really inexpensive, warm, quiet, and easy to build. Laura LaBree, Washington, June

Sheer curtains are an inexpensive source of bug netting.
You can find them near free at any resale shop or yard sale (people are happy to find someone who wants the darn things). With a little sewing, you can custom make an enclosure any size you need. To make it really bugproof, velcro closures at door and window work well and are also easy to sew on. Joyce Pierdinock, Herbal Voices, MI, June

(Comment:) We use curtains as netting and like them. However, we have been in a few places where there were tiny gnats (no-see-ums) which could get through. LLL has a paper, "Bug Free".

Mosquito repellant used before and after bite.
    If a mosquito bites, right away I touch or spray the spot with Cutters repellant. Itchy bump won't develop. Apparently Cutters breaks down a substance that humans are allergic to, which mosquitos inject to keep the blood from clotting. Other brands may also work. Double Dorje, Arizona, May

A complete covering of white prevents bee attack.
    I took a course on beekeeping. The less you look and act like a brown or black bear (the bees' arch enemy) the safer you will be. Bees, including killer bees, do not attack white. That is why bee keepers wear all white. Even a black pen top showing in your shirt pocket will invite a sting. My white dog was stung last year - just above her beady little brown eye. Bees go for my hair, which is brown. A net kept folded in your pocket can be retrieved to cover your head.
    "Killer bees": the name is an exaggeration, but they are incredibly hostile and very territorial. Their hive may be small, eg, a water meter box. They can pick up the vibration of you walking. Their territorial limit is said to be 50 feet - much farther than the limit of domestic bees. Ie, you can walk nearer to a hive of domestics without being attacked.
                                          Double Dorje, June 1994
Best defensive tactics against stinging insects?
    If I get too close to a bee hive or wasp nest and anger them, and some come at me, should I run away or stand still?
    Last summer I disturbed some wasps or hornets. Being on a fairly good trail, I ran, heading INTO the wind (blowing 5 ? mph). As long as I ran fast, I could stay ahead of them. But when I slowed for obstacles they caught up, at which times I batted my hands in the air at them. I had to run maybe half a mile before they gave up the chase. None seemed to land and I got no stings. Maybe they didn't really want combat. (There were only about a half dozen, so casualties would have seriously depleted their family.)   Bert, Oregon, November

(Reply:) I've heard that you are supposed to act like a flower. Don't flail. Stay calm. But personally, I'd run.
                                          Double Dorje
Comments on snake bite treatments.   Dec
    Most pit vipers are not lethal to otherwise healthy adults. If prevention fails, probably the best course is to seek professional medical attention. In the meantime, I suggest gentle local wound cleansing with mild soap and water, & minimal exertion (to reduce spread of venom and extent of tissue damage). Ie, I would personally do as much nothing as possible until antivenom could be administered.
    Some studies have shown that cut-and-suck treatments increase injury. Likewise ice treatment. I'm not aware of studies of electrical therapy. Jon Seaver, Michigan, Oct 1994

(Comments:) There is a high-vacuum extractor (discussed in March'91 MP/DP; sold by REI for $11 plus shipping; maybe also by Campmor and other dealers) that supposedly extracts most of venom WITHOUT cutting. Supposedly cutting, not sucking, is what often increases injury. A suction stronger than mouth is supposedly needed to extract most venom.

Yurts; housing restrictions; BLM land.
I would like more progress reports from people who build
yurts or live in them. What did you use for struts; cover;
yoke; ropes; etc.? I've heard some people use Sears snow
fences for sides and roof.
A second-hand yurt was sold in the Illinois Valley of
sw Oregon, summer 1994. I don't know price. New yurts I've
seen were gorgeous and well designed but cost thousands and
are technically not legal. Yurts may be great in Mongolia
where nomads are legal, but here a yurt is too bulky to move
easily without a car or yak.
With any kind of shelter, the big problem is finding a
place to live legally. Building permit requirements make a
home unaffordable whether it is a house or a yurt.
A great folly or oversight of this age, is homelessness
and landlessness in a world and country with so much land.
I or most any homeless person can build a house or yurt, and
manage a garden. Instead, many of us are on a "death march".
Even in the face of declining health, we must keep moving.
BLM land is pretty good for free camping, and there is
plenty of it, but it is all but invisible. Boundaries are
never marked. Exact locations are word of mouth. The maps
that BLM sells are crap.
The sweet and gentle manners of rangers and park keepers
change to arrogance and hostility the moment they suspect
they are dealing with a poor person who is there legally but
not on holiday - just deadly serious about staying alive for
a few months before moving to another site as seasons change.
                                        Double Dorje, AZ, May
(Comments:) Yes, the fantastic cost of houses and the lack
of legal alternatives is insane, especially so considering
the many low-cost (or free if scavenged) building materials
available. Obviously, except possibly in Tokyo and a few
other over-crowded cities, "homelessness" is not a housing
problem but a LEGAL problem: created by building inspectors,
big contractors, politicians, lawyers, and police - and by
some "environmentalists" who want 90% of population to die.
(Of course there are many different "environmentalists".
We think that what we do helps the environment. But we find
obnoxious the rich hypocrites who, while living luxuriously
themselves, claim that the planet or an area is overpopulated
and try to deny others living space. A few years ago,
thousands of them flew in jet airplanes (burning much fuel
and injecting a stew of chemicals into the thin stratosphere)
to Rio de Janeiro (a big, crowded city) where they no doubt
ate heartily (in a land where many go hungry) while pontifi-
cating about conserving resources and reducing pollution.
If they had been sincere, they could have stayed home and
conferenced via internet.)
However, Bert and I don't let the lack of a house get us
down. You and we and most houseless people have more and
better sheltering options than our ancestors thousands of
years ago when (eg) windows, if any, were oiled animal skins
- or ice. We sometimes worry about rangers or building
inspectors: our ancestors worried about hostile tribes.
Is lack of a house more life-threatening than is a
house? More houseless people may die from chilling (those
who don't know how to improvise insulation). But more
housed people die from housefires and earthquakes, and from
auto accidents commuting to work to pay for their houses.
Bert and I get house-sitting offers we pass up. And
when we accept, we do so because use of a pickup is included,

or so we can be in/near a city for a while; not because we want to live in a house. Our own shelters are smaller than yurts and quite crowded, but are more comfortable than were most houses we have sat. Eg, in winter our shelters stay quite warm naturally (partly because they are small) whereas most houses require stove tending. Holly & Bert, Oregon, Oct.

The criminalization of homelessness.

In California where an estimated million people are home-less, eight municipalities recently passed anti-sleeping ordinances. The city of Berkeley now forbids loitering within one block of laundromats, parks, and recreation centers; and has considered outlawing the carrying of more than one shopping bag ! Santa Cruz arrests people who sit on a side-walk, even if only there waiting for a ride or bus. San Francisco spent 450 police hours and $11,000 during 1993 to arrest 15 people for begging.

Why? "Visible poverty does discourage shoppers - especially those out to spend discretionary dollars that they could just as easily spend elsewhere. No one wants to run a gauntlet of panhandlers to get to a boutique...." In New York City, ad campaigns say that shoppers "have every right to be selfish and annoyed." Celine-Marie Pascale (from Utne Reader, Sept. 1994; sent by Guy Hengst)

(Comments:) Why don't all those "selfish and annoyed" shoppers simply say "no" to panhandlers? If they did, the panhandlers would soon quit. Refusing beggars, is less hostile than are anti-loitering laws, which not only threaten many who are not beggars, but may arouse sympathy for beggars.

This article, like most of the slick media, follows the official line that "homelessness" is the cause of panhandling. That encourages shoppers and merchants who don't like beggars, to persecute everyone who lacks 'proper' housing. Most "home-less" we know don't beg. And not all beggars are "homeless".

Perhaps the anti-camping and anti-sleeping laws are an attempt to goad the "homeless" into real crime, such as robbing to get rent money, so that frightened citizenry will support hiring more police and building more prisons.

Some consequences that officials might overlook:

Any city that prohibits shopping bags, knapsacks, or bike baskets, etc., threatens many thrifty, energy-conserving shoppers who bicycle or bus, or park a car one place while running short errands on foot; and makes a mockery of environmental preachings to conserve fuel and reduce pollution by driving less.

Any city that prohibits napping in vehicles, threatens many shoppers from the hinterlands who do one multi-day trip rather than many one-day trips; and makes a mockery of safe-driving preachings to stop and sleep when tired.

We say: Don't shop in such a city. Or shop less often. Remember that most shopping is discretionary, especially if you live in the boonies. If we had to, we could make just one supply run a year, perhaps hiring an unemployed person with pickup or van to help.

Some victims launch boycott campaigns to encourage reforms. Even just posting a few dozen copies of a well-worded warning, can upset merchants, who will then lean on the politicians and police. If doing that, some tips:

Warn; don't just complain. Most people are too busy to care much what happened to YOU. But if THEY feel threatened, they will try to avoid the threat.

Make many people concerned. Eg, while taking cardboard from a dumpster to shade her parked, well-loaded bike, a friend was questioned by police and asked for ID (not for her riding or for taking the cardboard, but because she "looked suspicious"). In retaliation, she composed a poster (which we helped put up within a 50-mile radius) which not only related her experience, but said she had heard that many motorists, especially people with pickups and vans (which includes big shoppers) as well as bikes, were often hassled there for petty or imagined violations.

Target a specific place. Eg, the poster's heading, in very big print, was: "AVOID DOWNTOWN CORVALLIS". Our friend did not know for sure that police were worse downtown than elsewhere in the city; or worse than police in Eugene, Albany, Newport, etc. But merchants in each city and neighborhood are in competition with merchants elsewhere. Though people can't easily stop buying, most can easily go to an outlying shopping center instead of downtown, or, if from out of town, to a different city.

After that poster, there seemed to be less hassling. H&B

Students choose autos and camping over dorms in Corvallis.

Are you tired of high rents? Or living in that roach hotel? Or dealing with the landlord from hell? Or of lugging boxes up three flights of stairs? OSU students have done everything from set up house in old civil defense shelters to camping out at Avery Park and the fair grounds.

After hearing rumors that some graduate students live in their offices at OSU, I managed to contact one person who was doing it. The setup is plain and simple: a foldaway army cot, a few personal belongings, a box of clothes, and toiletries adorn the shelf above the desk. How not to get caught? "Well, I know the exact timetables and days the janitors come, and when they come I just leave the office. They've never seen me sleeping in here. Sometimes I feel just like a rat living this way, but it's cheap, and I'm here all the time anyway, working on my research. When I first came here, I couldn't find a place that was affordable. I didn't want to pay a lot to live in a dump, so I tent camped fall term. Then, in winter, I moved in here as it was pretty wet and cold." The student plans to return to tent camping in the spring quarter. Favorite spots to camp? "Personally, I like behind the baseball field by Parker, but the fairgrounds are okay, too. Less hassles there."

Another student has been living out of his vehicle since spring of 1993. Why? "I wanted to conserve resources and not just monetary ones. I was only sleeping in my apartment so it was a waste of space." After an investment of about $1000 including building a "topper", his truck became home sweet home. "The first night was pretty scary. I would walk up and down the street looking for people that would attack my truck," he laughs. "Eventually, I got used to it. I just light a candle to read before I go to sleep." A senior in Environmental Science who also works two jobs, he has a busy schedule. Having facilities isn't a problem as he discovered Dixon Recreation Center (which is open only to OSU students, and ID is checked by a full-time receptionist). "Dixon is great. I just rented a locker for the whole term." His pad is 8x5': big enough for a bed and to store all that he owns. What to do when company visits? He laughs, "It gets pretty crowded. I usually visit people at their house." As for hassles from security, he says to date he hasn't had any

problems. "I also don't always park at OSU. I park in the
surrounding neighborhoods, in front of people's houses. I
change locations a lot." Would he recommend this lifestyle
to others? I really love it a lot. It's not a bad lifestyle
at all. Next time I want a bigger truck though," he laughs.
Laura Tesler (from Daily Barometer, April 25 1995

Mobile bed and storage.
     During my bachelor days, I traveled hither and yon in a
full-size pickup with cap on the back, and slept on it in a
folding army-surplus "D-ring" stretcher which has latching
hold-open bars. It is equivalent to a skinny, low canvas cot.
When not in use, it folded into a 7 ft by 6 inch package that
fit in one corner of the pickup bed. Jon Seaver, MI, Oct 1994

Last summer I lived in the woods along the McKenzie River.
     I camped more or less traditionally. I commuted to work
on the Eugene bus system. Friends of mine are headed to Baja
over the holidays, so I am interested in info on camping
there, for them. Kent Jones, Oregon, October 1994

More about living in van and working at resort near NYC.
     I was able to park close to an electric outlet, so I am
using an electric heater (ceramic) for warmth, and six 4'
fluorescent lights to grow stuff inside the cab section.
I closed it off with mylar curtains, and covered the windows
with foil and then a tarp to keep light in and for insulation.
     However, I am not content here. Too many people around
for me to "be myself". Also many petty rip offs. Also toxic
waste dumps nearby. Also NYC is 50 miles away, and a
potential danger. This summer I plan to travel to North
Carolina where friends with a nursery business have offered
me work. Next winter I hope to stay in southwest Arizona,
which might help my arthritic pains. Among other trades,
I have carpet installation tools and sometimes work as a
helper for $50-$100 per day. Eugene Gonzalez, NY, May

I live in a blue Chrysler mini-van for the time being.
     It has a tiger print steering wheel cover and a disco-
ball. I inherited it from my grandma last year. Although
I do not expect that she intended for me to LIVE in it, I'm
sure she would be delighted that it is being put to good use.
     I am sort of sick of people staring at it, though.
Punks hate it cuz it looks like a familymobile-bourgeous-
dream of the hip '90s, and everyone else thinks I am gonna
unload the two kids and the ski equipment from the back.
And when they see a bed in there -- ! Sue, NJ, April

My three children and I are living a mobile lifestyle.
     At present, we are in a car with a utility trailer. Fran
                                                          CA, June
I was living in a Subaru Turdmobile station wagon.
     I just got a Ford 138 WB van. It will be like a mansion.
                                                          Ed, NJ
I used to live in a truck box.
     Friends called it the coffin because it didn't have any
windows. Vince, Ontario, April

I will soon move into my "new" 1955 Spartan trailer.
     Info and ideas on space saving and energy independence
are welcome. Sue Harrington, Colorado, March

With trailer housing, you can avoid a disaster.

Some environmentalists want to forbid rebuilding in flood-prone areas of the Midwest, wildfire zones of California, and other regions that are frequently devastated. This would reduce the social cost of repeatedly providing disaster aid.

I suggest a more moderate approach: rebuild with a cluster of trailers which are individually small enough to be towed out of danger by the homeowner's car. I envision trailers that have two doors, one at each end. A covered connector fills the gap between the doors of several trailers, which together provide enough room even for a large farm family.

The cluster might be shaped like a wheel. The connector is a central "hub". Each trailer attached to it is a "spoke", providing each individual with a private room. The kitchen and bathroom could be either in the "hub" (if large) or in a "spoke". If still more space is needed, one or more peripheral connectors would join the far ends of "spoke" trailers to "rim" trailers, which could be connected also to each other.

This arrangement would occupy more land than a traditional house, but the vacant wedges between "spoke" trailers would have their uses. They would form play areas for small children that mothers could easily supervise; garden party areas with more privacy than a back yard; courts for outdoor games; etc.

Advantageous side-effects: Grown-up children could tow their trailer with them when they leave home; they needn't buy a house. Empty-nest parents would not be stuck with an overly-large house, nor with taxes on the value of its empty rooms. Ailing parents could more easily receive home care. Their children or other relatives could tow a trailer over and attach it, and thus be on hand for assistance without feeling either trapped or in the way. Visitors who brought their own trailer could also be present but out-of-the-way. Communes could be quickly assembled and, if discord arises, disassembled. Roger Knights, Washington, April

(Comments:) Other advantages: A home can be purchased gradually, trailer by trailer, as a family grows (or as possessions accumulate), and as finances allow, without going into debt. Unfinished trailer shells can probably be mass-produced and delivered at a much lower cost per space than a house built on site; and probably less even than can a mobile home (which, being much bigger, is expensive to haul far, and therefore is usually manufactured locally in small quantities). Each shell provides shelter immediately, and can be finished and turned into a bed room, kitchen, work room, or whatever, as the purchaser has time.

One disadvantage compared to a house: The trailer cluster has much more outer surface for the same inside space, and therefore more heat loss, or gain, or much more insulation required. This is a problem only if a family insists on heating or cooling their entire home. If, eg, during winter they are willing to crowd together in one trailer which is well insulated, and leave the others uninsulated and unheated to use as storage or during mild weather, it is economical.

(That is our usual arrangement, but with tents instead of trailers. One well-insulated tent is our cold-weather core dwelling. Other tents/tarps, not insulated, provide storage and mild-weather expansion space.)

For a flood-threatened farmer in the Midwest, where winters are long and very cold, I wonder if a large, well-anchored houseboat would be better than a trailer cluster, and maybe just as safe. H & B

Travel-Trailer Homesteading Under $5000.

In this 65 page book, Brian Kelling describes how he set up and equipped a travel trailer to live semi-permanently in the San Luis Valley of southern Colorado. Usually sunny and cool at 7500' elevation, "we average 50 nights a year in which the temperature gets below zero" F. With only 7" of rain/snow yearly, Brian hauls in water with his pickup. A photo shows only low desert growth nearby,but trees on a mountain far away.

His costs included $2195 for 5 acres, $1200 for a used 21-foot trailer, $825 for electricity (solar and generator), and $575 other. Not counted, was his pickup and power tools, that Brian considers essential. Land taxes were only $52 per year. Not mentioned is trailer's license, if required.

"A travel trailer (vs mobile home) is the best, because they're cheap, give all the comforts of home, and are easily transported by ordinary vehicle." Mobile homes are legal in his county. Travel trailers are not, but are tolerated by a lenient building inspector. (That could quickly change!)

Brian includes tips and some instructions with diagrams for choosing and setting up trailer, and skirting bottom; and for installing a septic system (the longest chapter!) and other equipment. "Slipping the upper (stove) pipe down over the lower pipe ... is the way it is usually done, and I did this when I first installed my (wood) stove. However, this allows condensation and creosote to flow freely from the joints, making a mess all over the outside of your trailer, and sometimes inside. Some people (especially in Europe) reverse the pipes, as I have done. This makes any liquids flow all the way back down into the stove. If you do this, make sure the 45 degree elbow out of your stove is a solid piece, not adjustable.... Another possibility is to install a piece of aluminum inside the joint where the 45 meets the straight piece. Make it long enough so the liquids drip into the stove (diagram in book). Don't use a regular piece of metal (for this)... I tried, and it rusted out."

Most of Brian's choices seem sensible. A few exceptions:

Flush toilets may be desirable in places that have both abundant water and dense population (such as London in England which is where they were invented). But not out in the boonies where you must build your own septic system. (There, shallow burials, widely distributed, are much easier, and are less likely to contaminate ground water.) And not in a place where water is scarce. Using a flush toilet in a thinly-populated desert where water must be brought in, seems insane!

Piped water makes sense if you use much water (eg, for a farm) and have a flowing source (creek or spring). But not where you must first haul it in. Especially not in a cold climate. "Travel trailers aren't really designed for winter living... Water pipes in them tend to run in odd-ball out-of-the-way places, and during extremely cold weather (below zero) I have sometimes had them freeze...."

The propane frig "costs less to operate than the cost of ice". But where nights are cold, most kinds of food can be cooled enough to keep several days simply by exposing the food at night and then insulating during the day. Of course, this won't suffice if someone insists on keeping frozen goodies.

Despite such criticisms, we recommend this book to anyone considering an RV, to help learn of the problems and some solutions. (Review by Holly & Bert of Dwelling Portably.)

(1995; Loompanics, POB 1197, Port Townsend WA 98368; $8 + $4 p&h; ISBN 1-55950-132-4. 292p.8x11 catalog of 800 bks,$5ppd or free with order.

Dwelling Portably
formerly named Message Post
POB 190, Philomath OR 97370
December 1995 (will be reprinted as part of the October 1995)

Shocking way to protect a vehicle.

There was an item in Mar'94 DP (now part of Oct'93) about parking a van in rough inner-city neighborhoods to avoid cops (who don't enter much? or are too busy when they do?) and then electrifying it to repel anyone else. We wonder if the writer has actually done this.

Imagined scene: a gang of kids comes strolling down the sidewalk, playing around. One shoves another, who falls against the van. ZAP! (How to make enemies and start wars.)

To avoid that, the van occupants could turn on the shock only if someone was trying to break in. Possible problem: most people have deep-sleep periods when not easily aroused.

I think the electricity could be shorted out by tossing a chain or metal cable over a bumper or trailer hitch. Electric fence chargers have problems in wet weather if even a tree falls across. But the burglars might not think of that, or might not have a chain along. Bert and Holly, October

(Reply:) I do electrify my vehicle. As you surmise, it is only turned on when I'm aboard at night, parked, and sleeping. It generates pulses, rather than a continuous output, so it won't grab someone so he can't let go.

It is fairly easy to set up with a farm fence charger. It might not be compatable with modern computer ignitions.

You are correct about grounding it out, but that will sound an alarm, allowing occupants to take other measures.

At night, my truck is parked in abandoned gas stations, deserted factory districts, or remote highway rest stops. In those circumstances, I assume that anyone who touches my vehicle IS an enemy. The least I will do is drive off. The cab is protected with Kevlar armor and Lexan windows.

So far, the worst that has happened is, a couple of rocks thrown at the truck after an attempt to break in. The attackers were surprised when they discovered that the windows could not be broken.

Electrifying vehicles is not new. The idea was pioneered in the 1960s to keep mobs from overturning riot-control vehicles. I have been experimenting with the idea since I was a kid after seeing the movie "20,000 Leagues Under the Sea".

There are some parallels between Captain Nemo (in the novel, not the movie) and my thinking. After a partially disabling accident, the state and the insurance companies cheated me. When one sees how the laws are used to disempower the ordinary citizen, one becomes an 'outlaw'. The stories in Oct'95 DP of hassles at Kauapea Beach and elsewhere infuriated me. I guess there isn't enough real crime to keep the storm troopers busy. That is why I park overnight in the most crime ridden (lawless) parts of the city. I can defend myself from criminals who are not in uniform. L.Smith, Wisconsin, Nov.

Criticism of the SRT-1 Survival Rescue Tool.

It is an imitation of the real thing, on a par with Chinese reproductions of U.S. Army gear. Badly cast. You would be lucky to cut through a few branches with it. The author of the report (in April'92 DP) certainly can't have tested it very rigorously.

Carrying it in an urban area would probably get you arrested. It would be considered "brass knuckles". L.Smith

Low-cost trailer parks are shutting down, stranding many poor.
    Life hasn't been easy for residents of Olivia Mobile Home
Park in Everett WA since it closed last June to make room for
a planned mall. Only a handful found space in other parks.
    Mark Gordon wasn't among them. He sold at a loss his
1973 14x46 Lamplighter mobile home (bought 5 years ago for
$3000), and purchased a 1972 Dodge Tradesman van for $600.
With nowhere to go, he squatted for a while on the site where
his trailer once stood. Behind the van, under a clear plastic
covering propped up by 2x4s, is his "living room". An oil-
stained tarpaulin hangs on one side to keep out the wind. A
blanket, tossed over what used to be his front steps, serves
as a table. He uses a toilet in an abandoned trailer nearby.
    Unemployed for 6 months, Mark, 33, last worked as a
quality-control inspector at a metal-plating plant. He has
been unable to find a new job because prospective employers
have no place to reach him. "I have no address. I have no
phone. I just keep filling out applications."
    Movers told Sharmi Daniel that her 1972 Greatland mobile
home would fall apart if they tried to lift it. So she left
it behind. Junk or not, it was home - and affordable.
Before moving to Olivia, apartment rent had cost $78 more per
month than her $546 welfare income. She has also been a
traffic flagger, teacher's assistant, and a dancer in a club.
    After eviction, the Daniels moved to a campground ten
minutes away by canoe on an undeveloped island in the
Snohomish River. With a 6-year-old son, they spent most of
summer in a tent. Sharmi's daughter left to live with her
father in another part of the state. "It's really embarrass-
ing for any 12-year-old girl to have to live like Robinson
Crusoe", Sharmi says. Sharmi caught pneumonia after a week
of rain. The family bathed in an icy river.
    Wallace Barnett, Olivia's owner, says the park had
become run down. Maintenance and taxes made it unprofitable
to operate. However, he says he felt bad for the tenants
and, as a humane act, left the park's water on.
    Never popular with nearby homeowners, trailer parks have
nonetheless been important enclaves of affordable housing for
America's poor and elderly. Building of trailer parks first
boomed during World War II to provide housing for workers
flocking to defense jobs in cities. Early trailers were
narrow, uncomfortable, and flimsy; and quickly took on a
negative image, which persisted even though later models were
bigger and better built - and called "manufactured homes".
    Mobile home parks, especially older ones with cheap rent,
are at risk. In WA since 1989, 22 parks have closed and 34
more will soon. Other states are losing similar numbers.
Some are being closed or condemned as their aging sewers and
streets deteriorate. But many, such as Olivia, are destroyed
to make room for stores and parking lots. Their sites, on
the fringes of cities out of sight of other houses, are the
same locales favored by discount retailers. Joseph Pereira
(much condensed from Wall Street Journal, 15 Nov 1995)

(Comments:) For the Daniels, a jug shower (Simple Shower)
using hot water, would be much more comfortable than an icy
river. (I assume they had some sort of stove for cooking.)
    We would like to inform houseless people about the jug
shower and other techniques for living comfortably without
expensive, elaborate equipment, but don't know how to reach
most of them. Many would not want our entire dwellingway.
(Eg, we are too remote for daily commuting, and even those

unemployed may hope their luck will change and they can resume profligate living.) But some techniques may be useful.

Housed people, too, can sometimes benefit. Their houses may stop functioning. Recently, high winds in Oregon knocked out electricity in some areas for long periods, and houses with electric pumps were without running water. Some people became so desparate (or smelly?) that schools put up signs: "showers open to the public after school hours".

Some 12-year-olds would love to live like Robinson Crusoe. But kids who go to school, become very fashion conscious, because, if they are different in any way, other kids will pick on them. Many kids may not only be happier but also learn more if they do NOT go to school. (There are many resources for learning at home, such as F.U.N. listed in OBP.)

I roam in a 1974 Dodge Long Van.

My habitat is north of San Francisco, routes 1 and 101 along the ocean. Robert Di Falco, California, November

I am going on the road this summer in my Toyota with camper. I could use some suggestions. Sharina, Texas, March

12-volt electric bunk warmer.

It is a pad you sleep on rather than under. Inside a cheap rectangular sleeping bag, it is highly efficient, being on about 30% of the time. A bunk-size model draws about four amps, so you need an auxillary battery for overnight use. But no carbon monoxide danger, no open flames, and no extra fuel to store. With it, I have no fear of -20° temperatures.

I've had one about 3 months, bought for $43 from Backwoods Solar Electric (8530 Rapid Ltn Ck Rd, Sandpoint ID 83864). Also check local truck stops. Electro-Warmth maker.
L. Smith, WI, Nov.

(Comment:) In cold weather, we use more than one sleeping bag, either one inside another, or opened up and spread on top. Seems easier than hauling around an extra battery and worrying about keeping it charged. Holly and Bert, OR, Dec.

Tips for fishing and for obtaining fishing equipment.

When fishing with bait, pools are easier than running water. Where a stream widens into a pool, fishing is usually best near the inlet. Drop live bait into the moving water to drift or tumble into the pool. Bobber optional. No weight.

In a pond or lake, fish near the edge of the water or in vegetation (such as cattails or reeds) using bobber and bait. Or fish near a sharp drop off without bobber.

Water levels in most impoundments (man-made lakes) are greatly lowered in winter, exposing much of the bottom. You can then harvest many expensive lures and other equipment simply by walking. Most plastic lures will look new after swishing in some soapy water. A few may need rubbing.

During low water is also a good time to study the shape of the bottom. Or drag out some brush and tie it down, to encourage fish to congregate there when water is high again.

Braided line is cheap. Buy 40 lb test or more. Brand is not important. To make it float (a plus) wax with a stub candle. Buy the best monofilament. Seldom will you need more than 10 lb test. 100 yards should last years, if used as 6-foot leaders added to braided line for fishing with pole. Store in dark, on original spool, with a little talc powder. Guy Hengst, Indiana, August

Simpler, more versatile bug bar.

Instead of forming a box-like enclosure ("Bug Free", LLL), I now simply sew netting (such as salvaged curtains) together into a flat sheet. Five yards on each side is ample for one person, adequate for two or three. The shape need not be a perfect rectangle: ie, if one curtain is a little longer, I leave excess (to avoid trimming and hemming).

With a crayon or grease pen (a felt pen might damage fabric), I mark diagonal lines from each corner inward at 45° angles (half the right angle). To suspend, I attach four ball ties, placing one tie along each line. (To form a ball tie, wrap netting over some roundish object or a wad of leaves, and tie between the object and the rest of the net. Drawing in May'95 DP.) If tied near the corners, the enclosure will be wide but low; if tied further in, higher but narrower.   Julie Summers, Oregon, December

tie-out cords

ball ties

net shown spread out

TOP VIEW

diagonal marks

SIDE VIEW
net set up

ball tie

Wintering in a Snugiup.

In mid November I built a shelter like the one in May'95 DP (also shown in 1995-96 Summary-Index) and have been living in it since. I used six plastic liners and two roofs. The top roof is cloth; the under roof is clear plastic. Most days the shelter stays warm enough to wear just a T-shirt and watch cap, or nothing. During one freeze I had to wear more, but stayed comfortable. This is with no stove. The shelter has stayed dry except for a little condensation on the front wall.

One problem: rain formed a puddle on the roof which had to be dumped frequently - a nuisance, especially at night. As instructed, I tied the roofs only at the sides and back; not in front. (Would Shelter Systems' clips be better?) My roof is not as steep as yours (because the slope is not as steep) which may be why a puddle formed. To eliminate it, I put three poles under the roof (but over the liners), spaced two feet apart, oriented up-down the slope.

Another problem: not enough light inside when heavy overcast. (Fine on sunny days.) Downhill is not entirely clear: a few tree tops protrude into "my" sky. To get more light, I rerigged the top (cloth) roof so that on cloudy days I can undo two ties and flip it back half way, uncovering the clear plastic under-roof. (If a low-flying aircraft comes over, I can flip the roof back down in a few seconds. But on cloudy days, most aircraft stay above the clouds.)

Another problem: muddy water splashed onto the front. I greatly reduced that by laying fir boughs (blown off tall trees on the next hill by a strong wind) on the ground in front. (I also made a bough foundation for my bed - comfy.)

I cook over a fire, quite far from the shelter, down near a creek so I have plenty of water. About once a week I cook a big pot of rice or spaghetti and lots of popcorn. Between cookings I first eat the rice (lasts a day or two) and then popcorn - plus nuts, sunnies, raisins, sauces/seasonings, and vitamins. I have not found much to forage (a few wild carrot tops). Come spring I will search further.

For next winter, I plan to get a propane cooking stove and put it inside my shelter - which I want to enlarge. I've not decided whether to widen it (which will require more poles and larger plastic), or to make several shelters the same size and interconnect them with tunnels. But how to line the tunnels so I don't get muddy crawling thru?   Emtu, Oregon, Febr.

(Comments:) With any structure, if the roof is not steep, irregularities will collect rain. Shelter Systems' clips would bunch the plastic less than do ball ties. Clothes-pin ties would bunch it even less. To form, roll edge of plastic a few times around a $\frac{1}{4}$" diameter stick, grip with a clothes-pin, and strengthen grip by wrapping rubber strap around jaws. Thread tie-out cord through spring of clothes-pin. (Drawing in April'92 DP.) Clothes-pin ties are usable only at edges. (Fine for a tarp or Snugiup but not for a dome.)

A larger shelter will be chillier, unless you close off part. Interconnecting several small shelters sounds interesting, and eases the avoiding of trees and disposing of dirt. I don't know a simple way to line tunnels. (I can imagine plastic held up by wands (flexible branches) steadied with cords. But not real simple. For safety, keep tunnel narrow, close to the surface, and arch ceiling. Bert, Oregon, April

Aborted test of a manufactured tent.

Seven years ago, to learn how the "other half" camps, we bought a Stansport dome tent, made in Taiwan, $30 on sale. Since then, it was never at hand when we could have used it to advantage. (For summer travel, we take just an insect net plus a dew tarp - which weighs less and admits more light.)

Finally, last summer, we were able to test it. It set up quite fast and easily, 20 minutes first try, by fitting the segmented wands together and inserting into sleeves.

But the tent STANK, probably from fire retardant. We did not move in, but left it set up and open to air out. Several MONTHS later it still stank, not quite as strongly. We wondered if scrubbing with a strong detergent would help, but did not have time. So back it went into storage. It easily stuffed into a 5-gallon pail after removal of the aluminum wands.

I won't blame the manufacturer: I suppose the fire-retardant was required by some government agency. (I wonder if it was the same stuff required on childrens' pajamas until found to cause cancer ! (I'd rather take my chances with fire.)

How was the tent otherwise? Like many commercial products, it seemed to have good detail design and fabrication, but poor overall concept. The fabric near the bottom was olive. But the upper portion and fly were off-white - conspicuous, yet not passing much light through the two layers of woven material.

(A better configuration would be a semi dome with one big vertical window under an overhang. Make the window out of transparent plastic and the remainder out of olive cloth. When setting up, face the window toward the most open sky.)

Light is not a problem if a tent is used only for sleeping. But even a summer trek may include cold rainy days when you remain inside. I suspect that chief executives of most camping equipment manufacturers have not done much camping. Bert and Holly

I saw a 30-foot yurt at The Slabs, east of Salton Sea.

You can still camp there free, year around, in anything you can tolerate. There are no facilities; just miles of sand and greasewood. Catfish in a canal near by. A grocery store four miles away in Nyland (a one-horse town).

The weather is pleasant from October until mid April. Many hundred come then, most with vehicles. Some incinerate their poop but some don't so there are flies. In summer the heat is extreme. Double Dorje, California, May 1995

If you care-take, take care not to get taken.

Some situations advertised, offer "free" use of a mobile home in trade for 25 hours of work PER WEEK. Outside income would be needed to pay for food and other supplies.

Actually, considering the fantastically expensive rentals these days, such an offer is not surprising. Translating into dollars, 25 hours a week at minimum wages is about $400/month: a typical rental for a mobile home with site and utilities.

But 25 hours per week is a huge chunk of your life.

The solution, is not to complain about greedy landlords, but to become more independent. Learn how to live comfortably without elaborate structures and utilities.

If you can provide your own shelter, you can find better deals. Many landowners who would like help, don't have spare mobile homes (or converted chicken coops), nor a spot to which a mobile home could be hauled. But they may have steep wood-lots where a tent (or?) can be put and not be in their way. For just a tent site, 5 or 10 hours PER MONTH is reasonable.

Some positions advertised are in "remote" areas. If only living space is offered, we're not interested, because FREE space is easily found in remote areas. When we house sit, we do so in or near a city for access to shopping or temp jobs.
H & B

Need portable dwelling space? Consider a burned area.

Forest fires are destructive but also beneficial. For ten years or more after, there will be lush growth, because the ground gets more sun and the ash neutralizes some of the forest soil acidity. This gives animals more cover and forage.

Most people avoid a burned area because it seems ugly or because the dense brambles impede hiking. But this provides privacy for us living light. Guy Hengst, Indiana, Sept 1994

(Comment:) After a burn there may be salvage logging and then replanting. I'd wait until that is done before moving in. Clear-cuts, too, develop lush growth, but often slash is burned some months later, so WAIT until replanted.

Tips for accessing cities from far away.

Any suggestions for living without a car in areas too far from town to bicycle for supplies? Hitchhiking is dangerous even for a male, and I'm female. Even cycling is too danger-ous here, as the main highways are the only routes to town.
Jaye, Washington, Dec.

(Reply:) We often had the same problem. Some possibilities:

To reduce the number of trips, reduce the weight by buy-ing mostly dry foods such as grains and beans. 50 pounds of brown rice will nourish you much longer than will 50 pounds of potatos (which are mostly water). The rice will also keep much longer (if kept dry), is at least as nutritious, and cheaper (per nutrients; not per pound). Avoid canned foods and beverages, which are not only heavy and costly, but often less nutritious than what you can prepare from dry ingredients.

Try to forage most salads. We also take vitamin C.

To further reduce trips, buy dry foods in quantity, a few hundred pounds at a time. (Check wholesale grocers, as well as asking for discounts at natural food stores.) Then, rent or borrow a vehicle, or hire someone with vehicle to help you transport. (Check ad boards for move/haul offers.) You will also need to get (eg) pails with good-fitting lids for storing.

Bicycle to town very early on a Sunday morning when most roads have little traffic, stay for a week at a temporary camp near town, and return the next Sunday. Best during spring and early summer when daylight hours are long. To allow a pre-dawn start and to shorten the ride, stash your bike and some bedding near a paved road, hike there a day or two before, and depart from there. Also stash bedding in pails near your town camp (to avoid hauling it back and forth on your bike).

There might be trucks coming your way fairly regularly, delivering to country stores, resorts, ranches, etc. One might be willing to drop off supplies, or pick up a pail you stash close to a highway pull-off. An independent trucker might even give you rides. (Company trucks have insurance hang-ups.)

On main highways there may be Greyhound or other buses. Though expensive, they are affordable if you don't use them often, and are cheaper than owning your own car.

Holly and I have hitchhiked some: most often me (a male) alone, but also together (including a few long trips to CA), and sometimes Holly alone. Our worst experiences: a very few rides with people intoxicated or driving recklessly. Holly was asked for sex a few times but, though she declined, never forced or threatened. Some women who hitch try to look like men. But, unless able to appear so even when in the car, might be better to look like a woman so you will have many ride offers from which to choose. Turn down rides with two or more men together, and with anyone who seems intoxicated.

If possible, locate near people with similar needs who are willing to run a few errands for each other when they go to town: eg, post and pick up mail, and buy small items whose needs were not anticipated. They might even share rental of a vehicle once a year to transport most of their supplies. Unless you know someone VERY well, better not direct them to your base camp. Arrange sites to meet or leave parcels at.

A possibility we haven't found desirable, but which might suit some: camp near a rural resident who goes to town fairly often and will give rides in exchange for occasional house-sitting or a little work. Likely problems: nasty neighbors; trips not scheduled in advance; different values, resulting in each party considering the other incompetant or crazy. Also, the settlers may feel they are being turned into chauffers, while the nomads may feel they are being turned into serfs.

Simple, cheap, high-energy travel/trail snack.

I make "cheapola" by mixing sweet molassas with dry oat-meal (the finer the meal the less I have to chew). Cheapola tastes as good to me as do most commercial granolas and candy bars yet costs only 1/6 as much (eg, oatmeal 35¢ and molassas 70¢ per pound at bulk food stores) and may be somewhat more nutritious: more fiber; less fat; less processed; less stale.

Some people add nuts, sunflower seeds, raisins, brown sugar, dried coconut, cut-up fresh fruit, etc.

Some stores don't carry molassas in bulk (and prepack-aged little jars are pricy). If so, I may snack on just dry oatmeal (not bad) maybe with brown sugar. Bert and Holly

"Raw" oatmeal has been cooked

Recently I've been buying 50# bags of rolled oats from a wholesale grocer. (Formerly I bought smaller quantities from a bulk bin at a natural food store, but switched when they raised prices.) These particular oats taste very good. They were bagged by Grain Millers in Eugene. I phoned their 800 number.

A man in their lab said: after hulls are removed, oats must be heated to 212° F to inactivate enzymes that would otherwise cause rancidity in 8-15 days. The oats are again heated for rolling.

After proper heat treating, oats have a nutty flavor. (I used to wonder why "raw" oatmeal tasted so much better than other grains.) Oats are high in oil: 8-15%. Vs, wheat 1%; walnuts 50%.

Rancid oats taste bitter/acrid, and cause a burning sensation in the throat. Some oats that sat in the lab 8 months after heat treating, still tasted good. Coarse-ground might keep no better than quick-cooking oats. Oats easily pick up odors. Eg, some shipped in a truck with residual perfume, were refused by buyer.
Julie, Dec

Sources for cheap or free equipment.

Most metal buyers have scrap bins that often contain bargains. I have bought stanless steel buckets, electric fry pans and other items by the pound at a small fraction of the original cost.

Big-city thrift stores trash or give away unsaleable items. If your cause sounds worthy, you can get trailer-loads. Al Fry, Idaho, 1994

Useful Reuse.

There seem to be two approaches to utilizing discards: devise special projects; or, keep a junk pile.

The projects approach can lead to creations like chain-mail vests from drink-can snap-top-rings (seen in book Re/Uses) - artistic but not too useful.

I prefer to wait for a need, then try to fill it from my junk pile. In the past month I have made: a replacement handle for a pot lid, from the case of an exhausted ball-point pen; circular knitting needles, from other exhausted pens (joined with cord); a pump-drill flywheel, from a typewriter-ribbon spool wound with strap cut from a bike inner-tube (for weight); rubber bands, from other inner tubes; moccasins, from a truck innertube; plastic gaskets, from margarine tubs; an awl, from a piece of bone; a desk-caddy addition to hold my sizzors, from a small carboard box that staples had come in.

My junk "pile" doesn't take up much space. The non-bulky items fit into a 5-gallon container - itself a discard that formerly held vegetable oil, with the top cut off for access (because it had only a narrow mouth) and holes cut to accept a cord handle. Julie Summers

Propane Notes

In this 11 page 8½x11 booklet, David Smith tells how he made heaters for various craft projects (kilns; heat treating metals; glass blowing) mostly from discarded household appliances.

Smith discusses tools, fabrication, connecting, adjusting, testing, safety; and lists sources for burners and parts.

"This or a regular stove should burn with a blue cone-shaped flame. If it's yellow, burners and ports are clogged or need adjustment. Pipe-cleaners work well for unclogging gas ports." If you use too much air, you lose heating power. "Start with a flame that's slightly orange and increase the air flow until the flame turns blue. In some furnaces there is an increase in the sound of the burners at this point."

"Regulators provide about 30 pounds output pressure from 80 pounds pressure in the tank. Typically regulators are set for a given pressure by a screw which adjusts the pressure a spring places on a diaphragm inside.... Tightening the screw DECREASES the pressure. Usually you will not need to adjust the pressure...." However, for supplying a Bunsen burner, designed for low-pressure natural gas, "a standard propane regulator will produce an output of less than a pound by replacing the spring with a stiffer spring...."

Smith does not use a sparker. "The spark might not come at the correct time and the electronic sparking units tend to wear out after about a year. I got the best results using a pilot flame to light the main burner." Some of Smith's heaters require continuous pilot lights.

(Reviewers comment: But a home cooking stove doesn't. On it, a pilot is unnecessary, wasteful of gas, and dangerous: a gust or momentary pressure drop could extinguish the pilot light and fill the shelter with an explosive mixture that any spark (static, or an appliance turning on/off) could ignite. On our stove, we use an exhausted propane lighter as a sparker.)

"I started working with propane when cleanup day provided me with free materials. I went around collecting all the old propane regulators, valves and gas lines from equipment I could find at the curb. I even picked up several tanks still filled with propane, though discarding (them) is against the law. I took apart an old gas stove for the valves and burner assembly...."

"Propane safety information. If any propane tank starts leaking, you must get it outside, into the open air, at once." "Check for leaks with a soap and water solution sprayed on. NEVER use a flame...." "Don't leave propane cylinders in a hot area, like a closed car. Keep your car ventilated when transporting." Don't transport in the trunk. "Paint white or silver. Dark colored cylinders can overheat in the sun...." "Store and use propane cylinders outside, or in well-ventilated shed separate from house or main building."

Criticisms. Though some items are repetitive, others left us wondering. "Compression fittings are not recommended because they are more subject to mechanical harm.... I feel better with flare fittings" (but no illo to help reader identify the two types). And the only two illos have kinky lines. (Does the jet really have little steps? Or is that merely how the computer draws?

1992, Cybernetics Design, 88 E. Main St #457, Mendham NJ 07945-1832. Order # 16719. $9 ppd in 1995. Revu by B & H

There's Something About a Train, #3.
This collection of freighthopping stories is informative and entertaining. Some are by women and most are recent (early 1990s). Includes a map of U.S. "main lines" from Rand-McNally Handy Railroad Atlas; and 14 book reviews.

Rail maps are not designed for hobos. "Neither show Roseville (just east of Sacramento), yet it is the biggest yard in the western states...." But maps do show what companies serve what routes, which is important. Eg, if in L.A. and heading north, go to the Santa Fe or Southern Pacific yards. Likewise, if heading east, try Union Pacific yard.

"Topographic maps show in detail the layout of rail yards. Topos can be found and xeroxed in map rooms of most university libraries...." But some are old.

Finding a train going where you want to, may be difficult. "I woke up thinking the train had ridden south all nite. Unfortunately, it had taken a turn east in Portland and headed back up to Pasco."

New freighthoppers (at least) depend on railroad employees for train info. Fortunately, many are helpful. "The yard workers, the brakies and switchmen and the like, are sometimes friendly, usually cooperative... They won't turn you in.... I think that bulls (security guards) must give the yardworkers shit, and so the workers don't like them...." "The shop is where the mechanics of the yard hang out. I've found the shop to usually be a pretty safe no-bull zone."

"The tower is the tall, narrow,white building, found in most train yards. Its height enables any person at the top to have a full view of the train yard. Telephones, radios, camera monitors (and hobo haters) are in them... We put our backs to the wall and inched past...."

"It was the edge of winter, and this time I was gonna be prepared with COVER-ALLS, mechanic-style. They are loose and warm and you can pass as a guy in them."

"Car selection is important - the train might not stop for six hours. You want a good hiding place, and not where cargo will squish you. Trains do this slamming thing, which you can't hear coming and you have to be ready for all the time. Underneath a semi-truck, good in decent weather; ends of a grain car, good;"tween intermodals,ok but no hidin.

"Empty boxcars are your best bet for concealment, and bulls do not care so much if you ride them." Nothing to steal.

"It's preferable to get on before the train moves out, but as often as not you will have to catch it 'on the fly'. Boxcars are difficult and dangerous; grain cars, piggy-backs, and gondolas (long rectangular car with short walls) are much easier cuz of ladders that are just a big step from the ground. Look way ahead, make sure you won't stumble on anything while running alongside, concentrate, match your speed...."

Beware of some container cars, a few gondolas, and spiners (a kind of piggy-back) which don't have floors.

"When you move around, always hang on and not too close to the doors of box-cars - trains jerk a lot. Sitting on the edge of a boxcar opening with your legs hanging out is dangerous and could prompt a train stop and unhappy visit from a pissed-off train engineer. Always

jam a spike or piece of wood in the sliding track so the door won't slam shut (and lock you in). Never stand between two rail cars. Always look both ways before crossing tracks, in yards especially, as single cars can be moving silently. When possible, sleep sideways near a front wall or with your feet to front in case of sudden braking...."

"In general, it is better to ride near the middle or rear of the train, as cars near the front are those most likely to be dropped off...." "When your train stops in big yards, be prepared to hop off on the side not being monitored, until the bulls are thru checking...." (Many more tips and cautions in book)

"The older non-punk freight hoppers were mostly homeless white males who traveled from town to town picking up food stamps.... They were very dumb, very racist, and hard-core misogynists." The younger, punk freighthoppers traveled summers, but usually had a home or squat to return to.

"Reno supposedly has some of the harshest anti-homless laws in the west. You can be arrested for walking the streets just looking homeless, hitch-hiking, or hopping freights...."

An article in Oct'81 MP(DP) said, "hitching is quicker but freights are more thrilling." But much depends on appearance. "Some people still score good rides but I don't - being somewhat weird looking and punked out...." One author thinks freighthopping is safer than hitching and maybe even driving.

One criticism: a third of the space occupied by photos most of which didn't print well or add much information.

1995(?), 87p.8x11, $6ppd, Hobos From Hell, POB 2497, Santa Cruz. CA 95063

Personal Defense Weapons
This book, by J.Randall, briefly introduces types, functions, history and selection. Not a training manual.

Desirable traits of a weapon: likely to be with you; unobtrusive; likely to disable assailant long enough for you to flee; easy to use; hard to snatch away; legal and acceptable to you and society.

Punching can hurt the deliverer as much as the receiver. Brass knuckles provide hand protection plus increased impact, but are illegal. A substitute: "C" link, made for joining chain/rope. Made in various sizes. Use as key ring.

From a high-powered slingshot with ½" or larger ball-bearing ammo, "a shot to the head ... can kill and a hit any-where else can be extremely painful."

A bullwhip excells at scaring off dogs. 8 to 12 feet. Shorter won't snap loud; longer not practical.

Steel-capped shoes are inconspicuous (some look like regular shoes); enable you to kick hard; difficult to disarm.

Other weapons discussed: firearms; knives; canes (if age justifies, good for jabbing); night sticks and heavy flashlights; tear gas (effect unpredict-able); electric zappers; bow and arrow (good for home defense); martial arts weapons (impractical); steel clipboard.

"The best way to defend yourself is to avoid having to do so ...(by) being able to look mean, serious, and prepar-ed...." Because the eyes can reveal fear, do not maintain eye contact.

To strengthen your hands' grip, punch and resistance to injury, Randall recom-mends squeezing a solid rubber handball.

As for 'iron hand' traning, he says, "By the time my hands became formidable weapons they ceased being good for much else.... Yes, you can break bricks but be unable to tie your own shoes."

How we dispose of feces when inside.

This topic is slighted in publications, because foraging and eating foods is more glamorous than what happens at the other end. And most of what little is written, assumes you are outside in pleasant weather with no one else nearby. But what do you do in bitter cold? Or when there's 6 feet of snow? Or at a gathering where your tent is near many other people and far from a stinking, fly-infested community latrine?

When Bert and I began living in the woods, we soon devised simple solutions. And we assumed everyone else had too, and that the subject was not worth discussing. We learned otherwise when we reviewed (in Oct'95 DP) a book about trailer homesteading. The author was in the middle of a desert and had to truck in water from miles away. Yet, with much labor and expense, he installed a flush toilet and a septic field !

Anyhow, here is what Bert and I usually do when inside during winter. We have only one small insulated (warm) room, typically 10 ft diameter. We also usually have a plastic shed adjoining or nearby, which is not insulated.

For me, the urge to defecate comes suddenly, with only a few seconds warning. If I have to wait, I'm uncomfortable. As compensation, what comes out, does so quickly, in less than a minute. So I shit inside. (Yes, in view of Bert. He is welcome to watch, but doesn't seem interested.) The smell soon dissipates, especially if a drape is raised.

Bert is different. The urge comes gradually. But he takes longer to get everything out - maybe ten minutes. So Bert usually goes to the shed to shit, so that he does not occupy much of the floor (and interfere with my activity) and smell up our shelter a long time.

Regardless of where, our procedures are about the same: put a few pieces of paper on floor/ground; bring a pee bowl within reach; remove any bottom clothes; squat over the paper; defecate; wipe; fold/roll the paper up around the shit; put in a container outside; squat over the water-catch basin; wash crotch; wipe off excess water. Further tips:

Shit-on/wrap paper. We often use slick paper from catalogs or magazines which has no other re-use. We may put an 11x17 sheet on the bottom with two two 8½x11 sheets criss-cross over it.

Pee bowl. Presently a plastic 4# yogurt container with snap-on lid.

Wiping. We prefer brown paper with no printing on it. We get much from 25 -50# bags that grains/beans come in.) We've also used news print. We never buy special wipe paper. We crumple/crinkle each piece to roughen it for better wiping. For hygiene, I wipe from front to back. If I will also wash, I may use only two pieces. If water is scarce, I may use 20 pieces, spitting on every third to provide some washing.

Disposal. We temporarily store the shit packages in a one-gallon plastic detergent tub we keep outside on the coolest side of our shelter. Putting a little dirt in the bottom may reduce odor. When full, we empty into our narrow-hole (±8" diameter) latrine, somewhat smooth the surface by pressing with a log or rock, pour pee over it to repell animals that might dig it up, and cover with an inch of dirt. When near full, we cover with 6" or more of dirt and tamp firmly. (Privies and wide-hole latrines were invented before contagious diseases were understood, and are poorer than narrow-hole latrines in every way but one: they're somewhat easier to dig.)

Water-catch basin. (Also used with jug-faucet for washing hands or dishes. See, "Running Water Anywhere", LLL.) This is presently one half (vertically cut) of a 5-gallon syrup or salad-oil jug, previously used for water storage, which sprung a leak in its other half.

Washing. I hold a squeeze bottle in one hand and squirt water onto my pubic hair. The water runs down and off into my other hand which splashes the water onto my anus while simultaneously rubbing. (More technique involved than I realized until I observed myself just now.) I also rinse after peeing, but that only requires squirting.

Bert and I have never lived IN a vehicle (vs car camping). But if we did, I think we would defecate just as we do now. Except, if I was sharing a bus with a large number of people, I think I'd like it to have a small room with a snug-closing door, an electric fan vented outside, and a waterproof tub-floor - so it could also be used for jug showers. Holly & Bert, Oregon

Common Poisonous Plants & Mushrooms of North America, 324pp 6x9,215 color photos

Nancy Turner and Adam Szczawinski describe over 150 plants, both wild and cultivated. Each entry includes photos, common name, species, family, description, occurance, toxicity (to animals and people), treatments (most assume hospitals), and notes. Plus a 19-page index (lacks entries such as "saponin" and "thujone"), and 99 references.

Children under 5 are "most vulnerable to accidental poisoning." (Elsewhere I read that during weaning, children necessarily fear new tastes less.)

The N.Am. plant most violently toxic is water hemlock (Cicuta spp.), It is mistaken for parsnip, carrot, celery.

The fiddleheads of bracken fern contain "high concentrations" of carcinogens and thiaminase (destroys vit. B1). Even though risks to humans "have not yet been fully established", it "should no longer be used." Ostrich fern (Matteuccia struthiopteris) fiddleheads safe.

All parts of nightshade (Solanum dulcamara) are toxic. Yet Adam recently found its leaves in a restaurant salad.

Comfrey contains liver-damaging alkaloids. But those who gather it should distinguish from more-toxic foxglove.

Many ornamentals are extremely toxic. At least remove flowers of such plants as castor bean and lantana - which develop fruits attractive to children.

As antidote to Indian hellebore, death camus, and water hemlock, B.C. natives eat lots of salmon oil.

1991, $55+$4p&h in'92. Timber Press, 133 SW 2nd Av #450, Portland OR 97204

We do most of our cooking over a one-burner propane stove.
The one-pound cylinders cost $2½. You can save money by
refilling them yourself from a 20-pound tank which costs $6-
$7 to refill. Use an adapter you buy or make, and, to refill
the small cylinder, turn the 20-pound tank upside down.
A Coleman stove comes along as back-up. I use Amoco
Silver (used to be called "white gas") in all Coleman units.
Never had any problems, but you got to be careful. Seldom do
we cook in the van, but I keep a fire extinguisher there anyway. Frank Dolan, West Virginia,Oct
(Comment:) There is also an adapter for connecting a 20-pound
tank to a stove made for the little cylinders, but it costs
$12 new. (Not seen used.) Better to buy a stove made for 20-
pound tank plus regulator. Check RV salvage yards.
If a camping trip is so short that a one-pound cylinder
would suffice, better to leave the stove behind and take
ready-to-eat foods (pinole, popcorn, cookies, etc.). H & B

How to withdraw water from a bucket without contaminating it.
I installed a small spigot about one inch from the
bottom of a 5-gallon bucket. Thereby, after I fill the
bucket, the lid stays on and the contents stay clean. I am
not repeatedly dipping into the bucket, risking contaminat-
ion. The spigot makes hand washing easy. The lid must be
on loosely for the water to run freely. Laura LaBree, WA,
June
(Alternative:) After sediment settles, we transfer the entire
contents at one time via funnel to plastic jugs. We half-
empty bucket by dipping with a clean bowl; then slowly pour
the remainder. As we use water, we take it from the jugs.
For washing hands, utensils and vegies, we partially
fill our "portable faucet", which is an inverted jug, filled
through an opening cut in the former bottom. To "turn on",
we twist the cap, thus loosening it and letting water out
through it. (See LLL paper, or Oct'81 MP(DP).)
Advantages we see for Laura's method: Less transfering
of water. Buckets are easier to clean than are jugs (which
gradually collect a grungy film on the inside).
Advantages we see for our method: Simpler equipment -
no spigot to procure or hole to drill. Jugs are more
plentiful (and expendable) than are buckets. Holly & Bert

When using a jug to shower, we REMOVE the cap.
Some people try just loosening the cap. But that does
not let much water out of an UNcut jug. (A jug used as a
faucet has a filler hole cut in the former bottom.) Holly

A child's inflatable wading pool makes a dandy tub.
Use both for bathing and for washing clothes. But it
will withstand only cool or warm water (not hot). Guy Hengst

Van remodeled to provide more storage space.
I am now living near the Pisgah National Forest in
western North Carolina. Luckily, my 25-year-old van broke
down near the home of friends. It is on blocks with the
engine out (clutch problems) and covered with a tarp. The
camper top is up so I have standing room. For a porch,
I put a wooden pallet by the door. I am re-doing the inside.
I got rid of the built-in sink and refrigerator. Easier
to wash dishes in a 5-gallon bucket or in my friends' house.
And any stuff that needs cooling, I keep outside.

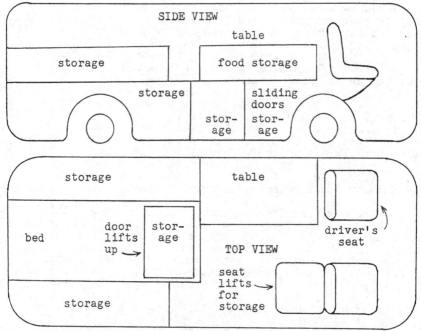

I extended the sleeping platform using ½" plywood, and have storage under the bed area. Now, all my things can be stowed away without jamming and breaking anything.

The van had a closet on one side that ran from the floor to the roof and completely blocked the long window on the passenger side. I cut it at window height and installed the cut half on the other side. Now I have an extra big window and a much more efficient storage area on each side of my bed.

The only materials I had to buy new were two 4x8' sheets of plywood, plus 20 small L-braces for attaching. I reused everything else, especially the pre-laminated. It looks good.

One of my best ideas: have sliding doors instead of swinging ones, so I don't have to move things to open doors.

I am plugged into electricity for my 75-watt light, corn popper for boiling water (etc), and a portable shortwave radio.

I am living on wages earned last summer, and some days I help my friends with their landscaping business.

The weather here in the mountains has been okay the past few weeks. One snow flurry left one inch which melted by noon. Nights 30-40°, days 50-60° a few to 70°. I am writing this during a rainstorm that's lasted 12 hours so far. Eugene
Gonzalez, NC, March

I have traveled many miles while van camping.
East of the Mississippi, I get reasonably secure over-nights in county hospital parking lots. And nobody has ever bothered me at river or ocean "put-ins" for fishers with boats. Boat ramps are usually quiet spots and sometimes in early morning you can get a fresh fish just by asking. Only one unpleasantry: a broken window and petty theft in New Orleans.

We often carry an old, battered aluminum canoe. Nobody wants to steal it, and with it we get to places often over-looked, such as the headwaters of the Green River and a stretch of the Colorado. The canoe is good for fishing, too.

We take along a weather radio and a small world-band radio. They keep us posted - and entertained: CBC and BBC are often funny, sometimes even on purpose. Frank Dolan, WV, Oct.

Selecting a vehicle for dwelling in.

Holly and I have little first-hand experience (some car-camping 20 years ago) but we get many reports from others.

For simply living out in the bush for long periods, a vehicle is a poor choice. Much better is some sort of back-packable or temporary shelter. It will be more comfortable, especially during cold or hot weather, because it can set directly on the ground (or, better yet, partially sunken) which moderates temperature. It will be safer, because it can be carried away from roads without leaving conspicuous tracks. It will be cheaper. It will be less trouble, without the legal problems (insurance, registration) or maintenance problems (keeping battery charged). A vehicle may be helpful occasionally for scouting and for hauling in supplies, but is best used promptly and then disposed of.

The only reason to dwell in a vehicle, is because you are moving frequently. Maybe you are traveling. Or maybe you are in a city and parking on the streets.

For traveling, consider a vehicle you already have, if any, because you may soon tire of travel. Or, you may discover an area where you want to linger. People who live in one place for many years, especially in a small town, get starved for travel and believe they can never get too much of it. But, like with any hunger, feeding brings satiation.

If you have a sedan, camping along side will probably be more comfortable than sleeping in it. During mild weather, all you will need is a sleeping bag or two, a foam pad, and a small tent with ventilation screened against insects. For easiest set up, get a tent that is self supporting - not needing tie-outs. Weather-proofness not too important: in a heavy rain or strong wind you can retreat to the car.

If buying a vehicle, sedans are generally cheaper than pickups or vans in comparable mechanical condition. A fairly big car may be best if fuel costs will be minor. (If you pay $500 for the vehicle, spend another $500 for insurance and licensing, and then drive it 2000 miles; even at 10 miles-per-gallon, fuel will cost only $250 - one fifth the total.)

If price isn't crucial, and if spending much time in the backcountry, I'd choose a pickup with canopy (NOT a big camper), because they have more ground clearance. Also, pickups are common in the bush and don't attract much attention.

For use mostly in cities, I might choose a van, for more room, a more weather-proof shell, and so I could move around inside without going out. The fewer windows, the better, because you may want to block them for insulation and so that people can't see in and light inside can't shine out.

Unless with a dozen or more people, I'd not get a bus, because it won't go as many places and because it is more conspicuous. For 8 people traveling together, I'd get a van but only ride in it, and set up separate tents for sleeping.

In these "interesting" times, when many folks are suspicious or resentful, especially of anyone who has more leisure or seems to be enjoying life more, the best vehicle for living in may be one that does not look like it is being lived in. Preferably not new, but not too shabby either.

Even people who can afford a $50,000 motorhome should consider: it will be a tempting target for robbers - **AND COPS**. And if police find one speck of an illegal substance

(which might have been tracked in; or planted by the police
themselves) or if they want to claim they SUSPECT the vehicle
is being used for something illegal (they need not PROVE anything), they can confiscate the rig, everything in it, and any
bank accounts too (so the victims will not even be able to
hire lawyers to fight back). And the police share in the loot.
      We have read idylic tales of motor nomading in big rigs.
But these stories seem to be from 20 or more years ago when
police maybe did not have as much power. Or, maybe the stories
were written for commercial RV magazines (which exist to sell
RVs and accessories) and left out the bad news.
      Don't buy any vehicle unless you are at least able to do
routine maintenance and minor repairs - or unless you have
loads of money. If not, hitch/bus/fly to your destination,
then buy a used bicycle for local travel.
      What I've said about hunger for travel, applies equally
to hunger for settling. Don't buy any land, at least not
until you have lived in an area for several years. Some folks,
after seeing a few beautiful sunrises over the mountains and
sunsets over the ocean, are sure THIS is where they want to
live forever; forgetting they might have once felt the same
about some other place. Realtors love such people.   H & B

Some engines seriously damaged if timing belt breaks or slips.

      The valves will collide with the pistons ! 1981 to 1992
engines at risk include all: Acura, Alfa Romeo, Daihatsu,
Honda, Hyundai, Mitsubishi, Nissan, Sterling, Volkswagon,
Volvo. Plus: Audi V8, diesel; BMW 2.5-2.7L; Chrysler Corp.
Medallion 2.2L and Mitsubishi built; Fiat 1.3-2.0L; Ford
Escort 1.6L, 2.3L diesel and Mazda built; Infiniti 3.0L; Isuzu
all except 1.6L; Mazda 2.0L diesel, 2.2L, 3.0L; Peugeot 2.2L;
Porsche all 4 & 8 cyl; Suzuki 1.3L DOHC; Toyota 2.2L, 1.5L,
1.8L, 2.4L diesel; Yugo 1.1L. (from J.C.Whitney 1995 catalog)
      What a crazy way to design engines. A friend said it's
done so the valves can be bigger or open wider, for more air
flow and thus more power at high RPM. But makes little
difference at normal speeds. I'd avoid those models. Bert

What's wrong with $750 bicycles?

      Many are not fixable with ordinary tools. Thus, to the
$750, add the cost of special tools - also their weight.
      Expensive bikes are more attractive to thieves. And, if
stolen, much more is lost. My $10 or $20 bicycles are less
likely to be stolen. And, at that price, I can afford to have
several, stashed in various locations. If one does get ripped
off, I'm not out much. Julie Summers, Oregon, December

LED lights, used on bicycle and in camp, conserve batteries.

      I like the flashers for riding at night, because I can
usually see well enough to ride without a light but cars may
not see me. I use a red light in back and a yellow in front.
      The yellow light can also be turned on steady. It is
perfect for peeing at night or finding things in my pack. It
attaches with a clip to my collar for hands-free use.
      The two AA batteries last 300 hours flashing and 60 hours
steady - much longer than in an ordinary flashlight. The LED
light bulbs are rated for 100,000 hours. Mine is Vistalite,
bought from Bike Nashbar for $12, but I assume they are sold
by most bike stores. Chris Soler, Washington, November

Rubber strap expedient fix of bike tire with bad bulge.

      Wrapped around tire and rim. After 50 miles, showed wear.
                                                    Bert

Dwelling Portably

formerly named Message Post
POB 190, Philomath OR 97370
December 1996 $1 per issue   Add 50¢ to check/mo under $6

Blowtube turns balky campfire into healthy blaze.
   Take an old tentpole section, or piece of
thin metal tubing. Flatten the exhaust end
to increase pressure. Place a handful of
small sticks on last night's faintly
glowing embers. A slow puff of air
through the tube aimed at the
embers, makes the fire burst into
life. Bridge, Utah, July

(Comments:) I have rejuvenated fires just by blowing with my
mouth. But if doing it often, a tube is nice for keeping
your face further from the fire and for getting the breeze
right where you want it. Other sources of tubing: discarded
aluminum lawn chairs; rolled-up paper (maybe dampen exhaust
end to resist fire); hollow stalks. Bert

Cow-tongue cactus may alleviate painful joints.
   Growing in Texas and Arizona (and maybe elsewhere), it
looks like a chain of cow tongues each licking the next. And
each pad is about the size of a cow tongue. Use a new bud
(new pad; not the fruit) when about 3" long. Imbibe some each
morning for about four days. Takes that long to act. Seems
to "grease up" the joints. An old Native American man told me
this remedy. Double Dorje, Arizona, 1995

(Question:) To prepare, Dorje suggests: put some in a jar,
refrigerate 24 hours, drink off the liquid (what oozes out?
or is the bud soaked in water?), refill jar, and repeat.
I wonder if this is done so the thorns need not be removed
from the bud. Can people who lack refrigeration just eat it?

Oxalis grows prolifically in the Pacific Northwest.
   And Nancy Turner and Adam Szczawinski mention oxalis
(Oxalis spp., wood sorrel (another name for it) family) as a
lemonade substitute, in Edible Garden Weeds of Canada.
   So I tried it. I picked a few handfuls of leaves and
stems, put in a pot, covered with water, and boiled about 5
minutes. The water had hardly any taste. The cooked greens
tasted sort of like spinach. Thinking I'd used too much
water, I repeated, using two cups oxalis and only ¼ cup water.
After boiling 5 minutes, the water was a beautiful dark pink.
It tasted very tart so I only sipped it. With sugar it might
have tasted like lemonade. I did add sugar to the leaves and
stems which then tasted somewhat like rhubarb.
   Nancy and Adam say, "The leaves are also a tasty addition
to soups and stews and, like the leaves of sheep sorrel (Rumex
acetosella), make a superb sauce.... They are also said to
make a delicious dry wine." Kirk, in Wild Edible Plants of
the Western US, says, "The leaves and stems may be eaten raw."
   However, I hesitate to eat much of the plant in any form
because of the high oxalic acid content.
   In appearance, oxalis resembles clover, and along with
white clover and black medic, is a shamrock (trefoil) - the
emblem of Ireland - indicating it grows there also. Each stem
is a few inches long and ends in three heart-shaped leaflets,
which are often somewhat folded along their central veins.
                                        Julie Summers, 1987

Another simple way to dispose of feces when inside.

Compared to your system (May96 DP), ours is just as effective and even more simple. We use two buckets. At least one, the toilet bucket, has a close-fitting lid. The other bucket holds a ready supply of dirt, gathered in summer when dry, and the clods are broken up.

A little dirt is first put in the toilet bucket to furnish the bacteria needed to break down the feces. After each deposit, a little dirt is sprinkled over the feces and wipe paper. A squirt or two of water will wilt the paper and cut down on the amount of dirt needed. This process is repeated until the bucket is full.

Then either: the bucket is emptied into a trench or hole and covered with at least 6" of soil; or the bucket can be tightly closed and a third bucket put in its place. In 3 to 6 months (depending on weather), the feces will be turned into soil, and can even be used as the covering. Alma Schreiber, CA, June

(Comments:) The chief advantage I see for your system: paper to hold/wrap the feces is not needed. The chief advantage I see for our system: bulky pails are not needed inside where we have little space. (Our insulated shelter only ± 9' D.)

Something not mentioned. Do you have a toilet seat that sets over the pail? Or do you place blocks on each side to raise your feet, and squat over the pail? Either would work.

Alternatives to flush toilets.

Flush toilets are a poor joke. They gobble up water. And if not warmed enough in northern winters, they crack.

I put efficient RV potties in all my mobile homes and living quarters. In colder climes I use the kind that does not need flushing tanks.

On lots without a $2500 septic system, I simply pull in a portable outhouse that looks just like the rental units. This keeps inspectors at bay and is usually legal with a little ingenuity - like you are gonna build soon and are working on the foundation. I pick these up from the rental places when they get too banged up to rent. ($100 up.) I scrounge the wheels or trailer cheaply.

In many counties, out houses are still legal. But building inspectors will seldom tell you that they are.

I once lived next to a gypsy camp where most of the population only spent the winter. Very few were legal. When harrassed too far, they would simply pull their trailers away for a few months. In summary, you don't need to conform if it is not affordable or to your liking. Al Fry, Idaho, 96

I am in a large 'wild' guava orchard in Kilauea.

I squat to pee or poop. I poop near my camp in a hole I dig, cover with soil and leaves (becomes fertilizer), wash anus with pee, and clean with water or leaves. Most third-world bush folk do likewise.

I bottle-bathe frequently by pouring quart or gallon jug of clean cool water over my naked body. Very invigorating now. I wash face, feet and hands in cold water to wake up or clean up.

This mini camp is only sleeping/dreaming space. During rains I hang a space-sheet-tarp over my bush hammock. During storms I get wet. Wild chickens forage and crow nearby.

Acclimatizing to nature is the simplest way to be warm, bug free or immune, energetic, and happy wherever we are. Micheal Sunanda, HI

Parents with unusual lifestyles should take precautions.
With the current trend to persecute those whose beliefs or lifestyles are different, especially in the Bible Belt parents are in danger of being accused of child abuse or molestation, having their kids seized, and going to prison.
I read in publications I receive: Over 50% accused of child-related crimes are innocent. Of those in prison, over 75% never saw their court-appointed attorney other than the only day they went to court. Over 98% were coerced by the state and their lawyer into taking a plea bargain instead of going to court. Two gentlemen who arrived here in prison the past month, are nomads but not for the next 10 or 20 years. They had a choice: plead guilty; or have their wives arrested and their children forced into foster care.
If you think you are safe because you have never had any problems or you have never been spotted by the law, remember: it only takes one trip to the emergency room and then, unless you pay cash right there, the police and state are involved.
I recommend: Never put your kids in school. Never take federal or state money to support your kids. Never let churches or religious groups know how you live. If changing lifestyles, always relocate at least several hundred miles from your last sedentary residence. Never stay in one camp more than a couple of weeks, and move on immediately once the authorities become aware of you. Keep your licenses in order.
Guy Hengst, IN ,Feb.
(Comments:) Thanks for your recommendations. Others: Keep school-age kids out of public view during school hours. And when in public view, try to look fairly conventional. To make dressing up less unpleasant, don't go to populated places often, and, when you do, beforehand try discussing them as if they were costume parties. (In a way they are.) If you go to an 1840s-style rendezvous, you will probably have a better time if you, too, dress that way. Likewise if you go to a 1990s city or public campground.
As for never staying in one place longer than 2 weeks. If living in a vehicle, that is probably wise. (If parking on the streets, moving several times a day may be wise.) But if in a secure backpack camp, and you have not been seen by anyone; moving less often will be safer, because each move to and preparation of a new camp might attract attention.
We would like more info on the cases you know about. How were the people living? What brought the police?
We have no kids of our own. But we hear from quite a few parents, and we know of no arrests or child seizures due to unusual dwellingways (which is not to say there aren't any). However, most families we hear from are in the Pacific states. Hasslings may be worse in some other areas.
Overall, portable dwellers who home/un-school, seem to have fewer problems than do house dwellers who send their children to school - and then discover their kids are being turned into fashion hounds (expensive!), tube boobs, and junk-food-junkies; or, if they resist, are despised and tormented by the other kids, and maybe beaten up or worse.

Your zine seems to becoming more passive as issues go by.
Yes, I could shave off my beard, never be nude outside a bathroom, and never express a contrary opinion. Don't go to Rainbow gatherings: you'll just be hassled. Don't defend your property (electrify your vehicle): you might antagonize someone. What next? Don't live in the woods: someone might think you are the Unibomber.

There is a point where rights unexercised become rights revoked. It's one thing to maintain a low profile because one is doing something quasi-illegal (squatting). It's another thing to blend in at any price. I have a friend who won't order books (ANY books) from Loompanics because then he might end up on a government "list". I told him, if we all got on as many lists as possible, then the lists would be useless for profiling anyone, or even for rounding up people.

Where would Blacks and Gays be now if they had never asserted themselves? Certainly more persecuted than they are now! The Amish have done pretty well at resisting public schooling and state-required registration of outhouses.

You don't need to be Freud to see that bigots and religious zealots are basically insecure. So they want to force everyone else to conform. That will ease their self doubts. Well, I don't intend to encourage their persecutions by always "lying" low and lying (denying) what I really am.

I haven't been lynched yet. If I am, I insist that you dedicate an issue to me as a martyr to the cause. L.Smith, Febr.

(Reply:) I don't think DP has become more passive. To the contrary, the Oct95 issue had perhaps the most activist article yet: about how one portable dweller, without great effort, launched an apparently-successful boycott of a city.

One problem with Standing Up For Your Rights. You can't really do that, unless you have a bigger and better arsenal than the cops and are willing to shoot it out. You are depending on the police and prosecutors not being as nasty as they could be. On one hand, if you have plenty of money for lawyers or if (eg) the ACLU happens to take an interest in your case, you might get an evil law overturned. On the other hand, the cops may decide to make an "example" out of you to deter other non-conformists. They beat you up, then charge you with "resisting arrest" - and your court-appointed attorney advises you to plead guilty.

Trying to defeat someone at their own game, is usually not wise. If a bull charged you, would you lower your head and counter-charge? Or would you climb a tree or hop fence?

Even if you are willing to become a martyr, most people aren't. By using boycotts, we can fight back without becoming martyrs. Blacks made effective use of boycotts. So did Gays (against Colorado when it passed an anti-Gay law). If we avoid a particular area, or if we earn and spend less generally, less taxes are collected. That hits politicians and police where they are vulnerable: in their wallets. Also, merchants will become unhappy and (better than you or I could) pressure the police to desist. Of course, a boycott by DP readers alone won't have great impact. But word gets around. We don't say, avoid all Rainbows. We do say, hold Rainbows only where people are friendly, or where there are no other people. Bert and Holly, Oregon, November

Rural deputies claim many people hide in the back country.
Clyde McLain, undersheriff for Crook County, told this story. "The sun was just going down over the rimrock and another deputy and I were heading back to town in an unmarked rig over this little dirt road. All of a sudden I looked up and saw a guy standing in the trees up ahead watching us. He was dressed in brown, camouflaged in the trees, and had a gun strapped to his hip." The deputies stopped and talked with the man, who turned out to be a benign fugitive, merely fleeing the company of other people.

McLain says some of the juniper-covered ravines and pine-lined mountainsides of eastern Oregon are dotted with little hideaways sheltering such solitary folk, living without electricity or telephones or nearby neighbors. Some, he says, are the law-abiding type, wanting only to be left alone. But others are hiding from the law. "There was one ranch out near Paulina in the middle of nowhere, and I can remember how eerie it was. As soon as you drove in, just for a split second you'd see 20 or 30 people. And then you'd see nobody."

A survey of law-enforcement agencies around the state, produced a chorus of agreement with McLain's view that it's easy for a fugitive to vanish into secluded mountainsides. (from The Oregonian, 1996; sent by James)

(Comments:) Why did all those "fugitives" stand up in plain view when an unknown vehicle drove in? And do they even exist? We spend most of our time in the woods, in areas more attractive than Crook County (which is far from any city), and we encounter few other woods dwellers. Maybe McLain just wanted his name in the paper, and would like more taxpayers' money to "protect the public" from "fugitives".

Furthermore, we and people we know are "fugitives" only from absurdly-expensive housing (though we also like living in the woods because they are attractive). I doubt that remote woods attract many desparados because, my impression is, most real criminals crave excitement. They'd get bored.

The original article, which included the line, "... back country is filled with reclusive souls like the Unabomber...", is typical of the sleaze delivered by the major media. Viewers and readers beware. Bert and Holly

An igloo or snow cave is more comfortable if lined.
The snow is fair insulation, but keeps the inside from getting much warmer than the snow's melting point (and if it does - drip, drip, drip). Insulations I've tried are either bulky to carry (foam) or tedious to gather (leaves). Other suggestions? (no name on this, which got separated)

Recently I designed a solar-powered knock-down pyramid.
I am also attracted to dome homes. Ross McKenzie, BC,June

Mud is an interesting building material.
Though not light or portable, in some situations it is inexpensive and easy to use. We built a 20-foot post-and-beam circle with shed-roof low to the north. We filled the low north side with 2-foot-thick mud walls and the high south side with windows. Three of us were very comfortable during our long, cold northern winter. On sunny days the door was open, and most nights the fire was allowed to burn out.

Mud could be used on a smaller scale in the woods. If carefully done, it could be very discreet and leave no obvious scar. Cob Cottage Co., Box 123, Cottage Grove OR 97424, offers courses on building with mud. Jai Loon, WA, 1996

(Comment:) In most situations (obviously not in a swamp or where drainage is poor), for a small structure I prefer to make a dug-out of some kind. (Eg, Snugiup, May95 DP) That way the walls are of undisturbed soil which may already be naturally reinforced with roots, instead of disturbed soil which may need reinforcement. A dug-out does require more digging, but if small that is tolerable. Bert, Oregon, Nov.

Dwelling Portably

May 1997 $1 per issue

formerly named Message Post
POB 190, Philomath OR 97370
Add 50¢ to check/mo under $6

Handy bike panniers easily made.

These are more widely available, easier to load, more durable, and easier to keep out of wheels than are feed bags (in LLL paper, "My two-wheel Truck"). Also more versatile: off the bike I use them to fetch water, launder, and hold things.

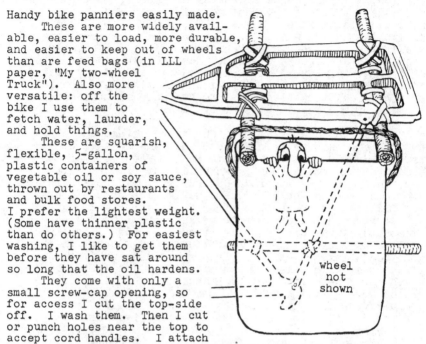

wheel
not
shown

These are squarish, flexible, 5-gallon, plastic containers of vegetable oil or soy sauce, thrown out by restaurants and bulk food stores. I prefer the lightest weight. (Some have thinner plastic than do others.) For easiest washing, I like to get them before they have sat around so long that the oil hardens.

They come with only a small screw-cap opening, so for access I cut the top-side off. I wash them. Then I cut or punch holes near the top to accept cord handles. I attach each end of the cord by passing it thru the hole in the pannier, and (not shown) up around the lip of the pannier and tie to itself. I leave extra length so I can adjust the height of the pannier after it is on the bicycle.

For hanging the panniers, I permanently lash two sticks to my bike's rear rack, at right angles to the wheels, about pail's width apart, and far enough to the rear to keep the panniers out of the way of my heels when pedaling. I lash the sticks to the rack's UNDER side, so they don't raise what is on top of the rack and make the bike less stable. Make lashing strong enough to take weight of the loaded panniers.

The pannier's handle slips over the sticks. To secure handle, I tie its ends to the rack, or pass rubber straps (cut from old inner tubes) around the sticks outboard of the handle, front and rear (which may also hold on a top load).

I also lash sticks to the bike frame parallel to the wheel (shown), to keep the panniers out of the wheel.

These panniers are not easy to cover (because their handles interfere). Therefore, if rain likely, I prefer square 4-gallon plastic pails with snap-on lids. But they are heavier and slightly smaller. (The square (viewed from above) pails wobble less than do round pails.) Julie Summers, Oregon, Dec.

Tent camping and working in southern Appalachians.

My stay with friends ended because of driveway improvements and inlaws visiting. I'm now working at an "exclusive resort community" and have a wonderful campsite in the woods nearby. I am using a Eureka Timberline 2-man tent. I sleep on my Thermarest Camprest in an old sleeping bag ($5 at yard sale). Outside my front entrance is a huge rock formation, over which I put a camo tarp to form a miniature porch.

I've found many useful items in a nearby dump, including a hibachi over which I cook dinners with oak firewood (less smoke). I use plastic 4-pound peanut jars to store things.

For pee I use a one-gallon Chlorox bleach jug. That brand has a wider opening (more comfortable). I empty 30 feet from camp. Does pee scare away animals? A few bears are around.

I make $8 an hour and work 25-35 hours/week. On the mountain side I build railroad-tie structures 60x40', which are filled with dirt to form level sites for RVs. Hard work.

In June, nights were 45-60°; days 70-85°. Now in late autumn, nights 30-40°; days 50-60°. Eugene Gonzalez, NC, Dec

Tent liner-ette improvised from large bedsheet.

When some unexpectedly-cold spring weather caught us in under only a plastic tarp, I rigged a double-bed-size sheet across the head end of our bed, suspending it with four ball-ties (like the insect net shown in May96 DP).

With heads inside the sheet-tent, our breathing raised air temperature 10-15°F over the near-freezing outside, allowing us to use bare hands for (eg) writing and sewing without discomfort. Our lower bodies remained warm in sleeping bags.

Enough air filtered through the sheet for ventilation. Moisture from our breath dampened the sheet, but did not annoy us because we touched sheet only when we reached outside. B&H

Further report on the Stansport model-723 dome tent.

We used it for a month last summer. The smell seemed less (see May96 DP) maybe because we were in it mostly at night when cool. With a net top beneath a built-in fly, and a double door (one netting; one fabric), ventilation ample. When closed, with two inside maybe 5-10° warmer than outside.

As a bug barrier, the tent was fine - even better than our home-made net-tent because of sewen-in bottom. The zippers (which we'd had doubts about) survived frequent use.

Though most days dry, a few were very rainy. The built-in fly shed fine. But much water came in the trough-like seam where sides and bottom joined. (We carefully kept ground tarp from protruding beyond sides.) To cope, we suspended a large, clear-plastic tarp above the tent. (If simply layed over, it reduced ventilation, causing condensation inside.) But the tarp with its tie-outs, nullified the self-supporting tent's chief advantages: quick set up; and no lines to trip over.
B&H

South slopes warmer, but beware if steep enough to slide.

For winter campsites, I prefer south-facing slopes. The steeper, the warmer when sun, because the light spreads over less ground. Also, downhill trees less likely to block sun.

However, if very steep, snow or wet soil may slide. A mostly-treeless patch extending up-down, in an otherwise-forested area, may indicate former (and future?) slides. (Some spots are treeless because soil thin. Sign: bedrock protruding. If rock firm, spot maybe safe unless much snow.)

How steep is too steep? That depends on soil and snow. I'm wary if more than one yard rise per two yards on slope.
B&H

Dwelling in a bus in Toronto.

From June 1992 until Oct 1995, I lived in a full-size (35') Chev school bus. I spent one year in New Orleans, and two years, including one milder-than-usual winter, in an industrial area of downtown Toronto. Another winter was too cold to live in my bus, so I stayed with friends.

The bus, which had not been on the road for two years, cost $1300 Cdn. I also bought furnishings I installed.

In Toronto, I fortunately found a parking spot that was near attractions of the city, but also had open space, trees, birds and animals.

Finding my urban oasis took some asking around. The property was practically abandoned. I discovered who the owner was, and wrote a letter explaining the advantages of me being there as a guard. Unscrupulous container trucks often dumped illegally in the area at night. Anyway, the owner let me stay, and then I never heard a thing.

I lived alone there, tried to be as discrete as possible, and didn't have many visitors. I kept the entrance blocked. I was on a deadend street and few people came there except for hookers turning tricks in cars. Though I don't object to their trade, I encouraged them to go elsewhere because many are addicts and hang out with Bad guys.

Metal is a good conductor of heat, so warming my "tin shack" was difficult. Accumulated snow would melt off the roof. I bought a propane RV furnace (forced air), insulated the floor with "Reflectix", covered the windows with plastic, and formed movable partitions by hanging thrift-store curtains with velcro, so when extremely cold the heat could be concentrated in a small area.

I slept warm and cozy in a quality sleeping bag with blankets piled on top. But getting out of bed was uncomfortable.

I experimented with a cheap, silver, heat-reflecting "space" blanket, and it helped. You are supposed to suspend it above you somehow.

I cooked on a propane camp stove. Propane is clean burning, relatively cheap, and widely available. I had a 100-pound tank. A friend with car helped me fill it - ± monthly in winter.

There happened to be an accessible city-water tap nearby, so about once a month I made 5 trips with a shopping cart and filled my outboard tank. From it, with an RV hand pump, I filled a low-cost water-filtering pitcher (Brita).

For cleansing, I collected rainwater into another tank, and used a standard easy-to-find car-windshield-washer pump (with switch, foot operated), some low-cost vinyl tubing, and jerry-rigged a spout beside a used stainless-steel sink. The sink drained directly under the bus. The pump's low flow was enough to wash dishes, vegies, face, etc. I bathed at a nearby public swimming pool.

My "porta-potti" toilet was adequate for one person and occasional visitors. To control odor, baking soda (sodium bicarbonate) proved most effective. I emptied it about twice a week in a nearby vacant lot, going at night to not be seen. I just poured out the contents and let the sun and rain dispose of.

Often my only night-time light was a candle, though I worried about carbon monoxide - deadly if vents shut tight.

Building the interior while living in it was frustrating at times. Best do as much as possible before moving in - otherwise you'll be living in a mess. Some knowledge of carpentry and metal working was needed, though this can be learned. Some ideas are in a 1970s picture book, Roll Your Own Home. Check libraries for others, eg, RV maintenance.

Moving a big bus down the road can be expensive. A bus/truck repair manual and mechanical abilities help. Even if you can't do a repair, you can diagnose. A repair shop is less likely to rip off someone in the know. Also consider step-vans, such as UPS and bakeries use. They are easier to park. Inside they are shorter but often higher.

I was never assaulted or burglarized. At first I worried, but gradually I relaxed. Toronto is a fairly safe city. Of course I kept the door locked, and when I went away I covered the windows. Potential thieves would be detered by the oddness, and by not knowing how many were here or if we had weapons or an attack dog. Other security measures might be: motion detectors that trigger a quiet alarm, or a camera; posted signs warning of dogs or electronic surveilance; or SECURITY VEHICLE.

One problem was height. I am six feet, and the ceiling inside was barely six feet in center, less at sides. Installing flooring for more insulation would further reduce height. This was one reason I eventually moved out.

In Oct 1995 I sold the bus and moved to Japan to be with the love of my life, a Canadian woman here on an English-teaching contract. I too now teach English, and we plan to stay until July 1997. Fred Spek, December

Most RVs are built to remain heated.

Freezing ruins all lines in RVs and trailers, including Airstreams. Some RV suppliers now carry a new plastic pipe that does not split when frozen. When I get an RV, I promptly replace all metal lines with rubber or plastic.

If without commercial electricity, to get running hot water is more trouble than it's worth. Al Fry, Idaho, June

Complex RV appliances are not reliable.

I once had a motor-home with a lamp, stove, oven, heater, and "instant" (no tank) hot-water heater, all propane.

The lamp and stove both had simple, manually-operated valves - and worked fine. The other appliances had thermostat controls and pilot lights - and all were perpetually troublesome.

The hot-water heater had additional problems. The main burner often blew out the pilot light, which required going outside to relight - in the middle of a shower! Also, an unexpected freeze cracked the tubing, causing a fast leak in an inaccessible spot.

Even house-size appliances are not reliable, I've heard. RV appliances are generally worse, because they must be smaller, cheaper, and (most important) fewer. To build something that is BOTH complex AND reliable, requires mucho engineering, which is affordable only if building millions (or if charging millions and selling to the government).

So, yes, DO do things simply. When you count maintenance, a (eg) jug shower using water warmed on a stove, is more convenient than a complicated "convenience". Chal, California, Dec.

More on RVs in May96 and May95 DPs.

Portable electric systems.

This is an update/summary of past articles, including Rob's in Jan91 and Hank's from Feb82 through Sept84 MP(DP).

If your base camp is remote both from power lines and motor vehicles, and if you want more electrical gear than a seldom-used flashlight or radio, you probably need a rechargeable battery plus a photovoltaic panel. (Other power sources: pedal generator; backpacking battery to where a charger can plug in.)

I still know of only two kinds of rechargeable batteries available: lead-acid and nickel-cadmium (nicad). Both contain toxic metals and corrosive liquids. Both produce explosive gases, especially if recharged rapidly. Both are easily damaged.

Lead-acid, especially, needs much care. If fully discharged, or if left long without recharging (they self-discharge), lead-acid batteries are ruined or seriously damaged. Even with the best of care, their life is only a few years. (Don't be confused by names given to varieties. Eg, "gell-cell". Any rechargeable battery bigger than a flashlight and less than $100 new, is probably lead-acid.)

Nicads are not damaged if not kept charged, and are generally longer life, but are very expensive. Even used nicads sell for several times as much as new lead-acids with equivalent capacity.

So, before buying, be sure you really need an electric system. For an occasional night light, a candle or even a propane lamp will be easier. (Yes, they are hazardous. But so are batteries.) To minimize use, during dark hours do things (eg, talk) not needing light.

Next, if such terms as amp-hours, volts and diode are like Greek to you, acquire some knowhow. Read Hank's series, or look for books in libraries.

If my system was very remote, and if I could afford them, I'd buy nicads. They are usually much less grief than are lead-acids. Otherwise, like Rob did I'd get used auto batteries. Though not tolerant of deep discharges, they are cheap, widely available, and (barely) light weight enough to backpack.

Suppose your system will be used mostly in winter when daylight is short. Each autumn, buy a used auto battery ($10-$15) from a dealer, or from a motorist who is buying a new battery. (Many do every few autumns to avoid winter problems.) The battery may no longer reliably start a cold engine, but should be near-fully charged (test all 6 cells with hydrometer) and be capable of holding a charge. (If, with no load, it self-discharges in only a few days, return it and get another.) With fair care, the battery will probably last the winter. If, then, you are away all summer and the battery is untended, it will self-discharge and be ruined. No big loss. Come autumn, trade it in (the metal is still valuable) on another.

A photovoltaic panel will cost $20 to $500, depending on size. Size isn't critical. But the panel MUST have at least 35 solar cells, wired in series, to generate enough volts (17 or so) to recharge a 12-volt battery.

(This assumes a system with battery. If powering equipment DIRECTLY, get a panel with about twice as many cells as volts needed. (Eg, 18 cells to power a 9-volt radio.) More may burn out radio.

The size needed, depends on your equipment and your sunshine. Some books tell how to calculate. Or you can buy a small panel and try it. If not big enough, add another. (Panels with same voltage can be paralleled.) Better a panel too small than too big. If too small, you can't use your equipment as you'd like. But if too big, fast overcharging may damage the battery as well as generating explosive gases (unless a regulator added: more cost/complication).

You will need a blocking diode (one-way valve) unless the pv panel has one built in. The diode prevents battery discharge back thru the panel at night. Frequently check battery with hydrometer. (A cheapo, with little balls that float or sink, is $1-2 at auto stores/depts.) When half discharged, shut off equipment until battery recharges. (Don't wait until (eg) lights dim. That will damage lead-acid battery.)

Radios take little power, tape player somewhat more, TV much more - especially color TV. Forget electric hot-plates, heaters, clothes driers, etc.: they need MUCH too much power to be practical.

If using a light several hours each night, a LED may be desirable, despite cost, because of efficiency and reliability. (Fluorescents are also efficient, but probably brighter than needed in a small shelter, and not too reliable.) If using a light seldom, ordinary small 12-volt incandescent bulbs (in auto stores) are cheap and adequate.

IMPORTANT. For safety, keep battery OUTSIDE your shelter, but near (to not lose much power in wires). Shelter from rain and sun, but ventilate space so explosive gases don't accumulate. B & H

Electricity in a bus.

I rigged a simple 12-volt system using a 100-amp-hour deep-cycle lead-acid battery (aka RV/marine). It looks like a regular car battery, but is designed to be discharged further, and may have different-looking connection posts. A car battery could be used, and they are cheaper and easier to find, but won't last quite as long. Keep a lead-acid battery warm, as they put out less power when cold. (The reason car batteries are so big, is for starting an engine when cold.)

Don't expect much power from just one battery. My loads were modest: a small stereo with AM/FM, cassette, CD; 8-watt fluorescent light ($15 from Canadian Tire), but the tubes can't take frequent switching on-and-off for long; the fan in my RV furnace; a windshield-washer pump used for water; and a 5-watt keyboard amplifier.

To recharge the battery, I bought a 22-watt (1½ amp full-charge current) amorphous photovoltaic solar panel. In winter it wasn't always enough, so I reluctantly ran an extension cord to the adjacent building to power a 12-volt battery charger. The cord also powered a 120vac heater I kept on hand for occasional comfort, or emergencies. I had to run the bus's engine occasionally, which also recharged some. Fred

117

Practical candle craft, and tips for easier use.

Candles are inexpensive, convenient light sources. I do not like candle light for reading, but it's fine for cooking and eating. CAUTION: burn only where ample ventilation.

I buy candles at yard/rummage sales. I seldom pay more than 25¢ for a big one (pound or more).

If a broad (eg, 3") candle burns long, a big pool of melted wax forms and may either drown the wick or spill over the side. To avoid that, I alternate two or three candles: I burn one until only a SMALL pool forms, then light another and extinguish the first to let its pool harden. But just in case wax spills, I set candles on a plate or pie pan. Any spilled wax usually pries off easily after hardening.

If a chunk of wax lacks a wick, I gouge a hole (with a narrow, pointy knife; though drill bit or hot nail works too) and insert a wick. Experts say, don't leave much air space around the wick; so, if the hole is overly large, I stuff wax shavings in beside the wick, and I may drip wax from a lit candle onto the wick to "prime" it. In any case, as soon as the new wick is burning, it melts wax that fills in the hole.

Some broad candles come with thin wicks that burn little craters in the wax until the flame is surrounded by wax walls that shade it. I insert (as above) a stouter wick alongside the original, or distribute thin wicks and burn one at a time.

An easy way to make a candle from small scraps of wax: put them in a shallow clear-glass jar and insert a wick between them. As the wax melts down, I add more pieces. I keep the level of wax near the top of the jar, so the flame doesn't heat the glass enough to crack it.

For wicks, I experiment with various cotton strings from my collection. Some work better than others. If too thin, I twist a length, then fold in half and let it twist itself into a 2-ply cord. To make thicker yet, I repeat to get 4-ply,etc.

I have also made candles from various animal and vegetable fats, and wicks from thistle or cattail down. I may form a wick by rolling the down between my hands and doubling (as above). (Tricky because these fibers are short.) Or I may mix the down with soft fat, glom onto an 1/8" diameter stick, and insert the stick as a wick into fat. If the fat is liquid I put a few pebbles around the stick to hold it up. Collect plant down when you find it: may not be in season when needed.

To extinguish a candle, I prefer using a metal bottle cap as snuffer. (Blowing may spray wax or leave a smoking wick. Pinching wick between moistened fingers may scorch fingers or get wax on them. Julie Summers, Oregon, November

I have been treating my engine with Slick-50.

I began at 70,000 miles. Now 217,000 miles and no major engine repairs on my 1981 Ford 6 cylinder. Under $20 when on sale. Steve Ronalter, Connecticut, May

Synthetic oil is the best thing to put in an oil can.

Fans on RV heaters will seize up in a few months using the usual auto oils. Two-cycle oil is next best for holding up under heat. Al Fry, Idaho, April

I keep an extra key tied in the laces of my shoe.

That way I avoid a major disaster if I lock myself out of my car while shopping, laundering, hiking or gold panning. Tumbleweed, CA, May   (Comment: A few times my shoe lace has broken without me noticing until I had walked many yards. I would tie the key so it hangs down into the shoe. H&B)

Equipping a vehicle for dwelling in.

Keep it simple. Don't install plumbing. Put in only what you can easily remove. That way you can use the vehicle for hauling, or use the equipment separately at a remote camp.

For a bed, plywood supported by crates may be warmer than the floor, and provides storage space beneath. Bedding used for backpacking should also suffice in a vehicle, except you may want more padding: wood is harder than most soils.

Though ready-to-eat foods are abundant in cities, in the back-country an ability to cook can increase food variety and reduce cost. A propane stove is usually best. (Campfire smoke could attract hassles.) Get one that connects to a 5-gallon tank. (Not to the little cans. The fittings are different.)

May96 & Dec96 DPs tell simple ways to defecate inside.
H&B

Bathing while camping in a city.

If without a vehicle, you may be on undeveloped brush-land, such as a river flood-zone during dry season, where you can shower with a jug (or whatever contraption pleases you). But if living in a vehicle, brush-lands may not be near by.

You might join a gym. But if in a city mainly to earn and accumulate money, you don't want to fritter it away.

In a van or bus, consider rigging a portable shower enclosure (eg, like March89 DP). You will need a big strong pan or tub to stand in and to catch the water, and a shower curtain (which may be rigged out of plastic) to intercept splatter. If your vehicle is too low to stand in, can you shower okay while sitting, squatting or kneeling?

Some public rest rooms have hot water. (McDonalds did.) Take along (eg) a cup for filling jugs. (Jugs won't fit under most faucets.) Holly & Bert, Oregon, December

Lives out of pickup more than in it.

Responding to John and to H & B in Dec96 DP. Yes, we still have our pickup with insulated canopy. But it is too small and usually too crowded with equipment to really live IN. We sometimes sleep in it a few nights when traveling or in cities. But usually we live OUT of it - using it as a mobile closet while doing most activities in our tent.

A few times I cooked in it (while Barb was elsewhere), but had to shift things around to make room.

Our original canopy was home-made, mostly of wood, with insulation built in. Despite frequent repaintings, the wood eventually deteriorated. I replaced it with a manufactured canopy, insulated with flexible foam held on by contact cement (which dissolves some materials - test), and inside that, plastic as a vapour barrier. The cement does not hold long (especially if pickup left parked in hot sun), so I have re-glue occasionally, at which time I also replace the plastic (which gets grungy). The pickup bed, too, has foam and plastic linings, layed in and duct-taped at sides. Hank & Barb
NM, January

Instead of fixing my van myself, I phoned a dealer.

I thought they would have all the parts and know-how needed. I said the van was old and described all its ills. The dealer said: no problem, bring it in. But after I paid $120 (double what should have been) for towing 50 miles to Asheville, the dealer refused to work on my van because of its electrical problems. So then I had to have it towed to mechanics who were willing. Three repair shops and $700 later it is running. I will wait until January to get insurance and new plates, because my rates drop then - to $135/6 mo. Eugene

Living out of a car in Appalachian cities.

You can live lightly and enjoyably in West Virginia. But not secretively in the mountains. At least not with a car.

I tried, beginning in 1982, but found it difficult. Rural residents and hunters spotted me faster than any search by police or chopper might. Even at night, if moon and not too cloudy, they saw my shiny metal before I could see or hear them. Suspicious of my wayward esconced vehicle, they reported their find and deputies soon arrived to run me out. I got so anxious that every time a bird landed on my car I relived a horror-movie scenario. So I opted for blending into urban confabrications. I have now lived out of my car continuously for eight years plus some summers previously.

In Wheeling, my home town, I easily made friends. After locals knew my plans and trusted me, I was in. At first, cops checked me out. But when satisfied, they left me alone. Sometimes they even offered advice on better places to park.

During my first year at WVU in Morgantown, everyone checked me out. After that they treated me fine, except for two WVU security guards who took a dislike to me, ran me out of buildings and parking lots, and issued trespassing citations. I complained to others on the force including the captain, and the harassment greatly diminished.

For warmth, at temperatures below 45°F I sleep with my head inside sleeping bag - completely covered.

To add insulation at night, I cut cardboard to fit and put several layers inside the windows. This also prevents frost from forming inside (which must be scraped off in the morning before moving).

Don't start the engine for heat. That not only wastes fuel, but rapidly wears cylinders while oil is cold.

To keep out insects when windows are lowered for ventilation, I cut fine-mesh hardware cloth (25¢/foot) to fit, and used magnetic strips (craft stores) to attach.

To keep rain out of lowered windows, vent-shades must reach all the way down the forward diagonals. (Most cover only the top.) A local sheet-metal business made me some awnings (working on them when business slack) in exchange for feedback. Also, J.C.Whitney sells some (four/$45).

While juggling in the park, I met a man who ran a salvage yard and used-car lot. Since then, whenever my car needed work, I visited him and he provided tools and advice to fix mine while he worked on his clunkers. In return, I sent him students looking for bargains. We have kept quite a symbiotic friendship over the years.

I earn extra income doing clinical and pharmacological research for a local drug company. Travelers can to, provided they have a phone number or local address.

I seldom use or want a computer, television, or phone. I make calls from pay phones. I prefer interfacing with real people. I also learn much from books; and from journals, magazines and newsletters I receive by mail. I get BBC via radio, and carry oldies cassettes.

I keep a permanent po box in Wheeling so my moves do not interfere with my mail, and I rent a storage unit where rent is cheap. (In Wheeling, you can buy a house for a song.) My unit is over 30' tall. I built four levels of free-standing shelves. (Lighter stuff goes on top.) A big unit does not react so drastically to day-night cooling cycles. (A small unit, especially a tin building, can over-heat and spoil things including electronics unless located in a sheltered spot.) So that is how I am heavy but light.

For the 23rd straight year, WV had the lowest crime rate in the U.S. (FBI) and Wheeling was again the lowest city. Only 5 murders in WV last year (most by out-of-staters). WV is among the poorest states and has high unemployment, which shows that poverty and crime don't necessarily go together. Laszlo Borbely, WV, December
(Comment:) Some Chambers of Commerce, I read, pressure local police to under-report crimes to the FBI, to make a city look good to prospective industries. So be skeptical of all statistics.

Living out of a car in New Orleans.

After completing degrees in Bio, Geo, Chem, and Physics at WVU, in Dec 1993 I drove south, just ahead of the worst winter in history. I had heard of jobs in Houston, but decided against Texas because police there often arrest single males to charge with unsolved crimes. Though transients and loners commit fewer crimes than do gregarious locals, prosecutors prey on them because they lack the connections and dollars for defense against bogus charges.

I stayed in New Orleans four months, living out of my car in high-crime neighborhoods. (The cops ran me out of up-scale neighborhoods, and threatened to jail me if they caught me there again sleeping in my car.) Almost every store had security guards at check-outs. Parking in wrong or risque places often elicited warnings or advice.

I met many locals including Cajuns selling door-to-door, enjoyed talking with them, and learned much. One fellow was sleeping in abandoned buildings without a sleeping bag. Temperatures dipped below 30°F occasionally. Then, just before spring, I read he perished from hypothermia. Only 40 years old.

I did not bother to rent a po box or beeper. I might have used a mail box at a vacated abode, driving by to pick up, though I'd try to get permission.

Seems 25% of population has left New Orleans due to dwindling jobs and much crime including 458 murders a year. As vacated homes are looted of appliances and construction hardware, neighbors get scared and move in turn. Due to heat and humidity, uninhabited dwellings succumb to mold and termites - often within a year. Laszlo Borbely, WV, Dec.

Travels With Lizabeth, by Lars Eighner
I was surprised to find dozens of books on homelessness in OSU's library. This was the most recent, spanning 1987 to 89, and perhaps the best. Lizabeth was the author's canine companion.

While Lars was living amidst a bamboo patch in Austin TX, fraternity boys cut some for party decorations. This exposed another squatter's tent to view of a hill-top mansion. The lady there had a wild imagination: the one 4x7' tent became, to her, half a dozen 6-man tents and the one occupant a well-armed para-military troop. The police rounded up the occupant and Lars (forcing Lars to walk, barefoot as he was, over the sharp bamboo stubble), and showed them to the woman. But the woman insisted an army was still in the bamboo. To satisfy her, the city sent in bulldozers and destroyed all the bamboo.

Though some homeless are alcoholic, drug-addicted, or insane, Lars thinks the numbers are greatly overestimated. "People who do not want to help, blame the homeless for being homeless."

"The purpose of welfare systems is not to help poor people, (but) to provide jobs for social workers and bureaucrats." 1993, 271 pages, Saint Martins, NY. Reviews in this issue by Julie Summers.

Government agencies seize children.
In response to Guy Hengst, Dec96 DP: I know of cases where, with no evidence of abuse, state "welfare" workers and cops took kids from families that were camping out; or were vegetarian, nudist, slept together, refused to immunize, or gave their kids freedom that someone claimed was "neglect". That happened to my family twice. We worked to get our kids back by proving NO abuse or neglect.

Two mothers I know had babies stolen because of home water-births. Took months to get them back, by which time bonding was broken. You never hear of these cases in the media.

A big threat, are laws that allow kids to be seized because of an anony-mous complaint, without requiring that the informer first confront the accused in court. In these state-kidnapping cases, children have no civil rights, and neither do parents unless they hire expensive lawyers.

Yes, schools train fashionettes, media addicts, treat pigs, and money hounds - afraid of raw nature. I am a homeducation teacher and partime parent. Homeducation is legal now and risks are minimal except in fascist regions that hate free families. Know the politics of any area you stay more than few days.

I usually like to meet any neighbors, especially if I'm with or near kids, to show I am responsible even though nude, natural, playful, and camping for free.

The recommendations of Guy and of Holly & Bert were mostly negative. Invisibility is good. But too much fear and caution can ruin a natural-camping experience, playing, and fun. Peaceful solutions to family wars are deeper than politics, hiding, or diets. We need to clarify our goals, values and needs (feelings) about children. Michael Sunanda, Family Peace Games, Hawaii, Dec.

Child "protection" has become a racket.
Favorite targets are low-income mothers who can't afford lawyers to fight the thefts of their children.

State social services get $4000 from the government for every child they put into a foster home. They keep 75%, and are not responsible for what it's spent on. Payoffs to police are common.

Child abuse cases are big business. For men to even be alone with under-age girls, is getting dangerous. One neigh-bor girl has sent four men to jail so far. Only two got off - after spending thousands to fight her false charges.

I am aware of families who have unpapered kids that get home taught, so that is still possible. Tom Van Doren, ID, Dec.

Cattle the most dangerous big animals.
Probably because they are common, and are less afraid of humans. Be wary.

I cut firewood with an antique pointcut pruner.

#120, made by N.K.Porter, Everett MA for pruning apple trees. With a vise-grip-like mechanism, it easily cuts 3" thick oak branches, without the noise of an axe. (Safer too.) It folds to 18" long. Eugene Gonzalez, North Carolina, Dec.

Sewing flesh is easier with suture needles.

Sold by vet supply houses for about 50¢ each, they are curved and have sharpened blade-like points. If you get a deep cut, they can save a $200 doctor bill. I use hydrogen peroxide to sterilize silk thread, needle, and wound; and put Bentonite clay over the wound to allow faster filling.

I have a fight-happy dog I have to sew up often (after subduing by sitting on him). Tom Van Doren, Idaho, December

Silicone caulking is good for waterproofing sewen seams.

Buy caulking that has a 20 or 40 year rating. A tube usually costs less than $10 and will last years. Spread thin with finger for most flexability and endurance. Guy R. Hengst
IN, 1994

Learning more about sealants.

In summer 1996 I phoned the Locktite Corporation tech advice number (1-800-562-8483). They said, their Black Rubber sealant is softer and more flexible than their Black Plastic. Both cure when the solvent evaporates.

Silicone cures by reacting with air. It can withstand 400°F, whereas rubber only tolerates 300°. (Sea-level boiling water 212°.) Silicone also has good moisture resistance and therefore is well suited for window caulking.

Locktite also has a clear vinyl sealant; itself vinyl.

I've used the Black Rubber and Clear Plastic to seal seams on vinyl upholstery repairs, and rain gear I made. The Black Rubber did not become brittle and crack (especially in cold weather) as did the Clear Plastic, and maybe adhered better. The Black Rubber also adhered well (for years) to a bike seat, where it was smeared over stitches in a flat surface; but poorly in the crevice of a rainjacket seam - eventually peeling out.

I have used silicone caulking on rubber boots, applying it over the stitching of a sewn repair, but it did not stay waterproof long. Julie Summers, Oregon, November

During winter, drink ample water - 2 or 3 quarts a day.

When cold air is warmed, either by a heater or by inhaling, it becomes drier and absorbs moisture from your lungs. (That is why a vapor cloud forms when you exhale.) Most sore throats and sinus problems can be prevented or alleviated by ingesting more fluids. Guy Hengst, Indiana, 1994

Fishing, hunting, and gardening in southern Appalachians.

Fishing is a 15-minute walk from my camp. Or when my friend isn't working, we use his canoe and motor to a lake. Smallmouth bass are biting on 4" "Power Slugs" (brown and pumpkinseed colors best) from Berkely (not CA) with a tiny split-shot sinker 18" above bait to keep it submerged 1-2 ft.

I started a garden but small animals ate the seedlings. While I was away for a few days, mice gnawed their way into my tent. Later, rats gnawed more holes. Sometimes at night I sit quietly at my tent entrance and kill rodents with a Wrist Rocket slingshot using .32 cal (9mm) buckshot. (I've had the slingshot 20+ years and am good with it.) I am overcoming an aversion to eating rodents.

I am also practicing with a compound bow, 50-60 pound draw, I bought for $115, plus $45 for sight and $60 for arrows. After getting over the fear of the bow string thwacking my cheek and nose, I have become accurate to 40 yards. But only once have I seen deer tracks nearby. The locals use dogs to hunt deer and boar, so the big game are skittish. Eugene, NC

Hawksbeard: another wild salad plant of the chicory tribe.

In May94 DP, Bert and I wrote about gosmore (Hypochoeris radicata), a wild green related to lettuce and dandelions. Last spring, in a recently replanted clear-cut, we came upon what we thought was a variety of gosmore, though the leaves were smoother, tenderer and generally less bitter - tasting very much like cultivated open-leaf lettuce. We ate handfulls of the leaves almost every day.

When we returned in mid summer, the plants had gone to seed and the leaves had dried up - unlike gosmore which is a perennial. A friend identified as rough hawksbeard (Crepis setosa). We have seen no mention of edibility, but we ate hawksbeard in quantity and suffered no ill effects.

Hawksbeard, gosmore and several other members of the chicory tribe (subdivision of daisy family) have (at least during spring) a rosette of basal leaves and then (if enough sun) yellow dandelion-like blossoms. But, unlike dandelions, the flower stalks branch and (in our experience) the leaves are less bitter. However, bitterness depends much on growing conditions. Generally, the more sun, the more bitter. All of these plants are tastiest before flowers develop. That makes identification difficult. So use caution. (Beware of tansy ragwort, a distant, poisonous relative with yellow flowers but more intricately divided leaves including leaves on the flower stalks (not just basal). Holly Davis, OR, Aug.

Don't swallow "concentrated energy" hype.

I've seen ads for "survival capsules" or "energy bars" which imply that a few pills or tiny wafers each day will furnish all essential nutrients. Nonsense! Though they might provide vitamins, such tidbits can't possibly furnish enough energy. A resting adult needs about a pound of carbohydrates per day; an active adult two pounds or more. Else s/he will lose weight, probably feel weak, and eventually starve. (Fat contains 2 times more energy than does carbohydrates, but eating mostly fat is not healthy.) Holly & Bert, Oregon, Dec.

Three compasses have stopped working, maybe from jostling.

I wear them around my neck and seldom take them off. The most expensive ($35), a Silva, lasted less than a year. Eugene

"Out There" Repair Kit

In a tobacco can, paint can, or Tupperwear container (etc.) with 12-16 fluid oz volume, I carry such items as: hot glue sticks, candle stubs, small Bic lighters, epoxy mix, super glue, small rolls of tape, plastic "snap" gasmets(?), small rolls of wire (10' each), small plastic clothes clips, spring paper clips, zip lock ties (4-6"), eyeglass screws, a few nails, assorted needles, assorted safety pins, razor (safety) blades, 2x2" sheets of sandpaper, assorted patches, rubber glue, rubber bands, rosin solder, vinyl glue, waxed floss, pack frame pins, tweezers, clear nail polish; with a Swiss (Victronix) "Champ" or Leatherman "toolbox" with various blades, files, other tools.

With these I can mend torn-off straps, broken eyeglasses, ripped clothing and pack bags, cracked water bottles, broken tent frames, and many other things. "Too heavy to hike with?" I would rather carry a little extra than abort a trip. Wildflr,

Dwelling Portably

formerly named Message Post
POB 190, Philomath OR 97370
December 1997 $1 per issue   Add 50¢ to check/mo under $6

How to make a small, smoke-free fire.

Because I'm locked up I'm forced to witness much stupidity. But I've also seen ingenious improvisations. In here, any fire must not draw the law's attention - and they're walking around. So this fire would also be useful in a populated area if you want to heat a cup of water without smoke. The fuel is single-ply, white, unscented toilet paper such as is in gas-station and fast-food rest rooms.

top view

Hold your hand flat. Tightly wrap the paper around your hand, about 20 wraps. Remove your hand. Roll the paper from the outside toward the center to form a "doughnut". You end up with a ring with outside diameter 3½"-4", inside 1½"-2", ht 1½"-2".

Set the "doughnut" on the side with the most irregularities because it needs to draw air through the bottom. At least, if setting it on a flat surface, make sure its bottom is not perfectly flat. Light the center. It burns with a hot flame, almost smokeless. To heat water, most folks here use a drink can, holding it with a 12" piece of string.

The only problem is extinguishing the fire. If you are not quick and thorough, you will produce lots of smoke. Most people here flush it down the toilet while still burning. I guess dumping a pail of dirt on it would work. Lance Brown

My philosophy for survival: fit in; be invisible.

What could be more different and offer more freedom? Anyone can be a baglady. But to be a baglady and not have it show, takes genius. For diversion I camouflage the baglady me and portable-ize my dwelling, making it simple and easy to maintain. And I work on my arrogance. I observe little creatures: wasps don't get caught in spider webs. D. Dorji

I have fifteen acres here I am taking care of.

I seem to be doing all right. I don't have a well yet, which would make local officials unhappy if they knew, so I keep them diverted. I'm from Los Angeles. When I get this chunk paid off, I'll move back to the West Coast. Donald, ARK

I have been living portably for a few years.

In tree houses, a school bus, and other ways. Soon, my friends and I will build an earthen ("cob") cottage out in some Oregon woods. Lee, Oregon, August

Tips for evading tracking dogs.

In the turbulent times ahead, the government may decide to round up nonconformists. Dogs that have been trained to track and attack escaped prisoners, would likely be used. The Texas Department of Criminal Justice now has 3500 track/attack dogs trained and ready to go. As an unwilling guest of the State of Texas, I spent 2½ years working with these dogs and have learned many of their weaknesses.

A human constantly sheds billions of minute skin particles. Bacteria break down the particles and emit odor. Though these bacteria thrive most in warm, moist areas such as armpits and crotch, they are present on the entire body.

These skin particles drift in the slightest breeze, so the tracking dogs usually run 3 to 10 feet downwind of a trail, parallel to it. The skin particles continue to drift until something catches them such as wet grass or leaves.

Heat, direct sunshine, wind, and low humidity favor the fugitive. The bacteria rot faster in the heat. The dogs are running with fur coats on and they don't sweat. The wind will scatter your scent over a large area and the low humidity will dry the grass and ground so there is no moisture to catch your skin particles that emit your scent.

Fog, cold, calm, drizzle/rain, clouds, dew and frost favor the dogs. Anything but a heavy thunderstorm will not wash away your scent. Moisture on vegetation will hold your scent. The dogs will stay cooler and have more endurance.

Most of the tricks you hear about for evading dogs are bogus. Putting pepper in your socks or behind you won't work because dogs don't run in your exact path. Nor do modern tracking dogs keep their noses to the ground; they run and sniff 8 to 10 inches in the air. Sure, you might incapacitate one or two, but they track in packs of six to ten.

What does work is a patch of fresh asphalt paving, but only if the whole pack gets a noseful. Fresh creosote railroad ties are also good. Any hard surface such as gravel roads or railroad beds will tear up the dogs' foot-pads and stop them. The easiest way to stop dogs is to keep them away from water. On a hot summer day they won't last 90 minutes without water. That fur coat is hot !

Do change direction frequently and irregularly. Make your turns sharp and approx right angles ($90°$). If you have time, overshoot your turns by ten yards or so, backtrack, and then turn. This will slow the dogs down but not lose them. Make lots of sharp turns, traveling at least 30 yards between turns, but not in a straight line for more than 5 or 10 minutes. I've timed my travel over a path, and then the dogs tracking me, and if I kept my corners sharp, the lengths of my segments varied, overshot and backtracked now and then, and walked a fair pace, I always gained time on the dogs. Also good is to walk toward an object that is obvious to the dogs, such as a building, woods or water, then backtrack exactly, and make a sharp turn.

Don't get in a pattern. I've seen dogs tracking someone who did 50-yard segments and $90°$ turns over and over. The dogs figured out what the pattern was and just intersected the corners, so the fugitive covered more ground than did the dogs.

A good dog handler will counteract most of your maneuvers, but each one will buy you time. If you change directions, change patterns, walk steady so you don't tire, don't panic, and pick terrain that doesn't hold your scent (hard dry), you can gain time until you lose the dogs for good. In wet grass, dogs can track you for 6 to 8 hours. In a dry field that has been plowed or harvested, dogs can track you less than 4 hrs.

If you get in the habit of following creeks, the dogs will run the creek bank, knowing that if they lose you, you'll be back. Likewise if you follow fence lines, ridges, or valleys. If you trend in one direction overall, you may find yourself boxed. Don't get in any habit: be unpredictable. Remember, you must outwit not only the dogs but their handler.

My own escape was semi-successful. I got all the way to Tennessee; then was busted because of a stupid mistake.
© Lance Brown, 1996 (originally in <u>Walter</u> <u>Mittey</u> <u>Papers</u>)

(Further tip:) At first, count your steps so you will know how long you are making each segment, to vary them. After a while it'll come automatically.

How track-attack dogs are trained.

At 6:30 am on a typical day, the Dog Sargent (S) arrives at the kennels. The Dog Boys (B), inmates who take care of the dogs, have been there two hours washing the pens and doing other chores. The S sends one B on a "puppy track" - a short track about 1½ miles long without much "work" on it, for training dogs 7 or 8 months old. "Work" consists of turns such as "stairsteps" and "boxes". "Not much work" means making the stairsteps 75 yards or longer and boxes 150 yards or so.

The S sends another B to lay out a full-sized track of 4 or more miles for training older, more-advanced dogs. The S tells B what pastures to go through and points to reach. (Eg: "work your way through the bull pasture to the lee woods, weave through the woods, and work your way to the windmill..." Sometimes B will leave the kennel on foot; other times he is driven to the starting point.

The S will run the puppy track while fairly "hot" - less than an hour old; and the full-size track when ±2½ hours old.

On the full-size track, the S takes the dogs to within a mile or so of where the track starts. Then he gets the dogs to "drag": run in front of S's horse in a left, right, left, right sweeping motion, with the sweeps about 150 yards long and about 40 yards between sweeps.

Eventually the dogs hit the scent and take off baying. The track is now about 3 hours old. Three-fourths of the time, the dogs take off in the correct direction. If they go the wrong way, S will try to turn them around by hollering at them. If they don't turn, he will start them again.

For the first 200 or 300 yards, the dogs overshoot badly and lose the scent a few times. But then they get "locked on". Before, they were looking for any human scent, but now they are tracking a specific person. That person can now cross the path of others and the dogs will search for his scent. They still overshoot, but not as badly.

Near the end of the track, B is supposed to wait 200 yds from his final destination until he can hear the dogs. Then he rushes to his tree or roof or shed, and puts on his "pack suit" to fight the dogs. When the dogs hit the "hot tail end", their baying becomes more frenzied - they know they are close.

Even though they are trained to fight, the dogs are not overly big or violent. I think they could be discouraged.

On one track I made, I followed a large ditch for more than a mile. The ditch was 12 feet deep and 25 yards wide with a small stream down the center. It was choked with willow, bloodweed, cattails, etc. Beside the ditch was a 50-yard-wide strip of 5" grass and then hundreds of acres of knee-high corn. The pattern I ran: down the center of the ditch for 150 yds; out and do a 150 yd box in the grass; back into the ditch for 150 yds; out and do a box on the other side; etc. I tried to walk in the water as much as possible and felt proud, thinking I'd fooled the dogs.

Wrong! From my waiting point I could see the whole ditch. The dogs headed for me like they were on rails.

Another day I did almost the same thing, but on a creek 30 feet across in places and chin deep. I ran 9 boxes off the creek. After following them the dogs decided: "Too hell with this. We'll keep running on this side and he'll come back." But I didn't. Took them an hour to decide they had lost me and to back track to where they re-acquired my scent.

If I ran an irregular pattern with overshoots and sharp

turns, the dogs ended up covering much more ground than I did.
Whereas if I ran a "lazy" track with gradual turns, the dogs
didn't overshoot and they gained time on me.

On one hot sunny day, 95°, I went from a creek up into
plowed ground, crossed into a pasture, and ran sort of "loose"
work: stairsteps about 75 yards and boxes 150 to 200 yards.
From the creek to a water hole was about 3/4 of a mile. In
that distance, two of the dogs overheated and had to be carried
to water. For this reason, most of the training tracks were
around water, or from waterhole to waterhole. Lance Brown, TX,
July

Story of an escape from prison.

One Sunday night in November I was in bed asleep. At
about 10 pm the police woke me and told me to go to work.
There had been an escape from another prison 15 miles away.
The police put 8 dogs, 2 horses, and us Dog Boys on a trailer.
I was there to feed dogs and horses, and keep the dogs from
fighting. They sent us to a pasture where we unloaded. They
"dragged" the dogs some. I sat in the trailer and watched.
At sunrise we went to an area near the prison.

As I learned later, three inmates had gotten into the
boiler room of the prison, tied up the inmate who worked
there, and knocked out the power. From there they cut through
the first fence and climbed over the second.

There, one escapee twisted his ankle. So he went to some
nearby trailers where the police lived and hid under one.

The second escapee ran 200 yards to the highway, crossed
it, and hid in some extremely dense woods, about 35 acres.

The third escapee also ran to those woods, skirted the
edge of them, then took off running down the highway.

The dogs got to where the escapees went over the fence
and took off baying after #2 and #3. When the dogs got to the
highway, one got hit by a car and the others scattered in
confusion. Early the next morning the dogs found escapee #2
in the woods. The police assumed the others were also there.

From the feds they borrowed a Blackhawk helicopter
equipped with infra-red, used to spot illegal immigrants.
By now there was a wall of police around the woods. The
Blackhawk went over and detected two heat sources. All that
day we Dog Boys sat around while the police tried to get the
prisoners out of the woods. They sent teams in, but they
returned empty handed. Finally, with the Blackhawk controlling from the air, a line of police, shoulder to shoulder,
walked through the woods. A medium-size doe came running out,
soon followed by a good-size wild boar. So much for heat
sensing. They wasted two days in the woods.

That night escapee #1 got caught when he came out from
under the trailer. Escapee #3 got clean away. Lance Brown,
TX, July

(Question:) Might tracking dogs be used to find "homeless"
people camped in such places as big, undeveloped city parks?

(Reply:) Virgin ground is a must for tracking. I'd say no
other foot traffic for at least 24 hours, mainly for the
initial pick-up and lock-on to scent. When training, I've
seen dogs try to lock on to a previous day's track, instead
of the new track. Dogs are most effective where very few
people are on foot.

I don't think dogs would be used in city parks. Too much
chance of tracking someone like the mayor's kid and biting.
I've seen dogs used one at a time on a tether, but that is not
as effective and there would still be too many "wild goose

chases". I'd say they'd more likely be used on rural squat-
ters. Lance
(Comments:) The dogs you worked with were trained to attack
whoever they ran down. But other dogs, used to search for
lost persons, do not attack (I hope). So they could be used
in city parks without endangering the mayor's kid. But, as
you say, too many trails. Seems like most rural areas would
also have too many trails. Some remote areas don't, but have
millions of acres of bush to crash through.

Anyhow, 90% of nonconformists probably live in urban
areas. Of the 10% who are rural, I expect 9/10ths could be
netted simply by going to their known addresses about 2 am.
The remaining 1% would likely be ignored during a mass round-
up (except for any prominant "trouble makers"), because the
government would be busy dealing with the others (millions?).

According to Tracking Dog (review in June 89 DP), the
oldest trail that dogs can track is about 3 days (less under
hot, dry conditions). So, in a situation where dogs might be
used, another way to elude them would be to leave more than
3 days before the dogs arrived. Holly & Bert, Oregon, Dec.

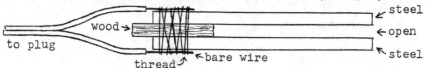

Jerry-rigged electric water heater for urban nomads.
The "stinger" requires 120-volt electricity so its
usefulness is limited, but it is simple and light. Parts
needed: a short electric cord; a small piece of wood (two
wooden matches, or a popsicle stick); some string or thread;
and two small pieces of steel (each about 2" x 1/2" x 1/16").

Place the wood between the metal pieces so they don't
touch, but leave some open space between the metal pieces
because electricity traveling through the water is what
produces the heat. Tie each wire to a metal piece.

Place in a non-metalic container of water so that most
of the metal pieces are submerged, and plug in. Within
seconds, water near the metal will bubble. In about three
minutes, six ounces of water can be heated to boiling.

The first few uses should be with a container and water
you can discard, to remove coatings and impurities from the
metal. After a few uses the steel should look rusty but the
water stays clear. Use glass or plastic container (NOT metal)
and don't touch the metal pieces or water while it is plugged
in. (I once saw an idiot test the water temperature by
sticking a finger in. He pulled it out fast !) Lance Brown

Turbine ventilators are more effective than RV-type vents.
Powered by the wind, they are frequently seen spinning
on factory roofs. The smallest fits on a 6" diameter stack;
ball about 10" diameter. Consider getting one if your shack,
vehicle, or underground bunker lacks sufficient ventilation.

If on a vehicle, install the ventilator so it can be
easily removed, and the end of the stack covered with a
plastic coffee-can lid. Don't drive with the ventilator on
the roof. L. Smith, Wisconsin, July

I currently live on a bus.   Nicky, Arizona, March

I live in my pickup.   Kelly, Kansas, October

Another possible use of trailer housing.

I am somewhat skeptical about the usefulness of trailers for housing to be evacuated in an emergency. "Mobile" homes that set for long become progressively less mobile as various extensions are built on and as the tires go flat, etc. Take a walk through any trailer or "mobile" home park, imagine you have a tow truck, and ask yourself: how quickly could I move them all? For midwest flood lands, seems better for farmers to put homes and important buildings on high ground, and commute to their riverside fields.

However, trailer housing seems fine for seasonal or annual moves for which there is plenty of time. As well as the traditional migrations north and south, there are environmental incentives for mobility. Oregon (and probably most states) has a growing conflict between preserving nature and providing homes. A state-wide law prohibits new construction on farm and forest land. But one result is absurdly high and rising costs of conventional housing.

Though that increases sales of Dwelling Portably, not everyone is willing or able to live in tents hidden in the woods (commuting problem) or in vans parked on streets (privacy problem - and if many did, the streets would jam). So, how can people live on (eg) farm land without interfering with the crops? Maybe in trailers. Most fields lie fallow part of each year, or every few years. So, park trailers in a fallow field during winter. Then, in spring when ready to plant, move them to pasture (if not used during summer), or to marshy areas (that were too wet during winter), or to mountains (that were too snowy during winter to commute). The trailers must be fairly self-contained (no water or sewer lines). But, no problem: compost kitchen and human waste and fertilize the fields - thus benefiting the crops.

On forest lands, after an area is clear-cut and replanted, partial shade will benefit the little trees. So bring in housing then (maybe not trailers with wheels, but just boxes, moved by the same equipment that moves big logs around). The boxes also serve as a sort of mulch, suppressing some of the weed growth that competes with the trees for water. Then, when the trees get big, move the boxes to a younger site.

Of course, to do this legally would probably require changing the laws: beyond the realm of most DP readers. But, if anyone happens to have an in with some politician or big media person, you might suggest this. Bert and Holly, Nov 97

Legal exemptions would make more rentals available.

Jim Turner, a small-scale landlord discouraged by too many bad tenant encounters, suggests what he calls a no-cost way to provide not only affordable housing but domestic "mentorship" for the needy: exempt owners who rent out rooms within their own homes from landlord-tenant laws. Then they would not have to give 30 days notice and undertake eviction proceedings to get rid of crazies and deadbeats, nor meet building-code standards for new rentals. "Overnight, you'd open up 200,000 to 300,000 units of housing," predicts Turner.

Should small shelters also be portable?

The need for lightness drives Dwelling Portably people to use materials (tent fabrics, sleeping pads, insulation, etc.) that requires petroleum industries and don't burn or decay without problem products. So what, since DPers use way less than do conventional householders? Also, DPers tend to scavenge or buy used, and use thoroughly what they buy; instead of buying new stuff on impulse that soon goes into attics.

Great. But someone still needs to develop alternatives, and those in small-but-not-backpackable shelters are in the best situation to do so. They are also better able to experiment, and draw on history for ways of using natural materials. They are also in a better position to affect environmental consciousness and policy in their communities than are those who are always moving on. Pluma, Small Shelter Council, TN 376, August
(Comments:) You assume portable dwellers are always moving on. Holly and I do most of our moving around within a home range 50-to-100 miles across (somewhat like traditional nomads. We might stay as long as 6 months at a winter base camp, and then several weeks each at a succession of lighter camps during the warmer/drier season, but seldom moving far.

Though DP folk vary, more seem to move mostly within home ranges, than move on and on never to return.

For experimenting and developing alternatives, portable dwellers seem better situated than are small-but-stationary dwellers. Both lack room inside. But, for projects needing much space, portable dwellers can temporarily move during summer to where outside space is abundant; while stationary dwellers are limited to what is close by. Likewise if special equipment is needed. And, for affecting community policy, if portable dwellers try something that stirs up more antagonism than is tolerable, we can move away until the hostiles cool down and forget about us. Whereas stationary dwellers live in perpetual fear of officialdom. They dare not "make waves" - else building inspectors or truant officers (etc) may notice them and come harass. Historically, most innovations were initiated by relatively-mobile artisans, traders, fishers, etc. Peasants, rooted to their spots and beholden to their lords, were last to change.

Socially, a big advantage of dwelling portably, is the ease of moving away from unpleasant neighbors. Though a stationary dweller may initially select a neighborhood for compatability, it may not remain compatable. People change, or are replaced. This is one reason why even people with big dwellings often strive to be portable: rent instead of buy; or sell one house and buy another. And look at some of the monster RVs on the road. So, if a shelter is to be small, why not also make it portable?

By the way, plastics don't require petroleum industries. They can also be synthesized from (eg) methane (producable by compost piles) or alcohol (I've read). Plastics are presently produced from petroleum only because petroleum is cheaper. (That will change as oil fields run dry.)

Also, synthetic end products are not always the most harmful. Petroleum-burning vehicles are nasty polluters, but replaced even worse polluters: horses. Between 1900 and 1930 in New York City, infectious diseases greatly declined, especially tetanus and tuberculosis (and this happened long after discovery of how diseases spread, and improved sanitation (mid 1800s), and before antibiotics were commercially available (mid 1900s)). Probable cause? Most horse-drawn wagons were replaced by motor vehicles, greatly reducing fecal dust and flies. Tetanus microbes breed in horse dung (which for some reason is much more dangerous than cow dung).

Holly and I usually use natural materials for framing (wood poles, instead of aluminum or PVC pipe), partly because they grow where we live (transportation only a few yards). But for windows and moisture barriers, we prefer plastic. If natural materials are heavier, they are environmentally better only if they occur at the site. Eg, a thatch hut is fine if the thatch grows close by. But not if someone must drive several miles to harvest it. That would burn more petroleum than goes into a plastic tent.

Comparison of portable showers: suspended versus hand-held.
May99 DP described an upright-jug faucet. Similarly, to make a shower, punch several holes and plug with golf tees.
The one real advantage of a suspended shower (either this one, or the devices sold): both hands are left free - a big advantage when scrubbing hands, vegies or dishes; but not important when washing your body.
Advantages of a unaltered hand-held jug (to shower, remove cap): Does not need tree with strong limb above and clear ground beneath. (Often hard to find.) Allows showering in patch of sunshine. Control flow simply by tilting jug (vs manipulating tees). Can use same jug to haul/store water. H&B

Vets use ethyl cyanoacrylate "super glue" to close wounds.
A formulation for humans is coming. Meanwhile, though super glue is NOT labeled for wound closure, weighing risks vs benefits, one might decide to have some for an emergency.
Jon

Pot with pail provides convenient wash basin.
I use a 2½-gallon pail, with rope tied to handle for easy dipping, to fetch and store water. I also keep clean utensils, plate and cup in it. A deep, sturdy, flat-bottomed aluminum pot is my wash basin. After filling from the pail, I set the pot into the top of the pail where it fits snugly whether level or tilted. Along with cleanser and towel, the pot with pail sets on the step of my van. Thus I can easily reach it to wash my hands without entering the van and touching door, sleeping bags, etc. A MUST when working on a vehicle while living in it. I use bandanas to wash and dry kitchen stuff, changing them daily.
On previous trips I didn't give much thought to cleanliness (I don't like washing dishes) and got sick a few times.
I also cook in and pan gold with the pot. Eugene Gonzalez, NM, Oct 1997

Simplified toiletry also diagnostic.
Though temporarily living in an apartment, I remain sensitive to waste. Eg, instead of the toilet (which needs much flush water), I urinate into a cup and pour it down the sink. I need only a little water to rinse the cup, and that cleans the sink as well. Instead of toilet paper, I clean myself with a thin rag and then rinse it. Dries between uses.
Added benifits of peeing into a cup, are seeing and smelling my urine. I am learning to use it as a diagnostic tool. Too dark, not enough water; too sweet, too much sugar (any form); too sour, too much acid producing foods.
Simple-living people need health awareness different than people who can afford expensive treatments. I appreciate readers' experiences maintaining health; as opposed to ignoring their bodies until they become sick.
I have noticed that usually (not always) before getting a cold, I ate too much sugar for several days. My first symptoms are very faint - in the nose, throat connection. Formerly, I ignored them - until too late. Now I immediately swallow about 4000 mg of powdered C, and go to bed a little early. I wake up fine.
More people (mostly older women) break hips in toilet-sitting cultures than where people squat. Doctors blame muscle weakness, and believe squatting keeps muscles toned. I now squat, even when using toilet bowls. Since doing so, I have

not had hemorrhoid troubles, which had bothered me for years.

By the way, when baking I mix into the dough about one teaspoon of vitamin C per loaf. Retards mold growth. Laura,
WA 981, Sept

How much vitamin C and how often?

Al Fry (in Dec97 DP) is only partly correct when he says 200 mg is all the body can use and any more is wasted. Linus Pauling recommended taking 90% of bowel tolerance, which for me is a whopping 9 grams. Pauling cited numerous studies. Eg, men who took 500 mg a day almost never contracted prostate cancer, and had much fewer urinary tract infections.   .

I find my point of diminishing returns and balance that with my budget. When finances are good, I take 500 mg a day. Otherwise, I bite the tablets in half and settle for 250 mg. If I feel a cold coming, I take an extra tablet or two.

On my generic vitamin C, bottled by Park Taft, it says: "Vitamin C often darkens in color; this does not affect the
potency." Lance Brown, May
(Comments:) Al Fry said, "at one time". I take a dab of vitamin C powder (maybe 200 or 300 mg) two or three times a day (except during blackberry season when I get plenty naturally). Supposedly better than taking all at once. Neither Bert nor I have had infectious illnesses for many years. (Why? Usually good nutrition? Generally low-stress dwellingways? Or being around many other people only during summers when flu (etc) at minimum? Maybe all of above.) H&B

Vaccinations and potential consequences.

The cynics (mentioned in Dec96 DP) who counsel "get everyone else to vaccinate their children but don't vaccinate yours", have grasped the concept of "herd immunity": a disease will spread only if there are enough susceptible hosts within a population. If few of your neighbors are susceptible, you are not likely to get exposed. On the other hand, you may face sanctions from the health or child service folks, which may change your assessment of risks vs benefits.

My wife and I are both registered nurses. She is an infection control nurse where she works. I have been a fire-department EMT in Detroit, an ER and ICU nurse, and nursing supervisor. Our children are vaccinated per health department recommendations. Of course, we live in a small town, and our children are in the local school system and therefore exposed to whatever the children of negligent parents bring to school.

I second Holly and Bert: do your homework. Consider the costs and benefits of your alternatives, and act according to your best judgement. Remember that adverse reactions to innoculations are very very rare. During 20 years in ER and ICU, I have never even spoken with anyone who has seen a reaction. On the other hand, I do not get influenza vaccinations, though my wife accepts them each year. Jon Seaver,
MI 488, Jan
(Comments:) This and other health topics are occasionally discussed in DP because risks for portable dwellers differ from risks for settled folks. On one hand, people who live in vans and go round to many gatherings each year, may be even more exposed to infections than is Jon and his kids. On the other hand, people with secluded backwoods dwellingways have much less exposure to most diseases (but possibly more to some such as hanta and Lyme). Most portable dwellers of both kinds may be less threatened by child "protection" folks: the van dwellers because they may move on before a kidnapping can be organized; the backwoodsers because no one knows they exist.

Therefore health, not law, is likely to be the chief concern.
Adverse reactions are easily identified as such only if
they occur soon after vaccination; not years later. Seems
like health problems among children and young adults have
increased. Causes? Junk food? Legal drugs? Illegal drugs?
TV watching? Environmental pollutants? Fast long-distance
travel (which brings exotic microbes)? Vaccinations? But
vaccinations are certainly invasive and should be undertaken
with caution. (A flier came for "The Immunization Resource
Guide", Diane Rozario, 2nd ed 1994, 60p."oversize", $12 ppd,
Patter, POB 204, Burl.IA 52601. "Detailed reviews of over
60 books" on the topic.") Holly & Bert, Oregon 973, June

Across the border in Mexico I managed to secure Claforan IV.
It is needed to treat third-stage Lyme disease, which
usually requires self-treatment as doctors don't seem to care.
                                                    Michael, July
Recipe for a herbal tea believed to boost immune systems.
Ojibway or essaic tea, which supposedly cures some
cancers, was mentioned in Dec96 DP, but not proportions of
the herbs. Laura Martin-Buhler (Gentle Survivalist Oct98)
uses as a preventive: 6½ cups burdock root (Arctum lappa);
16 oz sheep sorrel (Rumex acetosella) powdered; 1 oz turkey
rhubarb (Rheum palmatum); 4 oz slippery elm bark (Olmus
fulva) powdered; distilled water (quantity not mentioned).
Stainless steel pot, strainer, funnel, utensils. Cooking
time not mentioned. This makes enough "for several days".
Laura keeps the prepared tea in her refrigerator.

Experience sprouting various legumes.
I read both LLL's instructions and a Readers Digest
back-to-the-land book, and then pretty much came up with my
own method. Lentil sprouts were easy. But I couldn't get
garbonzo, pinto, or soy beans to grow well. I rinsed three
times a day, just as I did with the lentils, and they did
grow for a while, but always rotted before very big.
Mung beans are my favorite sprout, but neither of two
local health food stores carry the dried beans. I wonder why.
A store clerk said, soy sprouts are harmful. I was
surprised because I've seen soy sprouts mentioned both in
LLL's paper and in The Farm Vegetarian Cookbook. James Dawson
                                                    CA 954, July
Increasing the storage life of eggs.
Preparing for 4 months of camping this summer, I coated
eggs, both raw and hard-boiled, with water glass: sodium
silicate, available at good pharmacies. I haven't kept fresh
eggs, coated and refrigerated, past 60 days. I have eaten
hard-boiled eggs, coated and refrigerated, kept as long as 120
days. Water glass sealing of eggs dates back many years.
                                                    Brother Bat, May
A trick for opening screw-top jars with stuck tops.
Wrap a belt around the jar lid, put a stick or ruler in
the "crotch" of the belt (between it and the side of the lid)
and pull. Works much like those tools for loosening stuck
oil filters on cars. Laura, Washington 981, September

Oh, the thought of being able to camp and enjoy open places.
Listening to the wind; the sweet smell of it; the fire
burning down to embers; the starry sky; frogs singing for
mates and birds calling out.   For five years I've been locked
up and surrounded by people not of my choosing. I'm hoping to
go to a half-way house in June 99. Samuel Tucker, MI 498,June

Dwelling Portably

May 1998 $1 per issue

formerly named Message Post
POB 190, Philomath OR 97370
Add 50¢ to check/mo under $6

How to keep drawstrings centered permanently.

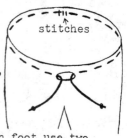

   Annoyed by drawstrings on sweatpants,
hoods, or parkas pulling out or getting
lopsided? There is a simple remedy. Arrange
the drawstring so equal length is on either
side. Then, at the midpoint of the drawstring,
sew a few stitches through drawstring and
garment. This does not interfere with
snugging up and tying the drawstring. Julie

Quick and ugly foam booties.
No pattern; no sewing; very simple. For each foot use two
pieces of foam: one the size of your foot's sole (or a little
larger); the other roughly a yard (or meter) square. Set the
small piece in the middle of the large piece, set your foot on
the small piece, gather the sides of the large piece up around
your ankle, and tie a cord around the bundle. Bulky but warm.

I have been sleeping on Thermarests for many years.
   Some I've had ten years; some five. The $100 mattress, "top
of the line", stays inflated for many months. I put it on the
bottom of my pile of three. The other two, each 2" thick, I
inflate a little every night to keep them (over) inflated.
I love them. I wish they were wider, but 26" is tolerable and
they are exceptionally light. Double Dorji, Arizona, April 97

Materials at hand form simple seats that add camp comfort.
   I used to think chairs were effete. Chairs certainly aren't
necessary: I can sit or sprawl on the ground, stoop, or stand.
But some sort of raised seat makes many tasks more pleasant.
   I've never bought a camp chair, nor built any of the complex
designs I've seen in camp-craft books. I like to minimize
possessions that cost much money or time - things I must carry
with me or protectively store. I've found I can quickly improvise
comfortable seats from natural materials at hand.
   There may be stumps, logs, or rocks I can use with little
modification. Or I may pile up big pieces of thick bark from old
stumps or fallen trees. (The bark, resistant to rot, separates
easily after the wood rots.) Or I may be able to support a chunk
of bark or a log on other logs, earth mounds, or other indigenous
features. At one camp, I hung a slab of bark from a slanting tree
to make a swinging chair - my favorite seat so far. Julie, Oregon

I plan to live in a tent at a nudist camp.
   While attending massage therapy school in Tampa. Much cheaper
than other housing. I had almost given up the idea until I read
DP. Though I may not want to live out in the woods, I think DP
will help me live more cheaply and simply. I tend to have very
different ideas from what is the norm in the Deep South, so mostly
I keep quiet about them. Lory, Alabama, October

Upholstery remainders become a ten-by-twenty-foot wall tent.
   I'm camping on private land with the run of near 600 acres,
in addition to 12 acres I share with my landlord's business. I'm
next to a pond in which I swam until October when it got too cold.
   For $80 I bought 300 yards of upholstery material from a
factory that builds furniture. All roll ends or flawed. Most
pieces only a yard long, but plenty are 2 to 7 yards long. I will
sew the tent on a treadle sewing machine I ordered from Lehman's.
   Meanwhile I'm living in a quickly deteriorating Wal-Mart
wall tent. I put a tarp over the top and as a windbreak, which
greatly extended the tent's life - else I'd be back under a tarp.

Since the end of July I've been splitting my time between my job and getting ready for winter. Short periods of intense activity as I acquired the funds for the next item needed, with long periods of inactivity between.

(Later.) I completed my tent. Unfortunately the temperature dropped before I could waterproof it, so I am dependent on the over-tarp/canopy for rain/snow protection. Most modern upholstery materials consist of a relatively durable fabric with a rubberized backing to which exterior latex enamel will adhere well for full waterproofing. I did paint some small pieces to test, and they are in much better shape than the exposed rubberized backing is.

To waterproof, add 2½ cups of water to a gallon of exterior latex enamel and apply with a 3-inch brush made for latex enamel.

Sewing tips: Use the 'Jeans' weight 'sharps' number 16 needles and size 50 or 60 polyester (dacron) or nylon thread to sew the tent. (Cotton thread will soon rot.) Guy R. Hengst, IN,
                                                            Oct & Febr

Evaluation of some widely-sold dome tents.

The June 97 Consumer Reports reported on tents and sleeping bags they had tested; about 20 of each. CR's "advice is mainly for casual campers (who camp near their vehicles) rather than serious backpackers who need ultra-lightweight compact equipment", and for people who camp only for short periods.

"After a summer outside, most tents were ready for the trash - victims of the sun's ultraviolet rays. That's because nylon (used for the roofs or walls) ages rapidly in sunlight." The only tent with "very good durability" in sunlight was Eureka Space III, a big cabin tent and, at $560, the most expensive.

Spraying the tents with Fabric Guard 303 retarded sun damage (how much not stated). One 16-oz can, $10-$15 (800-223-4303) does small dome; 4 cans big tent. Other brands tried, didn't work as well.

None of the tents blew away in a 22 mph wind, though the rain fly on a Coleman Sundome ripped.

CR tested two types of tents: cabins and domes. Of the two, domes seem the more useful to most DP readers because they can be erected quickly and are fairly light. (If staying in one place long, when erection time and weight aren't important, you can probably contrive a shelter better than any of the tents here.)

A large dome weighs 11 to 15 pounds; a small dome 7 pounds. After take down, a small dome is compact enough to backpack. A large dome is roomy enough for three; a small dome for two, says CR. Some manufacturers claim twice that many can fit in.

Features to look for: shock cords linking the segments of each pole; clips or brackets (rather than fabric sleeves) to attach tent to pole; seam sealant included with tent (apply it first time you set tent up); floor material that extends part way up walls; a rain fly with a peak over doors and windows (on some, the fly blocked window); at least one round (on top) window with a storm flap secured by a zipper with 2 pulls; FINE-mesh screens on door, windows and ceiling vents, to block gnats.

Of large dome tents tested, the 3 best, according to CR, in order: L.L.Bean Family Dome L377 $230; Eureka Sunrise 9 $230; Sierra Designs Mondo 5CD $500. All 3 rated excellent for rain protection (after seam sealant applied), and good+ for most other qualities EXCEPT durability in sunlight. Of the cheaper domes, Greatland (Target) Northridge 918093 $120, was generally good+ (except durability). LEAST durable: Coleman Sundome 9160E101 $135.

Good-to-excellent (except durability) small domes: Eureka Tetragon 7 $120; Coleman Sundome 9260D707 $70. NOT acceptable: American Camper Alpine 3 46471. Poles snapped while just setting.

Evaluating sleeping bags, CR found nylon covers and liners more durable than cotton; hollow-core fibers no warmer than ordinary polyester (but warned against half-poly half-"unknown-textile-fiber" mixes, which clump when washed); down warm and light, but absorbs moisture easily and difficult to dry. Manufacturers' temperature ratings were not accurate and generally optimistic. "Our thermal tests of 8 bags rated from 0° to 40° revealed only a 12° spread." (For full details, seek in library.)

(Comments:) To resist sunlight, instead of an expensive spray (and how long before it flakes off?), I suggest setting the tent in a shady place. If no natural shade, erect above it a cotton canvas tarp, or an over-roof formed of poles/branches/ferns/straw/leaves. Of course that will reduce light. But when brightness important, best not use a solid-fabric tent. Buy or make an all-net tent (eg, see May96 DP) and suspend a clear plastic tarp above.
     For go-heavy-and-stay-long camping, we recommend using 2 to 4 cheap sleeping bags, one inside or under the others. Cost less, and easier to wash and dry than one arctic-rated bag. If you sometimes use a sleeping bag as quilt, opened out, make sure its zipper extends across the bottom. (Some mummy bags don't.) A used bag of unknown history can be disinfected in a hot laundry drier. Critters such as lice can be killed simply by enclosing in a plastic bag for a month. Holly & Bert, Oregon, January

Further report on the Stansport dome tent.
     I reported in May 97 DP, the bottom-side seams leaked much. Later, stuck inside the box, I found "Stansport Tent Tips" which say: "... the sewing necessary in all tent fabrication can cause water leakage.... We strongly recommend that the new tent be erected before it is used and all seams treated with either Stansport seam sealer #344-F or Stansport silicon spray #DC-86."
     But Stansport did NOT include their sealer with the tent, costing a customer time and delay to purchase separately. More important: why didn't Stansport apply the sealant before shipping? Compared with sewing, the extra labor would be trivial. My guess: because the sealant would separate from the seam when the tent is folded for packing. (CR did not say if they erected their test tents more than once.) If Stansport applied the sealant, they'd get blamed. Whereas if the customer does, s/he may assume s/he did something wrong. The basic fault is a seam that needs sealing. (For a design that doesn't, see May95 DP.)

I made a very nice "space blanket".
     I affixed aluminum foil to a comforter I salvaged from a dumpster. It needed 2 cans of Elmers spray-on glue and some touching up after the first night's sleep, but I'm quite pleased with the results. Kurt Wettstein, Illinois, December

How long-distance sport backpackers minimize weight.
     Ray and Jenny Jardine of LaPine Oregon have finished their third through-hike of the Pacific Crest Trail, Mexico to Canada, in a record 95 days. To average 35 miles a day, they carried homemade gear weighing only 8½ pounds, not counting food.
     Ray's 28-ounce 8x8' tarp is roomier, lighter, better ventilated, and better rain protection than are most tents. It has withstood 60 mph winds, and has no zippers to jam or poles to break. Ray sewed 2 pieces of 1.8 oz urethane-coated nylon together along what becomes the ridge line, seam sealed, and added tabs and reinforcements where lines attach. $15 plus 4 hours sewing.
     For a ground-sheet they use a trimmed 4-layer space blanket ($15). Even though it gets poked full of holes, it doesn't pass too much moisture. Pack, and running shoes go under it as pillow, which also keeps the shoes from freezing. They look for cushy campsites that haven't been compacted by other campers, but also carry pieces of closed-cell foam cut to torso width and length ($15). Though not enough insulation for sleeping on snow, the Jardines find some bare ground almost everywhere, even in winter.
     Believing that a sleeping bag's under half is not very insulating, they made quilts, each 79x58", 3 lbs, from synthetic insulation sandwiched between 1.1 oz breathable nylon. $17 + 8 hrs sewing. One side white; one black. In sun with black side up, "it'll dry within minutes."

They usually sleep in all their clothes for warmth and mosquito defense. A piece of netting sewen to the head-end of the quilt provides face protection. If weather too warm for the quilt, they wear a nylon jacket and pants, and apply repellant to face.

All this goes in a 12-oz knapsack they made from 1.9-oz coated nylon, with shoulder straps of Cordura-coated nylon and Beva Lite #2 foam. With such light loads, frame and waist belt not needed.

They buy polyester dress shirts and light-weight nylon socks. For those who sweat a lot, Ray says plain old polyester is better than high-tech wicking fabrics, and in rainy conditions dries faster. They make lycra shorts, Thermamax pants and shirt, and fleece and nylon jackets. Each costs about $8 and 4½ hrs sewing.

For rain they carry umbrellas, lightened by removing springs and trimming handles. In deserts the umbrellas, covered with (aluminized?) mylar to reflect sun, provide shade.

They carry a basic model Swiss Army knife, no soap, no deodorant (attracts bears, says Ray); floss and shortened toothbrush but no toothpaste. Total cost: $135 per person.

But Ray warns: "Hiking with minimal equipment requires much greater proficiency. Until you have that, always carry backup items. Always prepare for the worst that nature can throw at you." Tina Kelley (Seattle Times 97/6/26,shortened; sent by Roger Knight)

Bicycle panniers strengthened by adding cord around bottom.

My original design (May97 DP) had the support cords attached only to holes in the panniers. Recently, while carrying a very heavy load, one of the holes ripped out. To repair, I cut a new hole further down. I also tied an auxillary cord, to the support cord and around the bottom of the pannier, to take much of the weight. A rubber strap, horizontally around the pannier, helps keep this cord in place. Julie Summers, Oregon, July

Mount pannier-support sticks over or under the bicycle's rack?

If the sticks are put on top, the lashings that hold them to the rack can't stretch and possibly break under load. David French

(Reply:) I had said, I put the sticks under the rack, so they do not raise a load placed on top. I now think the effect on stability may be negligible. But something I didn't mention: sticks under the rack, leaves the rack's spring clamp (if any) usable. Also, the rack's top is left flatter, for better support of some loads.

If the lashings have enough wraps, they won't stretch or break. The extra weight of lashing seems negligible. Julie

Report on self-stick patches for innertubes.

I bought an Advent Speed Patch (tm) kit for $2 at a local bicycle shop in August 1997. Distributed by Service Cycle Supply, Commack NY 11725. The kit contained 6 patches 1x1", and one piece of sandpaper that size, in a mini-ziplock bag.

I used one in Sept. It held okay even though a bit of one corner, where backing and patch had separated, did not adhere. The backing seems to separate easily at the corners, just from moving around in the package. After noticing this, I transfered the patches to a plastic 35mm film can.

A more expensive brand was packaged in a hard plastic box. The store clerk thought that only under very wet conditions (heavy rain) would a patch with separate cement be more apt to hold.

I've had opened, carefully-recapped tubes of cement dry out - discovered only when needed to fix a flat! Thus the appeal of self-stick patches. But I don't know how long they will stay good.

Both kinds are over-priced - considering I find all the inner tubes I need (including some with no leaks) in bike-store dumpsters. But a patch kit is lighter and less bulky. I usually carry both: one extra tube; and a patch kit (with both kinds of patches). Julie

Porcupine(?) bit tires of bikes stored over winter in woods.

Many punctures. Good to have extra tubes in critter-proof jar.

Acorns are high in energy and many other nutrients.

   Oak trees grow from Maine to California, yet few people know
how to make acorns edible. The best way: shell, then cover with
warm (but not boiling) water. Let set. When the water becomes
brown, change it. Repeat until the water stays clear. Maybe 5
changes over 2 days. (The tannic acid is what makes acorns bitter
(and would cause a belly ache) and turns the water brown.) Then
(eg) grind them and make acorn pancakes - or experiment. Lance

Almost every wet area grows some cattail.

   Young green shoots can be steamed, boiled, mixed in stews,
or eaten raw in salads. The cattails themselves (top portions of
stalk) are excellent in spring when tender. The roots are a
typical tuber that can be baked, boiled, or added to a main dish.
   One thing that worries me about cattails is their ability to
thrive in polluted areas and filter pollutants from water. In an
emergency that might not deter me, but for day-to-day consumption
I'd select plants growing in relatively clean water. Lance Brown

More about wild salad plants of the Chicory Tribe.

   I've noticed that several "false dandelions" seem less bitter
than true dandelion (Taraxacum officinale); enough so for the
leaves to be palatable and even delectable raw, at least during
winter and early spring, and in shady spots later. I wondered if
the difference was due to species or to growing conditions.
   This February I came upon what I think is gosmore (Hypochoeris radicata) and dandelion growing side by side in a spot which,
then, was getting little sun. The leaves looked quite different:
gosmore had little or no indentations; dandelion had indentations
half their width, and were longer and less fuzzy. No flowers, so
identification not certain. Gosmore tasty; dandelion too bitter!
   (Correction to May97 DP.) Last summer we returned to the
same area while the hawksbeard (Crepis setosa) was blooming. We
found that, unlike gosmore or dandelion, hawksbeard DOES have some
leaves on the flower stalk as well as basal leaves. The hawksbeard
was much less prolific than the summer before, being crowded out
by various perenials, indicating it is an EARLY pioneer. Holly, OR

Ramen-noodle soup-mix provides cheap no-cook snack.

   I crunch the noodles some, add half the seasoning pack,shake,
and eat. The left-over seasoning I use with dinner; or save.
   Ramen noodles contain much sodium (especially the seasoning)
so I would not try to live off them. But an occasional snack is
tolerable, because I don't often eat salted foods or add salt.
   I've seen these soups on sale ten for $1. (If each 3 oz, ±
53¢/lb.) Not as cheap as some bulk foods, but much cheaper than
chips which is what I'd otherwise snack on. Lance Brown, Texas

(Comment:) I've also eaten these after moistening with warm-to-
hot (but not boiling) water sun-warmed in a jar or jug. Quite good.

What device do you recommend for cooking food in a car?

   A friend and I plan a road trip, summer 1998. We won't be
able to start a fire every evening, and would like to be able to
cook inside (after we tire of eating cold snacks).
   We plan to shower at beaches and parks; wash our clothes in
laundromats and dry on a string in the car.
   If we need cash, we plan to stay in a town a few weeks and
get jobs. What skills should I learn for easy employment? I've
been a store cashier; also baby sat, washed dishes. Anne, NY

(Reply:) I've never cooked inside a car, and don't know what if
any device would work well. If all you want is a little hot soup
or drink, there are 12-volt emersion heaters that plug into a
lighter socket. Though more efficient than hot-plates, they do
take much electricity. Maybe okay if driving much, heating little.

Personally, I'd rather cook outside. Some waysides and city parks (which are usually free unless overnighting) have barbeque pits. Collect some firewood enroute in case woods near barbeque are picked clean. I've heard that fast-food shops have a rapid turn-over of employees. Bert and Holly, Oregon, January

Leaky fuel joint almost caused disaster.
I've used my MSR-XGK stove thousands of times without mishap. Then last night after refueling I didn't tighten down the fuel bottle. A few drops leaked out and caught fire.
At first I wasn't sure which way to turn it to tighten the connection. But to loosen it would be disasterous. So I quickly took the stove outside where I shut it off.
A few burning drops landed on the floor of my van but soon went out. A few drops landed on my legs and also went out, but today I notice blisters. Ouch !
The XGK does not support a pot well. Its "legs" swing around too easy (on mine anyway). So I use an old auto license plate (with plastic previously burnt off in a fire) bent around the burner for pot support. If the pot is small, I put a Backpacker adjustable grill under it. Eugene Gonzalez, Arizona, October

Hot springs may spread diseases, but can be disinfected.
In my area there are half a dozen natural, free, hot spring pools I have used for years. Last year several were contaminated by outside visitors with new hybrid virus strains to which I lacked immunity. I picked up sinus, throat and other ailments repeatedly. Now I take sterilization iodine (available from vet and stock suppliers) and treat pools I suspect. Al Fry, Idaho

I hope to join or start a kayaking community.
We would live on the coastlines of the Americas, migrating seasonally. I like caravans, but not piling into pickups and driving around. Not cost effective. Rolf Hardiek, Utah, Nov

Two old Solar Showers developed leaks around the fill holes.
I discarded, and bought a new one at K-mart for $10. Eugene

(Comment:) Have you tried using unaltered plastic jugs for showers? (Remove caps.) For years we've used nothing else. Jugs work fine and save buying (or making) and storing unnecessary gadgets. The first few showers may seem awkward, until motions become easy.

In a trailer, how to install plumbing so it does not freeze.
May97 DP said, "Complex RV appliances are not reliable."
SO TRUE. I gutted my trailer and threw out all the original appliances. I put in a simple stove and a gravity-feed water system. I put all my plumbing (plastic) INDOORS, with removable sections for clean-out and repair, connected with flexible (rubber) fittings. I sloped the pipes more than usual, to have quick, complete drainage so no water remains in them to freeze.
Last winter, my neighbors' new $40,000 trailers froze up. Not mine, even with outside temperatures to minus 80°F.
On very cold days I sprinkled some salt down the drain. Helped prevent freezing. Last winter I used 12 lbs table salt.
I engineered my drain system so my waste water flushes my toilet. Saves much water. By mounting bath tub 6" above floor.
If wintering in snow country, add a foot+ to the plumbing vent sticking above the trailer's roof. Otherwise, snow will cover vent and vacuum-lock plumbing, causing it not to drain. Happened to my neighbors last winter.
If buying a trailer, look for an older model with twin I-beam frame and two axles. David French, South Dakota, May97

(Comment:) Put salt down a drain only if the plumbing is plastic or tile. Might corrode metal. If using much salt, look for non-food-grade (sold for industrial uses). Cheaper than table salt.

When rebuilding a van or bus into a motorhome:

For framing, instead of wood I use slotted steel to which I can easily bolt. Bolts and nuts hold more reliably than nails/screws, and allow easier transfer to a future vehicle.

I "module" everything for easier changes or replacement.

I color-code wire and pipe systems for easier maintenance and fixing. I prefer "marine grade" electrical and plumbing parts because they are designed for long life in rough environments.

Before refitting a vehicle, make an accurate drawing of its floor space, and maybe even build an interior model with modules to scale, to find best arrangement and avoid costly mistakes.

I use bungee cords and small nets to secure loose objects, which otherwise become flying missiles during a "very sudden stop". (Once a heavy mug went through my windshield.)

Even if the vehicle seems large enough to live in, carry along a large tarp or tent to provide extra space when parking in the boonies at one spot for quite a while. Even a modest dome tent serves to reserve a space when away a few days. A tent also provides personal shelter when the vehicle is in a repair shop. (Saves renting an expensive motel room.) Wildflower, CT, Febr

I am not homeless. My HOME is homeless.

So says Guinea Apollos. She lives in a 1964 school bus, purchased 3 years ago when her income could no longer pay the rent of a small San Francisco apartment. She equipped the bus with stove, sink and spice rack; and brightened it with family photographs, potted plants, crocheted afgans, and window curtains.

Although Guinea is as poor as many of the thousands of homeless on the streets, she believes her bus sets her apart. Some officials agree. They are considering a project that would stop the grim cat-and-mouse game that Apollos and many like her play with police. The city may build campgrounds in the port area, far from residential neighborhoods, where hundreds already park. Showers, toilets, laundries, a community room, and social and health services would be provided for car dwellers, who would be responsible for maintenance and security. With homeless shelters filled every night and hundreds more sleeping parks or business doorways, pressure is mounting on officials to do something.

Sleeping in vehicles is presently illegal in SF between 10 am and 6 am. But typically, police move people or tow cars only if residents complain. One day last month, police ticketed 58 vehicles parked along one port-area street and later towed 17 of them. A few days after the sweep, some had already returned.

Mike Waters, president of a charter-bus company whose bus yard is there, periodically asks police to move the campers along. "We've seen the street lined solid with campers, trucks and cars. They like to park here because they can get fresh water from our spigots. Most seem harmless, but some have dogs who chase my employees." Waters opposes building campgrounds. "I think it will be a waste of taxpayers' money. Some of these people have psychological problems and belong in supervised care. The others probably wouldn't have anything to do with such a place." Mary Curtius (from Seattle Times 10/22/97; sent by Roger Knight)

Life on the streets of downtown Eugene.

When 14-year-old Olivia arrived in August, the mall seemed better than her mom's house. Mom drank and Mom's boyfriend was abusive. Olivia had much to learn and learn quickly. Her first night was tough. She didn't know where to sleep. A young girl asleep outside was an obvious target for sexual predation. Or if a cop found her, she could be locked up - it's illegal to sleep outside or in a park after 11 pm. The "mall rats" (other kids) told her green, newspaper-recycling boxes were good. That's where Olivia slept her first night. She removed some papers, flattened the cardboard boxes, climbed in, and covered herself with papers.

The veteran mall rats also told her which restaurants, such as IHOP, would let you stay all night, until the 5 am breakfast crowd came in, if you paid 99¢ for a bottomless cup of coffee.

Olivia learned where to snag free food boxes (Catholic Community Services, St Vincent de Paul, Looking Glass); where to clean up (public restrooms downtown); and how to get around town (LTD central bus station). Above all she needed safety; provided by other mall rats who looked out for her - her street family.

The true mall rats were kids who had nowhere else to live, and were able to get along with each other. Kids who didn't - who refused to share food when they had it, stole from the other kids, or narked to the cops - were ostracized, sometimes beaten up. They wound up back with their parents, in foster homes, or jails.

In July, life on the streets had seemed attractive, not only to teens from bad homes, but to wanna-bes, rebels and thrill-seekers to whom a teen-only world, without parents and responsibilites, seemed preferable to the drudgery of school and rules. But by December the number on the mall had plummeted along with temperature.

Homeless runaway teens are becoming more visible. The Northwest's relatively mild climate and grunge image are attractive. Brett Campbell (condensed from _Eugene Weekly_, August 1997)

States vary in regulation of home schoolers.
Low-regulation states do not require parents to initiate contact with officials: ID, IL, IN, MI, MO, NJ, OK, TX.

High-regulation states require parents to send notification, test scores and/or professional evaluation of progress; and may require corriculum approval, parental qualification, or home visits by officials: ARK, MA, ME, MN, ND, NV, NY, PA, UT, VT, WA, WV.

Intermediate regulation states: those not listed above.

Recently, on standardized tests, 5400 randomly-selected home schoolers averaged 80; compared to 50 by state-school students of similar ages, races and wealth. (0 to 100 scale.) NO correlation between regulation level and achievement level. Now ± a million home schoolers in America. Brian Ray, Home School Research Inst., Salem OR, 1997?

Fix-a-Flat caused tire to thump.
Fix-a-Flat is goopy-glooey stuff in a pressurized can used to temporarily seal punctures. You are supposed to later have the tire fixed at a service station. Instead, I plugged the leak myself but used too much Fix-a-Flat (2 cans). A "thump" developed and got progressively worse. At first I thought a brake cylinder had seized and tried to fix it. But the thump remained. I finally went to a VW specialist who found the problem. Eugene Gonzalez

I sleep in my car under tule netting.
I drape it over me if there is even one fly or mosquito inside. I also use it to barricade each open window: I open the door, drape the netting around the outside of the door, over the top, and back out through the window; then close the door. That leaves a gap between layers at the bottom, but few if any skeeters find their way in. Won't stop gnats. 59¢/yard at fabric stores.
D.Dorji

I use spring shades as window covers and awning on my car.
I have one for every window. I don't want to look up from my bed and see a face, cop or otherwise, leering at me.

While parked, if a window is open for ventilation, I lay a spring shade on roof, overhanging window, as awning. I anchor by setting a bean bag, rocks, or food cans on top of it.

A spring shade goes from dish size to window size in one swoosh and weighs only a few ounces. Auto stores/depts sell for about $7. Cardboard would work, but not be as light nor fold so neatly. Double Dorji, Arizona, June

Dwelling Portably

formerly named Message Post
POB 190, Philomath OR 97370

October 1998 $1 per issue   Add 50¢ to check/mo under $6

I have taken the first steps to a more mobile and free life.
     I purchased a used van in good condition: ideal for the
open road. Also, I have been using only a pager with voice-
mail for the past two years, instead of a home phone. And, to
top it off, I have been receiving job offers in my chosen
field (a fast food) from people I know who will pay me under
the table. Bill, New York 139, June

More about trailer housing on Mid-west flood-plain farms.
     In response to your objections (in Oct95 and Oct97 DPs):
Farmers would place fewer attachments on their trailers than
do trailer-park residents; knowing that emergency mobility was
why they chose trailers instead of permanent houses. And
mortgage insurers could restrict attachments. To avoid tire
problems, put run-flat or solid-rubber tires on trailers.
     Even without such measures, a farm's six-trailer home
could be made ready to move in half a day at most, and moved
to high ground in another half day. In most floods that would
be quick enough, because there are usually days or weeks of
warning: true of the Upper Mississippi floods a few years ago.
     Your suggestion that farmers commute to their fields from
homes on high ground, is common in Europe and might be good in
many flood-plain situations here. But trailers would be a
better choice where: (1) Severe floods are rare, and are
preceded by long warnings: consequently infrequent trailer
moves would be less burdensome than daily commuting.
(2) Unattended farm equipment or animals may be stolen or
vandalized. (3) No high ground near by to commute from (as
in the upper Midwest). (4) The family prefers a home with no
close neighbors (instead of in a cluster of houses on hill).
     Trailers could be phased in naturally AFTER a flood, as
on-site emergency housing for victims. This may already be
done sometimes. (Long after a flood, the ground is too wet
for conventional rebuilding. Or infrastructure was destroyed,
as in Central America after the recent floods.) So victims
could/should be encouraged to continue living in trailers.
     Trailer housing would also be advantageous in beachfront
areas subject to storm surges - the most damaging result of
hurricanes. Warning time is usually ample. Roger Knights, WA

Isolation did not foster individuality.
     Pitcairn Island, a speck in the Pacific, is famous as the
refuge of the sailers who in 1789 mutinied on the ship Bounty.
     Today it is inhabited by 38 descendants of those mutineers
and their native Polynesian spouses. The island has no autos,
sporadic electricity, and only a few simple appliances. No
ships dock there, though some pause to trade for mementos.
     Is Pitcairn an idyllic haven? No, says Dea Birkett in
"Serpent in Paradise". Much on the island appealed to her:
the islanders' physical skills, good looks, and courage;
their pleasant demeanor; their curious language (a patois of
Polynesian and 18th-century English); their religious
devotion (they are 7th-day Adventists); and their friendly-
ness to her. But after several months she began to see that
envy and rivalry existed on Pitcairn as elsewhere, that
everybody watched everybody else, that gossip was the most
popular pastime, and that individuality was impossible in so
small a place. Not without some regret, Birkett had herself
ferried out to a passing freighter and headed home to London.
(from Parade 22Nov98; sent by Roger Knights)

With a bicycle, is a sidecar better than a trailer?

Responding to December 1997 DP, page 7: yes and no.

With a sidecar you can sit on a bike without having to balance it. While underway you can reach into a sidecar for goodies, or to adjust an auxillary motor or engine. You can add a top cover and sleep in it or on top. A brake cable can reach the sidecar but not a trailer. A sidecar can't fishtail or jacknife as can a trailer.

On the other hand, a trailer is cheaper, easier to start with, narrower, and tracks directly behind the bike.

As for forces sideways due to bike not tilting: no problem with 20-inch wheels. Kids are rough on bikes, yet I've repaired hundreds of bicycles and never seen a 20-inch rim bent by side forces. Even better are 20-inch BMX wheels. More spokes, thicker spokes, and wider and stronger rims. I've used many on trailers I've built for people. The only rims I've seen bent by side forces, were 26-27 inch, and they only with forces of a 300-400 pound load. If bent, you just kick them and they snap back into shape.

I have been in third-world countries and seen many bicycles with sidecars. David French, South Dakota 577, March

(Comments:) For items accessed while moving, a small handle-bar basket suffices me. Why can't a trailer be covered as easily as a sidecar? Or slept in? (Maybe make it just big enough for head and body, with pull-out extension for legs.)

For abrupt stops, have brakes applied by springs after pulling a release cord? Disadvantage: must stop and dismount to release. But mostly used on long hills, and emergencies.

All our bikes (old) have 26-27" wheels. I've seen no adult-size bikes with 20" wheels, except folders. Big wheels have less rolling resistance. (Enough less to matter?)

Yes, with a trailer, jackknifing might be a problem. But with a sidecar, might spins be a problem, set off by unequal braking? Eg, after partly missing a puddle, the sidecar rim is wet while the bike rims are dry.

In a third-world city I might prefer a sidecar.   If most traffic bicycles and moving at bicycle speed, the width is not as hazardous. And, with many petty thieves, a sidecar would be less easily stolen from at stop lights. But on North American streets and highways, I believe I would prefer a trailer. Makes me a slimmer target. Holly & Bert, OR 973

I plan an extended bicycle trip of the U.S., Mexico, Canada.

I will leave between September and December. How can I make money along the way to keep me going? (How do I parlay my skills into successful bartering or day labor, for food, shelter or cash?   Will I get a good reception doing this?)

How do I learn to dwell more portably? (Currently I do lots of camping. I also stay with other cyclists.)

How do I meet up with like-minded people? (I've done several long tours, mostly skirting the cities in favor of rural places, and have met nice farmers, Amish folk, laid-back suburbanites, etc., but no real counterculture people like I imagine read Dwelling Portably. Jerome, OH 452, June

(Reply:) If you camp for free and eat economically, you should not need much money. One summer, Holly and I biked several hundred miles to a Rainbow gathering in northeastern Calif, and made more than enough money picking up drink cans along the way. (5¢ deposit in OR. Now in most states?)   We ate mostly bulk foods (much dry oatmeal); some bread and marge.

Departing in autumn, you will encounter cold weather (unless you winter in southern Mexico), and the additional insulation may reduce portability. You might TRY (best test beforehand) using only one light sleeping bag, augmented over and under with leaves, moss, crumpled newspapers, or whatever, gathered locally. What you have been doing to meet people, sounds effective. DP readers are very varied. No one method of meeting people will work with all. Bert & Holly, OR 973

I lived on my bicycle for three months during summer 1985.
Saved much money on rent. Had fun too. Washed at the river, and when I went swimming in the lake. (Dr Bonners soap works well in cold water.) David French, SD 577, 1997

Lives in and travels with trailer from Midwest to Southwest.
After retiring, I traveled to Yuma AZ and spent the winter there. In the spring I returned to MN and SD where I have ties. This Midwest summer has been strange. My little travel trailer suffered a hail storm in MN. Only cosmetic damage - the skin looks like a bad case of cellulite, but the insurance company considered it a total loss and paid off the loan, so in essence I got a free trailer.

I plan to return to Yuma in September, leave my trailer there, and drive on into Mexico in December with my canine companion. My son lives in Mexico City, so I plan to get as close as common sense allows: the pollution there is horrid. I've done research on retiring in Mexico, and talked to friends.

Incidentally, there were a number of Oregonians in Yuma. I hate to say so, but they seemed red-neck. Maybe it was their age, or maybe it was me. I wouldn't want to live among them. Supposedly, Oregon is beautiful. But what about the political/ social climate? Are some areas friendlier than others? That is true of Minneapolis and Rapid City. I guess us non-traditionals just have to nose around to find our place. Vardo, SD 577, July

(Reply:) I can't say from personal experience (our contacts are either too selective and unconventional, or too fleeting). But based on statistics we've read (eg, Abapa Freer), per capita, Oregon has more social/political non-conformists of most types than does any other state. Hippies, punks, gays, greens, reds, libertarians, pagans, atheists, whatever.

Us non-conformists are not evenly distributed. Most are around Portland (biggest city); Eugene, Corvallis, and Ashland (university cities); and some coastal areas. The rest of Oregon may be more like Idaho than like the above places.

If you live in an area where there are many non-conformists, the upside is: you are more likely to find people like yourself. The downside is: some narrow-minded people feel threatened by all the "weirdos" around - more so than where non-conformists are scarce and may be regarded more as curiosities than threats. (South Dakota?) Holly & Bert

I found a nice place in an otherwise-uncampable area.
It has picturesque scenery, remarkably friendly people, and will let you stay there occasionally in a tent or RV in exchange for some work. It has a sweat lodge, features trading events, and is non-profit, dedicated to wildlife. For info: Silverado (or Belle Santos), POB 5434, Bisbee AZ 85603.
Michael, OR 970, July

I have been living homelessly on the East Coast a few years.
Soon I will be moving to the Pacific Northwest; toting a backpack with all that I own in it. Eric, VA 229, February

Dwelling Portably

formerly named Message Post
POB 190, Philomath OR 97370

May 1999 $1 per issue   Add 50¢ to check/mo under $6

I use a Sierra Designs "Flashlight" tent.

I have had three since 1983. My first two, the smaller
model, are still in use by friends. I now have the larger
model. I sewed a 4" extension on the edge of the fly so as to
cover the tent's seams. Recently I tried ironing on tarp tape
over all the bottom seams. So far the tape is holding well.
(Seam sealant is expensive, toxic to breathe, and a hassle to
apply.) I've had good experience with these tents. But I take
time to care for them and I keep them out of direct sunlight.

Many years I traveled by motorcycle or bicycle, living
outside 6 months or more per year, mostly in drier, eastern
Washington. But I've also used the tent in wet climates and,
with my modifications, it does well. Laura LaBree, WA 981,Nov

Bike rack made from branches.

This autumn, at a yard
sale, for $5 I bought
an old 3-speed. It
had sat unused for
years in a garage and
both tires were
deflated, but it was
otherwise ride-able.
No basket or rack.
It had a step-thru
("girl's") frame,
and while playing
with sticks to rein-
force the top, I
realized that two
sticks, criss-crossed,
and extending back-
wards, would also
provide a rack.

For the two main
sticks, I used ± 5/8" diameter
green willow branches, because they were prevalent where
I was. For the other sticks, smaller diameters. (I prefer
western red cedar (Thuja plicata) when available, for its rot
resistance. I also prefer dry wood, for lightness. But green
wood will gradually dry.) I did not peel because I liked the
bark's color for camo when stashing bike, and I lacked time.

The main sticks were curved, so I mounted them bowing
outward in the rear for greater rack-width. (I later replaced
them with straight, aluminum ski poles I found in a dumpster,
which were lighter. Both worked fine.)

Later, I sawed off the front extension, because if bulky
objects were put on it, they interfered with steering. Also,
the rack not turning along with the handlebars, visually
disconcerted me (though I might have become accustomed).

I lashed the rack together and to the bike with rubber
straps cut from discarded (holey) bike innertubes. Multiple,
tight wrappings gave a very strong joint. Time allowing, I
may cover the joints with duct tape. Otherwise sunlight will
deteriorate the rubber. Julie Summers, Oregon 973, Sept 97

Tip for cutting innertube into straps with uniform width.

I first cut along seam, then in half, and half again until
narrow enough. (Halfing easier than cutting narrow off wide.)

When lifting a bicycle over a fence.
Goes easier if the handlebar or front wheel are fastened so they can't pivot. Safer, too, so the handlebar won't pivot unexpectedly and poke an eye. I tie twine to the down-tube, at the point closest to the front wheel. Then I loop the twine around the wheel-rim and tube a few times and tie again.
If encountering many fences, to save time I might leave the twine permanently fastened to the down-tube. Julie, 1996

Shifting gears on a three-speed bike.
If shifting from low to medium is unreliable, try this. Shift from HIGH to medium, and then adjust the indicator rod so its shoulder is flush with the end of the axle (seen through an observation hole in the sleeve part of the axle nut).

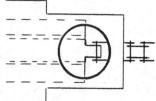

Then, whenever shifting to medium, always go FROM HIGH. (If in low, go first to high, then med.)
The reason: There is a spring that gets compressed when shifting down, and expands when shifting up. I guess it weakens with age or rust and does not expand the same each time. But when compressed, it necessarily moves the same each time, and hence returns to where it was adjusted.
When I am done riding, I leave the gears in high, to release compression on the spring. Julie Summers, 1992

Loading a bicycle for stability.
Put heavy items low and toward the center. I strap (eg) grain sacks in the triangular frame section, if they are narrow enough to not interfere with my legs. I put next-dense items toward the front of panniers; somewhat lighter objects rearward; and lightest bulk (sleeping bags; foam) on rack. (This assumes the panniers cannot swing. If they can, I put only light things in them.) Water bottle and in-route food go in handlebar basket along with excess clothes as removed. Be sure straps don't dangle where they could catch in wheels.
If you wear loose long pants, strap bottoms snug so they can't snag on something and prevent putting a foot down. H & B

Don't be blinded by a bungee.
If the bungee is stretched, and you lose your grip or the bungee breaks: WHAM ! No telling where the hook will go. Instead of bungees, I use rubber straps, doubled to provide loops. There is usually a projection to put the loop over. (If not, I may permanently mount a strong hook.) Julie, Dec.

I love to bicycle, but fear for myself when on the road.
One year, when camped in eastern Washington, I rode 34 miles (round trip) to town once a week. Several times I was almost killed by unyielding motorists. Laura, November

Suggestions for safer bicycling on roads.
Well-known precautions include: being visible (bright/ light-colored upper-body clothing); wearing helmet (cheap at thrift stores); riding single file; riding slow or walking where gravel ; not arguing right-of-way, especially with anything bigger; checking tire inflation and wheel fastenings often; and avoiding busy streets if there are bike paths or low-traffic byways. Some less known or less heeded:
Never ride faster than you are willing to crash. A tire may blow, an axle break, or a deer dart out unexpectedly.

A long down-grade before an up-grade tempts me to let bike gain speed. Risky!

On a two-lane road lacking wide paved shoulders, avoid double passing. Ie, do not get passed simultaneously by overtaking and oncoming vehicles. Anticipate passings, stop, and get off of pavement. Also be wary when on curves or summits where an overtaking vehicle cannot see what is oncoming. Some cyclists believe they have as much right to the road as motorists and refuse to get off: forcing overtaking vehicle to either slow to bike speed, or try to squeeze by. That is not only dangerous, but angers motorists who then may agitate for anti-bike laws.

Bert rides some highways I won't, by alternately sprinting and resting. During pauses in traffic he sprints; then when the next "convoy" comes along, he gets off and lets it pass.

If you must stop (other than briefly to let traffic pass or to check bike), get completely off the road and OUT OF SIGHT. Don't be a "sitting duck" for motorized predators, uniformed or otherwise. A stopped vehicle (of any kind) is an easier, more tempting target than is a moving vehicle. (Last summer, on a secondary road, Bert and I stopped for a mid-day snack, well off the road but visible from it. We were not on posted land nor near any building. We were clean and "decently" dressed (not bikini weather). As we stood by our bikes eating/drinking (not smoking), a county cop drove in and began interrogating us: "Where you coming from?" "Where you go going?" After his first questions, we mostly ignored him and busied ourselves putting away lunch remnants. Maybe that was a good tactic: at least he soon left. Why did he accost us? We were easy prey: already stopped where he could park off the road. (Stopping ON that stretch of road would be hazardous: no shoulders; few pull-offs; many blind curves.) He may have hoped we were affluant sport-cyclists (many use that road) who would pay a fine no matter how wrongful, rather than go to court. But when he got close, he saw our old bikes and non-snazzy clothes. (Local police don't like to fill jails with poor "hobos" who can't pay fines.) That was the first time either of us have been hassled in over 20 years.)

The safest time to travel is usually very early Sunday mornings, especially in late spring and early summer when days are long. Few motor vehicles, no/ little frantic commuting-to-work traffic, and most police are sleeping after scoring on party-goers the night before. Next safest: early Saturday morn. H&B

Camping with horse and milk goat.

Horses aren't for everyone. They are BIG strong animals and can easily panic. For beginners I recommend donkeys.

I've worked with horses most of my life and spent long periods in the back country with one or more pack horses.

One horse can carry 150 lbs: enough for a very plush camp. I usually have along a cast-iron skillet and dutch oven. I prefer wool blankets to nylon sleeping bags, and a horse easily packs all the wool I need. By eating mostly whole grains and foraging greens, I can stay out months without trips to town for supplies.

Move the horse often, to not overgraze one spot. I use a 50' picket rope.

If necessary, I can hide my camp, horse and all. During the day I keep the horse in woods or brush; then, after dark, put it in open pasture to graze.

I don't get hassled in National Forests because I keep moving. And most Green Meanies like horses. The only place I've ever been hassled was on a state beach in California; and there only because I was still in camp at noon. I could have avoided trouble by moving early. But I recommend staying out of California no matter how you travel.

In populated areas, I've camped along the edges of highways. A horse changes people's attitudes. Many strangers are friendly and helpful, offering pastures for grazing, back yards for camping, and gifts of hay. On the road, people stop and give me money. I've taken long bicycle trips and never had that happen.

I live in a horse-drawn wagon-camper during cold weather. I mostly park it on a friend's private property. I don't like using it on highways because car drivers are crazy and in a big hurry. But I know quite a few folks who do.

I often have a milk goat along. She forages as we hike and turns brush and leaves into a high-protein drink. A goat can't walk as far or as fast as a horse or human. But I do more wandering than treking and am willing to wait for the goat as she's got the lunch with her. A milk goat can't be used as a pack goat, as she needs all her energy to make milk. I've found that one horse plus one goat work well, and keep each other company if you need to leave them briefly.

I hope more people use horses as their main transportation. The oil-burning-auto lifestyle is most damaging of Mother Earth. Dancing Bear, ID 834, Jan.

Two kinds of police at Mexican border.

The regular U.S. Border Guards were polite and efficient, and did not seize or damage the anti-biotics I had bought in Mexico (which, though legal in and manufactured in U.S., are almost impossible to obtain in U.S. (because U.S. MDs, fearful of serious side-effects that could bring law suits, won't prescribe?))

But also at the border were specially assigned police, probably all from the Drug Enforcement Agency though they often wore uniforms of various other agencies including Forest Service. All looked similar: wiry males, tobacco-stained, and contageously nervous. And all were trouble: sticking dirty knives into sterile factory-sealed packages.

I have heard the DEA may be withdrawn. Meanwhile, best remain in Mexico while taking any medicines bought in Mexico. Michael, Oregon 970, December

Be careful with ID and credit cards.

Do not carry them on your person, especially not where you might be robbed. If you have only cash, the robber will take it and hopefully let you go. But if you have credit or bank cards, the robber has an incentive to kill you so you can't report the theft while he, or an accomplice who resembles you, cashes them or makes purchases. (I've never seen store clerks examine ID carefully. If they did, ID would be seldom usable, because most people's looks change too much.) Also, if the robber is "wanted", he may desire your ID so he can impersonate you if he meets cops.

If driving, keep your drivers license hidden in the vehicle where you can get it if police stop you and demand it. But not on your person. Likewise with a credit card: retrieve only when you arrive at the store. (We recommend not having credit cards. They incur high charges, and encourage impulse buying and excessive consumption. H & B)

Some cities and states try to require carrying ID. But such laws have been ruled unconstitutional when appealed. Police would like everyone to carry ID so they can process subjects faster, levy more fines, and improve promotion prospects. (The police might also like everyone to be tatooed with a number, like in Nazi slave-labor camps.) The police don't much care if more people are murdered as a consequence: in fact, the more crime, the better for police - as long as most sheep citizens respond by voting more funds for police.

I've heard, some airlines require ID, even on domestic flights. Boycott them.

Most foreign nations require ID for admission. I would not go there, at least not for recreation. If interested in some far-away place, I can learn more easily, quickly, economically and safely through books, zines, recordings and videos than by actually going there for a few weeks. Or, if I seek live novelty, I am more apt to find it nearby because I can better search nearby. Most major cities and some smaller ones have ethnic neighborhoods, stores, festivals, etc.

However, if you must travel abroad, keep your passport and other important papers hidden next to your body. Also carry small bills in a wallet or purse for surrendering to a robber.

If stopped by police, make sure they ARE police before giving them anything important. Gangsters often impersonate police. When you check their ID by phoning their (supposed) headquarters, look up the number in a phone book. (Do not merely call a number they might give you.) Steve, New Mexico 880, November

Helping lost children survive.
A child can get lost anywhere. I live in a small town on a cul-de-sac where everyone has several acres. One morning, a young girl who lives some distance away, became lost and wandered to within 50 yards of my neighbor's house, only to die at the gate to the yard. To help avoid such tragedies, have each child:

Wear red or orange outer garments.

Carry a whistle. It takes less energy and can be heard farther than a voice.

Carry a clean trash bag. And teach: If becoming cold or wet, put bag on over head, after making hole for face.

Once you know you are lost, hug a tree. If you stay in one place, you'll be found quicker and can't be injured by falling. If scared, hugging may calm you.

If at night you hear a sound, yell at it, but remain where you are. If it is an animal, you will scare it away. If it is a searcher, you will be found. (Fears often cause children to run.)

Hundreds will search for you. Do not fear them, or feel ashamed of getting lost. (Some kids, afraid of strangers or men in uniform, or of parents' wrath, hide and don't answer calls.)

Try to pick a tree to hug near a clearing. If you have spare energy, make a big SOS in the clearing out of broken shrubbery, rocks, or by dragging foot. Whether or not you do, when you hear a low-flying aircraft, go out into the clearing and lay down, outstretched, to look bigger from above.

For retention, make these teachings into a game. Ken Larson, GA 301, 1997

(Comments:) I like the trash bag idea but have doubts about some others.

Among thick foliage, which absorbs high frequencies, a voice may be heard farther than a whistle. Also, around here, a common bird call sounds identical to many whistles. Teach: call or whistle in groups of three.

Red does not show well in twilight or dense woods. Wear orange or bright blue (which, unlike orange, can't be mistaken for autumn foliage). Or maybe best: blue bottom with orange top.

Hundreds will search? Don't count on that unless you're a VIP. Even if they do, foul-ups may delay search many hours. (Instances reported in Signpost zine.)

Do not fear? Most kids are taught to fear strangers, and such fears may also be instinctive. Unrealistic to expect an abrupt change of feelings.

Hug a tree? May be best if weather is warm or if child has ample clothing. If not, the child may die from chilling before being found. (Would tree-hugging have saved that young girl?) Also, a tree with big dead limbs is dangerous in wind, and a lone tree or tree taller than nearby trees is dangerous in lightning. Instead, I would equip the child with bright ribbons ALL THE SAME COLOR (which can be cut from worn-out plastic shopping bags) and teach: During daylight, keep moving and try to find your way to other people. But, as you go, tie a ribbon every 20 paces or so. Under each ribbon, form an arrow (can be just ⟩) with foot-rub or broken branch, to show direction of travel. Searchers are much more likely to cross such a trail than to happen upon a motionless child; and once they do, they can easily follow it to the child. Also, that helps child detect if s/he is walking in circles.

City and Suburban Survival: Tom Brown's Field Guide (with Brandt Morgan, 1984, 266 p., Berkley, 200 Madison Av, NY 10016)

"No amount of insurance can guarantee that we won't lose our homes or jobs, but if we know how to fend for ourselves, we will be able to enjoy our lives whatever the outward circumstances."

"Some survival situations are so dismal that if we stop to consider all that is left to endure, we will be overwhelmed by despair.... The only way to get through, is one moment at a time."

In crises, many people make wrong choices. Eg, many die in fires because "they were too modest to leave the house without their clothes. Don't be afraid to act boldly."

You can slip a few pages of flattened newspaper "inside a meagre jacket (front and back) to create a weather break..." For sleeping, a newspaper spread over the body serves like a blanket.

"Good heat insulators ... contain a lot of dead air space that can trap and hold the heat." To increase insulative qualities of paper or other thin material, crumple, or put in separated layers. "Even fir springs can have a tremendous warming effect (within clothes) if you tie off your cuffs to keep the stuffing in."

As umbrella, Tom suggests: "Take a cardboard box (found in dumpster) ... and hold it, spread flat, over your head...." "Many other useful shelter items can be found in dumpsters and alleyways. Boxes, packing crates, plastic sheeting, and other untainted debris can be used in much the same way as furniture to form a protective shelter." Eg, a hut made of mattresses.

"There is no way for the human body to warm a whole room, much less an entire house. If it's cold and you have no additional heat source, make a small shelter - the smaller the better" - within the house if it is warmer than outside. But never have flames of any kind inside a mini shelter.

"Almost any open flame can be made more efficient by enclosing it in a metal container. Instead of quickly escaping, the heat ... collects and radiates through the walls of the container, casting its warmth in all directions. This is what stoves are all about." If making one from a coffee can, "to create draft, punch holes around sides at both ends...." The heat from 3 candles may be enough to boil a cup of water.

To make "canned" fuel, roll up a strip of corrugated cardboard (as wide as a tuna-size can is high) and fit it snuggly into can. Pour in paraffin, leaving ¼" of cardboard sticking out for lighting. (Review by Julie Summers)

A way to dry a small quantity of kindling.

When the whole world seems wet and I plan to build a fire later that day, I gather some tinder and kindling (for least damp, I look under leaning trees or logs), put loosely in an extra T-shirt (or wrap in paper), and place inside my upper garments next to my body. In a few hours (if not too wet or too much or too big chunks) my body heat will dry it.

To ignite still-damp kindling, I place a candle beneath for a few minutes. Conserves lighter or matches. Once a fire is well started, it will burn quite wet wood. To partially dry, I place the next pieces near the fire.

Body heat can also dry (eg) cap or mittens.   B & H, Dec

Butane lighters survive wetting well.

They are temporarily disabled, but okay after drying out. Some lighters I had stored a few years still work fine. Whereas "waterproof" matches, after long storage, light unreliably or not at all. They seem to absorb moisture.

All butane lighters I've had, worked fine except for ones with the confounded "child-proofer". But it can be pried out.
Julie, Oct

Brief suggestions for building a winter shelter.

Designs in past DPs include: Tleanto, Sep85; Hillodge, Apr92; Snugiup, May95; Twipi, LLL. However, I usually tailor shelter to site, rather than follow plans exactly.

Choose a site sheltered from: wind and lightning (avoid ridge tops); water (avoid gulch bottoms; flood plains); big animals and people (avoid houses, campgrounds, cow pastures, easy-hiking terrain; also read May95 DP). Generally best: south slope (for solar heating) but not near top (windy) or bottom (cold sink). If possible, prepare site before hunting season, but wait until after hunting season to move in.

Cut as little vegetation as possible. Digging is usually easiest when soil is moist but not soppy. In this area, best done the previous winter or spring.

If rain or snow expected soon, erect roof first. If you will depend on rain water, think about how roof can catch it.

Use mostly materials occuring at or near site. If you will only sleep in the shelter, all natural stuff may suffice. Otherwise, I'd also use plastic: for window; and perhaps an under-roof to intercept leaks and sifting debris.

Make one wall entirely or mostly of plastic and face it toward the most open sky. (That is simpler, and better for light, than are little windows all around.) Hang plastic vertical or (if reflections might attract attention) with bottom further in. At least 2 layers spaced $\frac{1}{2}$" to 1" apart.

For the other walls, and ceiling, use anything fluffy that can be easily contained. Eg, bags of leaves or moss; or inner and outer wattles (interwoven branches) with insulation between. CAUTION: don't put weight where could fall on you !

In most areas, the best floor is earth: smoothed and packed, and maybe covered with semi-stiff plastic (eg, linoleum): easier to wipe than is limp plastic. Earth stores heat (or cold) and warms a shelter in cold weather (and cools it when hot): much more comfortable than a raised wooden floor. If water seepage may become a problem, ditch around.

For warmth, the best entrance is from below, so heated air (which tends to rise) does not escape when hatch opened.

If using combustion inside, be very careful, not only to avoid setting the shelter on fire, but to provide enough ventilation. (Carbon monoxide is sneaky and deadly. People have been killed by candles in air-tight tents. However, every site-built shelter of ours has been leaky enough for candles and a propane stove without extra vents. A bigger problem has been mosquitos infiltrating during warm weather. We often need an insect net hung inside, at least at night.)

If in an unfamiliar environment or type of shelter, have a back-up shelter handy. Bert & Holly, Oregon 973, January

Blockage of trailer's heater nearly kills movie actress.

On location near Reno, Jenny McCarthy was in her trailer. "My heart started palpitating.... I got dizzy. I was nauseous and started convulsing. Everything was going black."

She collapsed to the floor but managed to crawl to the door, open it, and tumble out. Oxygen was administered in the ambulance. The hospital released her later that day. The doctor said, the convulsions indicated she was near death.

The crew had taped plastic tightly around the trailer's bottom to keep the water pipes from freezing. That blocked air circulation to the heater. Carbon monoxide built up and seeped into the trailer. (From 29 Dec 98 National Inquirer,
sent by Roger Knights)

My dog and I live in a 1979 Chevy van.

We are relatively safe and comfortable on 3 acres of wooded residential property on the fringes of Chattanooga. By being here, we provide some security for the owner's two vacant houses. But I'm free to go away for long periods. I have enough privacy to be nude when temperatures permit.

My only source of income is occasional climbing for a tree-care service. My casual employer reaches me via phone with answering machine located inside one of the houses.

I could move into the house for more living space. But I am happier in my little box on wheels. Everything is within reach, and the small kerosene heater makes the inside toasty even on the coldest nights. Jimmy, Tennessee 374, February

I have lived year around in my 26' Nomadics tipi over 4 years.

I plan to relocate out west. Paul, VA 228, Feb 98

Live cheap and portable. Have nothing government can seize.
    I have lived on a farm since I graduated in 1971. Took
me until last year to pay it off. All 640 acres. I worked
night shifts and day shifts and farmed, and had a wife and
family. It seemed to make sense: my ancestors had done it
and I was trained to.
    Now I am 45 and look back with an emptiness. I'd wanted
to camp and travel and maybe even sail a boat to taste the
variety and wonders of the world. Instead, all those years
were spent complying with government farm programs: do this,
do that; plant this, plant that. Once you have a big stake
you can never leave. You will not own it; IT WILL OWN YOU.
    I encourage DP readers to stay small. Limit possessions
to things that are portable and concealable. I have become
defensive because of a bitter divorce I never wanted. But
because of money and possessions I was forced to play the
game. Roger, Kansas 677, November

I have been living "primitively" off and on for ten years.
    For the past 7 months, I've been in the Kiamichi Mtn
Wilderness Area on the Oklahoma/Arkansas border in Ouachita
Mtns. No electricity or running water. Sharon, AR 719, June

Backwoods nomadics: problems; solutions.
    Here are questions Bert and I are asked. Our answers
apply to OUR way of life. What works well for us here, will
not necessarily work for someone else, somewhere else, or in
a different portable dwellingway. (There are many kinds.)
    Do you gather/hunt most food? Or buy? Income sources?
    Sometimes we forage much; sometimes little; depending on
season and opportunities. We forage mostly fruit (berries) and
salads. Most calories come from purchased foods. Grains cheap
if bought in bulk. Occasional short, low-pay jobs suffice.
    How do you handle medical emergencies? Snake bites, etc?
    We have not had major traumas. Minor injuries we treat
ourselves. We do have (eg) "Ship's Medicine Chest and Medical
Aid at Sea" on microfiche for consultation. But we emphasize
prevention: hike carefully to not break limb or step on snake;
avoid constipating diet that might cause appendicitis; and
sleep/rest plenty to keep immune system potent. Prevention is
more important than response, because even someone living next
door to a hospital will die if injured badly enough. In a few
cases I might die while a house-dweller could be saved. But
overall, most house-dwellers are much more at risk. Eg, they
commute daily in frantic rush-hour traffic, to pay for their
houses and for the vehicles needed to commute. Each year,
traffic accidents kill MANY more people than do snake bites.
    How often do you move? And how? Only with backpack and
bike? Or motor vehicle too? Do you lug typewriter along?
    We move quite often (maybe 5 or 10 times) during the warm
dry season when we need only light equipment; seldom during
winter. Like some traditional nomads, we move mostly within a
home range ± 50 miles across, where we are not far from cached
supplies. We own no motor vehicle, but sometimes borrow,
rent, share or hire one to (eg) bring in much food supplies.
    Our typewriter remains with winter-base-camp equipment
and thus may move only once a year and only as far as our base
camp moves (seldom far). If we will be away from the base-
camp area most of the summer (usually), we pack away things
that rodents could damage: into plastic pails, trash cans, or
barrels. (The plastic barrels (olives or pickles were shipped
in) are stronger and seal better than trash cans, but aren't
as available and don't have as wide openings.)

Do you camp alone? Or with a group? How big? Clumped or spread out? If spread, do you visit? Hold gatherings?

Sometimes we camp alone; sometimes with others, depending on proximities and activities. If with others, we spread out, with camps ± a mile apart for easier tolerance of differences. We don't visit each other's camps (apt to annoy) nor try to gather everyone together (difficult). Each pair of families who wish to interact, choose a spot to meet at or to leave/pick-up items lent/swapped/bought-for. For us, winter is better than summer for interactions (other than chance meetings at events), because we have more free time then, and because we move less often and know farther in advance where we may be. (Most winters, some fairly mild dry days here.) Population unpredictable. (Sometimes zero: all are elsewhere.)

H & B

A simple home-made washing machine.

Salvage a 5-gallon pail with lid. Cut a hole in lid big enough for the handle of a plunger (a rubber bell-shaped device sold for unplugging drain pipes). Add plunger, clothes, water and soap (or whatever you wash with). Close lid. Voila ! Patricia MacKenzie, NY 130, February

(Comment:) Instead of plunger, may use any smooth stick with fork on end in pail. (Julie's tip in Apr92 DP.) The lid with hole (new idea) prevents much splashing of water out of pail.

To pour into a narrow-mouth container.

One way to avoid spilling: use a funnel. But suppose the opening is narrower than the funnel's spout. Or suppose you don't have a funnel along when (eg) you are hiking and want to pour some iodine solution from your crystals bottle into your canteen.

Fortunately there is a neat way. I suppose chemists use a glass rod to guide the flow. I use a grass stem or twig; or finger if opening is wide.

Hold stem vertically. Place bottom of stem into the container receiving but without touching its opening. Place the lower lip of the source in contact with the stem. Pour slowly. The water will flow along the stem. Julie Summers, 1997

Another way to make a faucet from a plastic jug.

Poke a pin-hole near the bottom. Fill with water. When ready to wash hands, loosen the cap. The weight of the water will force a small stream through the hole. When done, tighten the cap. If the cap is airtight (if leaky, add a plastic liner), the water will stay inside the jug. David French, SD

(Comments:) Compared with Julie's inverted-jug faucet (in LLL Packet), advantages we see for this upright-jug faucet: Hands don't touch spout. If spout is above the bottom, any debris may settle to the bottom and not interfere with flow or stoppage. (With inverted jug, debris may get between lip and cap, causing leak.) Cap-thread size doesn't affect flow. (With inverted jug, thread size critical; new milk jugs have threads too fine.) A jug is easier to tie to a tree or pole when it is upright. Unscrewing of cap isn't critical. (With inverted jug, if cap is unscrewed too far, it comes off and dumps all the water.)

Advantages we see for an inverted-jug faucet: The jug need not be strong. (A milk jug, left full of water, was collapsed by a vacuum after a slow leak developed.) The flow stops immediately when the cap is tightened. (With upright jug, the flow continues until a vacuum builds.) Flow rate is more easily adjusted. The jug is easier to clean (if filler hole big enough for hand).

A naturist park with portable dwellings.
(This is fiction. Any similarities to real places is not admitted.)

Valley View Park is located part way up Maple Mountain near Varied Valley, 50 km (30 miles) from Central City.

To minimize initial costs, property taxes and building-code hassles, Valley View has only portable structures.

The facilities dome, 16 meters (or yards) diameter and 5 m tall, consists of an open geodesic framework on which are layed various covers. On hot days: reflective tarps overhead and on the west for shade, with insect netting on other sides. On cool days: clear covers toward sun, with insulation on other sides. At night: complete insulation.

The dome contains: small pool; salad garden; communications center (phone, fax, etc); library (mostly fiche); frig (solar powered); and the Eatery.

The Eatery's fare is free to members but rather monotonous: plenty of rice, oatmeal, popcorn, and beans (etc) and seldom much else. The vegetarian menu minimizes cost, frig space, and clean-up. Members may bring own foods, including meat, into park for own consumption.

Though residence varies with season, the park is the usual home of more than half its members, and a weekend/holiday haunt for most of the rest. A shuttle van, towing a trailer with bike racks, drives down and up the mtn twice a day (which is a long tedious climb for a cyclist), connecting in the valley to bike paths and a city bus line. Once a week or so, the van goes all the way to the city for items too big for bike or bus. Few members own motor vehicles: parking space is scarce and NOT free.

Residents set up various portable dwellings in wooded or brushy areas of the park. With food and facilities at the dome, little personal space is needed. Bitter cold is rare. When it comes, some members take their bedding to the dome and crowd in. With the dome heater going full blast, and the pool emitting stored warmth, the dome almost always remains above freezing.

To allow disturbed environments to heal, the park is divided into two zones. One year, camping and hiking are limited to the first zone; the next year, to the other; with some overlap for moving.

Nudity is encouraged within the dome. At its portal, any clothes worn outside are removed and left outside, and a shower is required. The dome is usually warm enough for naked comfort. (The more-active or less-heat-tolerant occupants often need dips in the pool.) But in the dome, as elsewhere, clothing is optional, except: only garments that are kept inside may be worn inside. That helps keep out vermin, dust and associated pathogens; and minimizes pool water filtration and changes.

About half the members are women; more than at most naturist parks. As inducements, women join free. Men pay nearly a thousand a year: high, but with most everything else free, no one needs steady employment. Most of the funds buy food supplies for the Eatery. A few members garden and provide seasonal fresh vegetables, or do maintenance, instead of paying money.

Some women use Valley View only as a free campground, and never go to the dome where they would have to shed their shrouds. Some nudist members resent "subsidizing textilists". But most tolerate that, expecting those women will eventually either be tempted enough by the dome's freebs to overcome their inhibitions, or will leave.

(This is the first of two parts. In next issue: Valley View's youth-oriented synergistic competitor & how it differs)
H & B

More than a tick about ticks.
Lyme is a devastating disease and difficult to cure. To avoid infection, discover ticks before they bite (best) or soon after (next best). Disease transmission usually requires several hours. Here is what we now do if hiking or working outside during tick season.

To best detect ticks, wear as few clothes as possible. Choose light color so ticks will show. (Ticks I've seen were dark: brown or reddish brown.)

Carry any bedding or extra clothes enclosed in plastic bags.

Promptly investigate any irritation. View through a hand lens. (Some ticks are pinhead size.) If hiking solo, have two mirrors for viewing all body parts.

Frequently stop, remove any clothes, and inspect body carefully, both seeing and feeling. Check lumps. Unlike most scabs and moles, ticks when attached can be flipped from side to side. Inspect clothes, turning inside out.

At end of hike, remove any clothes, inspect body extra carefully and, if possible, shower BEFORE entering camp area or any dwelling. If you don't have time then to scrutinize clothes, put them in plastic bags until you do have time. Best not enter any shelter while wearing clothes you have been hiking in, without first inspecting them.

Kill any tick by burning, or by crushing between rocks. (Tick is tough.) Don't get its body fluids on you.

If a tick bites, remove promptly by grasping with tweezers, improvised tweezers (from stick) or fingernails close to its head. Try not to squeeze its body. Pull gently and maybe twist a little to hopefully remove in one piece. (Dabbing with oil or hot match did not budge ticks we tried that on.)

Suck wound using a short pipe or (eg) film can with hole in bottom.

Wash wound with (eg) iodine solution, hydrogen peroxide, or soap and water. (I don't know how much sucking and washing help, but they seem worth doing.)

With hand lens, inspect wound for any remaining head parts. Dig out with sterilized pin or thorn.

Not all tick bites are noticed: be alert for symptoms regardless. Michael, a former lyme patient, says: only a third of cases show a bulls-eye rash. More common: stiff neck; flu-like cold that doesn't go away. Lab tests for lyme are not reliable. If symptoms, promptly seek antibiotics (eg, minocycline). MUCH easier to cure early.

I've read, nudists get fewer tick bites. Nudity helps several ways:

Ticks are easier to see on most skin than on most clothes (at least on skin lighter colored than the ticks).

You need only inspect your body; not also clothes with many irregularities.

Ticks are easier to feel crawling on you, if no clothes clinging to or rubbing you (but ticks crawl slowly and do not tickle much, so also look for them.)

Ticks are easier to feel with your fingers if clothes are not in the way.

You can more promptly check a sore if clothes removal isn't necessary.

Ticks usually crawl around looking for cover before biting. Clothes are cover. A tick may eventually bite regardless. But the more it crawls around looking, the more likely you are to discover it before it bites.

When hiking nude (except shoes and sunshade hat), Bert and I have seldom if ever been bitten. Ticks get on us but we find them before they bite. When wearing only shorts, most bites have been under the shorts.

During 25+ years of camping and hiking, mostly in the West, Bert and I have found maybe 100 ticks on us. Most (maybe 80 of 100) before they bit (and this was before doing everything suggested above). Of those that bit, most were felt quickly - some before they got firmly attached. With one exception (a juvenile), all ticks were discovered before they had fed long enough to bloat. The ticks included all stages but mostly adults. We encounter most during warm months. But this year, Bert found one on a mild late-Dec day.

For clothing, some authors recommend tight fits, apparently hoping ticks won't crawl under them. Such clothes are not comfortable hiking or working. I prefer loose fits, so I can feel inside clothes easily and remove clothes easily. A light forest green looks natural yet contrasts with ticks.

As for repellants, anything toxic enough to dissuade a tick, I'd rather not have on my skin. Also, repellants won't stay on long, especially in hot weather when sweating or showering.

Be kind to lizards. I've read, the California fence lizard has something in its blood that not only safeguards the lizard from lyme, but also disinfects the tick. (Range? Other lizards? I don't know.) But that may be why lyme is less common in West than East. (However, other tick-borne diseases lurk in West - and East.) Holly & Bert, OR 973, Jan

Grandmother's bug repellant.

She mixes: 1 oz white tyme oil; ½ oz each of lavender, citronella, patchouli and cade oils; 8 oz any clean vegetable oil. She may bottle in little vials, or mix with 2 gallons red cedar shavings and put in small plastic bags.

To keep out mosquitos and flies, put a few drops in little tea light candles, or near a light bulb or other warmth.

For roaches, do like for mosquitos, and also use roach baits.

For ants, follow their trail to where they are entering. Block their path with a heavy line of oil.

For fleas, put a big handful of the cedar shavings under pet's bed-padding.

For moths, put some cedar shavings in cloth bag and hang in closet.

Spiders couldn't care less. (Maxine's Pages, Crystal Rain Research Agency, GA)

Cedar: Tree of Life of NW Coast Indians, Hilary Stewart, 1984, 192p., 47 photos, ±600 drawings (clear,accurate,detailed), Douglas&McIntyre,1615 Venables,BC V5L2H1

Cedar so permeates NW coast Indian culture, "it is hard to envision their life without it." Red cedar (Thuja plicata) is lighter green than conifer companions. Mature trees contain thujaplicin, a fungicidal oil that resists rot. A fallen tree may remain sound for a century. Because its "loose, cellular structure creates air spaces," it insulates better than do hardwoods.

The wood was made into totem poles and dugout canoes; or split into planks for boxes, chests, and huge houses.

Bark was harvested from trees "about 2 handspans wide". Only during spring and summer, when sap was running, could the bark be removed, in long, vertical strips. (I remove bark only from fallen trees. Some fall naturally, especially beside streams where their roots get eroded. Some are left behind after commercial logging. Removing bark from a live tree kills or injures it - depending on how much of the circumference is removed.)

UNseparated bark was used as bark boards (a popular trade item - threading with salmonberry sticks prevented curling), storage boxes, cooking pots, canoe bailers, and emergency canoes.

For other uses, inner and outer bark were separated with knife, then pulled apart. The bark might first be bent every 4 handspans to crack the outer bark, which made separation easier.

For baskets, mats and rope, inner bark was separated into layers and split in width: eg, 1" wide for coarse matting or 1/16" for fine baskets. To split with speed and precision, 2 razor pieces were set in a wooden handle. (NW Indians had iron-tipped tools (of unknown origin) for centuries before Capt. Cook came in 1778, but apparently they were scarce.)

For quality clothing, inner bark was softened by shredding: fully dry bark was pounded, then twisted. Oil on the hands helped soften. Clothing of yellow cedar (Chamaecyparis nootkatensis) is tougher than red; thus more valuable.

Withes (branchlets) were used as fastenings. Twisting made them flexible. For quick use in the woods, the withe was twisted right on the tree, with bark left on. Better: heat withe; remove bark; reheat; then twist. Split withes were used for lashing, sewing, rope.

Cedar roots, split one to 8 times, were used to make coiled baskets which were often waterproof. Roots were straighter in rock-free soil. About 15 feet from base of a big old tree, a woman dug down with a digging stick, 2 feet or more. All women made baskets, but the most expert were spared some household tasks so they could devote more time to their craft.

Formerly, and still in Britain, all conifers were collectively called pines. When early explorers spoke of NW coast Indians using "pines", they meant red or yellow cedar. Review by Julie

Holders improve access.

I use holders with multiple compartments (also called caddys) for kitchen utensils, craft tools, and art supplies. Those that revolve are nice. I've bought them inexpensively at garage sales, and even found a perfectly good one in a dumpster. But I wanted more than I was finding, so I began making my own. My home-mades don't rotate: duplicating that feature seems not worth the effort.

I make them from discarded plastic bottles. Ones with square cross-sections fit together without the gaps that round bottles leave. Clear film canisters hold small items. In cities, I find bottles at recycle centers or in recycle bins behind eateries; in the boonies, at impromptu dumps.

I cut the tops off with scissors. Then wash. Then punch holes for joining. I use a paper punch or revolving leather punch. Where punches can't reach, or when I'm without them, I use a narrow-bladed knife. But cutting flexible plastic is tricky. An alternative: melt holes with a hot nail, held with pliers or vice grips and heated over a candle or stove. Finally, I fasten the cut-off bottles together with twist ties, string, or rubber straps.

I prefer several small holders to one big one. Easier to pick up and move, and fewer compartments to search thru.

These holders are so helpful and easy to make, I even construct them when light camping if I expect to be at one place more than a few days. Julie Summers, OR 973, 1996

Bivy/storage boxes desired, especially for sleeping in cities.

A bivy box is big enough to sleep in when the top is raised, but closes quickly and then is weather proof, mouse proof, and very low profile. Closing takes much less time than does taking down a tent and stuffing bedding into pails. Easy close-up is especially advantageous when camping on remnant brushlands in urban areas, where a tent left set up is likely to be seen and vandalized.

A bivy box is light enough to transport as a bike trailer (lash on wheels and hitch) or to backpack empty. Or it may stay cached, semi buried, with only the top above ground. If slept in, to avoid condensation the box must be insulated. Even for storage, insulation is desirable; else moisture will concentrate on inside top or bottom (depending on temperature).

I've looked at big plastic boxes (for carrying/storing tools in pickups). About $17 on sale. But not big enough and not insulated. How weather and mouse proof I don't know.

Then there are tent-trailers, made to be towed by vehicles as small as big motorcycles. They expand for living

in, and close up for towing. Much too big for human-powered
transport (lightest a few hundred pounds). But that type of
structure might be miniaturized.
   If foam ice chests are made giant size, they might
serve after strengthening the outside with fiberglass.
   A wooden box would not be good. Ordinary wood quickly
rots when in contact with soil, and mice eventually chew
their way in - assuming the structure doesn't warp enough to
let them simply stroll in. Fungicide-treated wood is available but may be toxic to humans as well as to fungus.
   Maybe best: something of molded plastic, mass produced
for other uses, that could be adapted. Bert & Holly, 1997

(Comments:) Insulating any shelter is pretty easy. 4x8 sheets
of ½-inch-thick insulating board sell for about $6. Available
faced with aluminum (which blocks moisture). With foam core,
it cuts easily with razor knife. I've used it in trucks.
   Or, to insulate a tool box, maybe "bubble wrap"?
   I believe very cheap coffins are made - for cremations.
But I think they are only heavy cardboard.
   Perhaps some sort of shipping container would do. L.Smith
                                                   WI, Apr 98
Henry David Thoreau wrote of bivy boxes.
   I used to see a large box by the railroad, six feet long
by three feet wide, in which the laborers locked up their
tools at night; and it suggested to me that every man who was
hard pushed might get such a one for a dollar, and, having
bored a few auger holes in it, to admit the air at least, get
into it when it rained and at night, and hook down the lid,
and so have freedom in his love, and in his soul be free....
You could sit up as late as you pleased, and, whenever you
got up, go abroad without any landlord or house-lord dogging
you for rent. Many a man is harassed to death to pay the rent
of a larger and more luxurious box who would not have frozen
to death in a box such as this. (from Walden, ± 1850; sent by
                                                   L. Smith)
A new hotel concept for rucksack tourists.
   The cabins of modern Danish ships accomodate four people
in 85 square feet (eg, 8½x10'). Two-tier bunk beds are
arranged so the upper ones fold away. They provide real
comfort, including private bathrooms, but without pretensions.
   My idea is for a hotel on the same lines, in the city
centre where visitors most want to be. The small floor area
allows prices to be low even in an expensive part of town.
   The walls and ceilings of the units would be made in one
piece by spraying fibre-reinforced cement into moulds. The
resulting shells would then be bonded onto floor slabs of
reinforced concrete, and outfitted before being taken to site.
   Managers are of the same social group and ages as the
guests, who they treat as equals. They are friendly but
without acting as servants. Each manager has charge of a
section and, within limits, runs it as own business. The
managers are the only permanent staff, minimizing costs
during slack seasons. When the place fills, a manager may
pay guests to help with the cleaning and other work. Thus,
the availability of help is proportional to the need for it.
   I have researched this idea in depth. Unfortunately,
the public health rules make it unworkable. Nicholas Saunders
(from Institute for Social Inventions, London; sent by Roger
                                                     Knights)
I seek information about freighthopping and nomadic living.
   Willis, Georgia 311, November

A naturist park with portable dwellings - Part 2.
        120 km (70 miles) away across the valley, nestled between
two hills, is Bushy Gorge Park: the synergistic competitor
of Valley View (described in May99 DP). Some differences:
        Valley View is mostly families, with adults 25 or older
plus their young children (few teens or early 20s), and Valley
View does not stress body shape or muscle power (it includes
some heavies). In contrast, Bushy Gorge is mostly singles,
13 to 25; with few younger than 10 or older than 30. Though
there is no age limit, male members must pass, initially and
annually, fire-fighter fitness tests - quite a few pull-ups,
push-ups, etc. (Waivers, given mostly to new young applicants,
require members' unanimous consent.) As men approach middle
age, most either can no longer pass the physical, or they lose
interest in the youth-oriented activities. Women need not be
athletic (though many are), but most of them, too, eventually
lose interest. A few stay on - often in house-mother roles.
        Valley View is open to visitors only a few days each
year. Bushy Gorge is always open, but confines visitors to a
separate area. Members may visit visitors, but not vice versa.
        Valley View allows alcohol and some other drugs "in
moderation". Whereas Bushy Gorge, to avoid "underage" hassles,
absolutely bans alcohol, tobacco, and other restricted or
illegal substances. But, conveniently, the park is bordered
by public land, and what happens there is of little concern.
        Valley View is usually quite quiet. Bushy Gorge is often
noisy, with live concerts weekends, or stereos blasting.
        Not surprisingly, aging members of Bushy Gorge often move
to Valley View. And, not surprisingly, Bushy Gorge occasionally "raids" Valley View (tacitly ignoring visitation rules)
and lures away its young with tales of the fun going on at
Bushy Gorge - far from domineering parents and other old fogies.
                                                            H & B
What abode will you abide ?
        There seem to be conflicts of interest. Holly/Bert's idea
of dwelling portably is what you can carry on your back into
the woods. Whereas for me and many readers it is: what can
I drive - and live in ? Perhaps we are as fascinated with
vehicles as the Indians were with horses.
        But obviously, from the letters DP receives, not every-
one wants to endure years of wage slavery to buy a factory-
built RV. Anyhow, they are built to be used only two weeks
a year; not lived in. The ones I've examined were shoddy,
sloppy, and not well thought out.
        I think there is a niche DP could fill: between using a
vehicle to just transport camping gear (pickup truck), and
building a rolling house with flush toilet and generator, etc.
        My interest: how to live out of a vehicle simply and
cheaply. My vehicle just serves as a shelter. The exterior
is deliberately drab, to elude rogue D.A.'s seeking plunder,
and, more importantly, to avoid theft by unofficial criminals.
        Laws are easily circumvented; especially laws concerning
vehicles. L. Smith, Wisconsin 532, 1997

(Reply:) This conflict of interest arose soon after DP (MP)
began. The decision then (in Feb85 MP): MP is primarily about
portable (backpackable) dwelling, but many of the techniques
are also useful to people living other ways.
        Anyhow, I wonder how fillable your niche is. DP has had
short articles by various people on how they outfitted their
vans, but not much detail. Detailed plans may not be worth-
while, because every make of van has different dimensions. B&H

(Comments:) Quite a few write that they wish to live out of a van or school bus, and then ask how. Of course, this is somewhat silly. Who knows what facilities they want, versus portability. And it does smack of the "ask the expert" syndrome so prevalent today. How will any new ideas be generated if all we do is copy someone else? What happened to Yankee ingenuity? Maybe what they really want is a fully-equipped RV, but they don't have the funds. But, still, I will encourage them.

My own rig just grew out of sitting in an apartment and thinking: I'll need storage of food and clothes, room to lie down and sleep, and perhaps a light to read by. Trying to keep it simple is harder than imagining ways to do it. I now realize I will never make it to the Salton Sea with four golf cart batteries aboard (240 pounds) - which are only powering two 8-watt fluorescent lamps, a blender, and a radio. Ah well.

I am writing this at the harbor in Milwaukee. It is deserted nights and weekends, and I have a nice view of the waters. Soon I'll be leaving for the beautiful shores of Lake Superior, far from the summer tourists up from Chicago.

L.Smith, Apr98

Chilly sleeping bags chill desire to camp.

In spite of our good intentions, we brought civilization with us: cooler, dehydrated foods, medicines, creams, deodorants, state-of-the-art sleeping bags, and reading material. Still, we reminded ourselves, few people of our age would sleep in a flimsy tent in the cold mountain night.

This campground is developed, yet has a remote feel, with trees, boulders, meadows and logs between the widely-spaced campsites. On this spring day, only 10 other campers are in an area with spaces for 75. There is a narrow, fast-paced river with falls, and wildflowers fill the meadows.

The animals are quirky. The ground squirrels are cute, with their glossy tabby fur coats: eating seeds and nuts from their little front paws; or standing on their hind legs staring at us. But they scamper obnoxiously close. Barry spent lunch time scaring them off with a stick, or throwing water at them. At times he was almost surrounded by those shrewd scavengers. While we were both busy elsewhere for a moment, they gnawed a banana and chewed on a unopened soup cup on our picnic table. One persistant fellow crept up to the woodstove and gnawed open my USED tea-bag. He shook out the tea, tried to chew it, then threw it down disgustedly.

At noon, warmed by the bright mountain sun, we talk bravely of future camping trips: how   we'll streamline the food supply from overly-complicated cooking of scalloped potatoes, to instant or dehydrated soups and stews.

Around 3 p.m., the sun is already sinking behind other nearby mountains and I'm cold. I briskly walk to our tent-cabin, where lay two inviting sleeping bags on their hunks of foam, with colorful rugs, blankets and pillows placed around them. I quickly change into long-johns.

At 7 p.m., with dinner finished, Barry starts the bon-fire. I sit before it with wine. Barry pops Jiffy popcorn.

One hour later the scene changes. After dousing fire and blowing out candles and lantern, we lay shivering in our sleeping bags, anxiously listening to the night sounds. The full moon hovers above and casts white eerie shadows through the thin tent walls. I toss and turn.

Two hour later, awakening from crazy, frightening dreams, my heart is beating madly. I have to pee again, so I go through the procedure of putting shoes on, unzipping the tent, stepping outside, and rezipping. I spot an animal. Seeing me, it freezes. It is large; cat-size. It has a bushy tail (no, not a skunk.) A red fox? It hesitates, then scurries behind a boulder. I hurry back to the tent.

More shivering, tossing and turning. The night creeps slowly forward. Finally, we squint our eyes at the approaching pink dawn. My head pounds as Barry scuttles over to the stove to boil water for tea and coffee. I pull up the sleeping bag, absolutely frozen. But the morning performs her magic show, with bird choruses widening in the crispy fresh new day. Ironically, the most lovely early morning I've ever seen. Now I lean forward my exhausted shivering body and sip grateful gulps of sage tea.

Later, after the day warms, we sleep like zombies for a few hours. We've made up our minds to enjoy this day: do some hiking and cook a nice dinner - then raze the tent and head for home BEFORE the shivering terror-filled night comes.

Until now, the few campers here have given each other a wide berth. But, right as we finish our fry pan of cheesy potatoes and tofu dogs, a pickup backs into the NEXT campsite. The two occupants immediately hook up their CD player AND television. As we pack our gear, we are treated to a blasting sports report, plus hooting and laughing.

As we pulled out, heaving a sigh of relief, at the gate we notice a new sign: "Warning - some ground squirrels are contaminated with fleas which carry BUBONIC PLAGUE."

We have come to the conclusion that campers we're not. Nature is a bit too hard on our aging bodies.

EPILOGUE. It's 7:30 p.m. I put down my book for a moment to view the golden setting sun out the screen windows of our beloved tent-cabin. We will probably leave it up here in our BACKYARD all summer. (From "Notes from Campsite 30", Essay #8, © 1998 by phyllis hordin, CA 921

(Comments:) Many things are difficult at first. MOST people have unpleasant experiences the first time they camp (or do anything very new).

To sleep warm, use two or more sleeping bags if necessary. They need not be "state of the art" (unless you are a competition trekker who needs to eliminate every ounce possible). Cheapo bags are fine. Just have ENOUGH.

For convenience, keep a pee bowl (or jug) in your tent.

To avoid obnoxious animals, DON'T go to developed camp-grounds. Animals there have learned to scavenge. Far from human activity, we are seldom bothered by creatures bigger than mice (which are easily trapped).

Yes, do simplify food supply and preparation. Even in our winter base shelter, with jug faucet and sink, and propane stove on 5-gal tank, and where our two bodies usually keep inside air above 60°F, we seldom use the stove oftener than once a day. When light-camping during summer, we may cook only once or twice a week. Holly & Bert, Oregon 973, May

TVP is one of the mainstays of my diet.

Texturized vegetable protein is dehydrated soy protein. Available in most food co-ops in several sizes, from flakes to chunks. Light weight, and cheap: ± $1 per pound.

I've been totally vegetarian for 24 years. I don't know if it has improved my health, but it hasn't harmed it. L.Smith

(Comment:) At times we have bought whole soy beans. Much cheaper than TVP. Roasted, they have a pleasant nutty taste.

But HARD - not easy to chew. They can be ground along with
wheat to enrich bread. At first, soy improves the flavor.
But after a few weeks, DELETING soy improves the flavor. Is
there something in soy our bodies don't want much of? H & B

Santa Claws leaves us a high-protein Christmas present.
     In January 1998 we found the deer on a water trail, only
a quarter mile from our winter base-camp. From the marks, we
think a cougar ambushed it. (Suppose I had come along before
the deer?) Quite fresh. (One day old?) Only liver and part
of one hindquarter had been eaten. We took all we thought we
could eat before it spoiled (cold spell, fortunately), but
left some for the cougar in case it returned.
     We don't hunt much. We don't like harming animals that
aren't harming us, find hunting boring, and think a steady
high-protein diet is unhealthy for most adults. But, like our
ancestors, we happily scavenge. One risk with road-kills and
predator-kills: you don't know if the prey animal was sick.
So cook thoroughly. And, at least with mammals, don't eat
brain or spinal cord (mad cow (etc) disease, which, we've
read, cooking does not inactivate). Holly & Bert

Someone came seeking an Easter dinner. It was not a bunny !
     The first sound of our visitor: gentle rustling of the
curtains at one end of our shelter. Not loud. A chipmonk or
lizard ? But, peering through the translucent plastic, Bert
glimpsed something big ! No guns on hand. We grabbed knives.
     The creature moved out of sight and circled our camp -
amazingly quiet. (Except for a small terrace in front, our
shelter was surrounded by thick brush.) Finally the animal
stalked across in front, profile silhouetted against the sky,
only a few feet away. Four footed. Much bigger than a coyote
but smaller and leaner than most bears. And bears are usually
NOISY. So are dogs. A cougar? The same one?
     We both growled, deeply. It took off. No sign of it
since. Why did it come? We had not recently eaten meat.
But I had been menstruating. Had it smelled me ?
     Since then, when hiking solo, we carry wooden spears
(which are also useful as staffs in some spots). When hiking
together (attack less likely against two), we carry knives.
                                            H & B, May 1998
(Comment:) I was reluctant to publish these two reports,
because they are NOT typical experiences. Bert and I have
camped full time for over 20 years, and part time before that,
and have not had any other close encounters with big animals.
We don't want DP to become like the sensational "adventure"
magazines which feature the freaky. However, anyone who lives
in the bush (or anywhere) a long time, will sooner or later
have some UNusual experiences. Holly & Bert, Oregon 973

Don't scavenge vending machine discards - unless desperate !
     (In response to Laszlo Borbely's article in Dec97 DP.)
I've been in the vending business off and on for 20 years.
Venders buy only the cheapest meats, bread, and other foods.
A small vender buys his food from a kitchen distribution
center. Refrigeration from the kitchen to his facility, and
from his facility to the machines ? Maybe, sometimes - if
not inconvenient. But usually, just throw in a cooler - and
by the time the driver reaches his last stops, the food is
warmer than your mother's heart.
     Health safety switches, that prevent vending if the
cooling fails, are often bypassed. Expiration dates on food
are usually coded; if not, they're made illegible with a
drop of paint thinner.   L.Smith, WI

Dwelling Portably
(formerly named Message Post)
POB 190, Philomath OR 97370

November 1999 $1 per issue   To be reprinted as part of Aug

I have been using canvas shoebags as caddys for years.
    I usually hang them on walls. Each consists of twenty
6-by-4-inch pockets, fairly well reinforced. Unlike vinyl ones,
canvas bags are repairable. Skilled sewers might make their
own out of heavy cloth.
    A shoebag is very portable, because you can roll it up,
tie the ends, and transport without losing anything.
    I got the idea from Carl Franz books: On and Off the Road
Cookbook; or People's Guide to Mexico. L.Smith, WI 532, August

Cyclists use newspaper as wind-break.
    During mountain stages of the Tour de France, helpers and
fans wait on summits and offer flat newspapers to riders, who
stuff them in their jerseys to help keep upper body warm during
descents at speeds over 50 mph.
    During the 21 years I lived in n. Cal, I carried a spare
paper for crisp morning commutes. Worked well. Dave Parish, FL

I freighthopped several times during the 1970s.
    West of the Mississippi; sometimes alone, sometimes with
a male companion, once with a female companion.
    Talking to frequent "hoppers" is the best way to glean
info. I was told which cities were most dangerous to go into,
either because of the railroad "dicks", or because more of the
people going there were desparate and willing to give you a
shake or a sore head to gain your goods.
    Many of the hoppers had alcohol problems, but not in a way
that alarmed me. Most were helpful, witty, knowledgable, and
more than willing to share info, food or spirits (both kinds).
Some hoppers were migrant workers. I was there for the "fun of
it" and to experience some areas that are rarely visited except
by trains and wildlife.
    I suggest, walk to the nearest train yard and just watch.
See who's who. If you spot someone about to hop, ask a few
questions. Follow your instincts: if you question someone's
character, be friendly but move on quickly - you will live
longer. Many railroad employees such as brakemen and engineers
were friendly and helpful when I asked which direction a train
was going. One railroad dick in Reno even took me to breakfast. But I suspect my being a woman accounted for his
kindness, as he had a stiff reputation among the hobos. The
railroad dicks can make your life unpleasant, and there were
several stories of physical abuse by some of them.
    That was 25 years ago. Maybe some particulars have
changed. Ask around the yard: that is the best way to learn.
And don't ride mail trains unless you have great faith: they
go recklessly fast. Once was enough for me. Laura LaBree, WA

(Comments:) We have never hopped. Once I was tempted to. I
was in s. Cal hitching north, not getting rides, and saw a
freight go slowly by. But I felt I did not know enough.
Getting on and off (especially) can be dangerous if one does
not know how (as can many things).
    For campsites in cities we generally avoid "hobo jungles"
near railroads, not because we dislike hobos (those we've met
we liked fine), but because hobos are a target for cops.
    May 96 DP included a detailed review of a book about
freighthopping, by Hobos From Hell. Various peoples'
experiences, most recent, with some detailed advice. B & H

How dangerous is camping?

Traveling and camping for extended periods has long appealed to me, but I have yet to do much of it because of all the contradictory reports I've heard about cougars. Do they ever come into your camp? What do you think would be enough protection if camping in remote areas of the Coast Range?

Also, could one be arrested if a forest worker came across a campsite that seemed like it had been there for months, in a National Forest or on timber company lands?

Krista, OR 973, Oct

(Reply:) We do not get media, so I don't know if many attacks by cougars have been reported. Two years ago, a cougar came very close to our shelter. We both growled, which scared it off. (Account in Aug99 DP.) We have had no other close encounters in the woods with big animals or hostile people in over 20 years. If meeting a cougar, advice I've heard: look big; stand tall; never run. And, when hiking, observe carefully: cougars like to ambush their prey.

Since our encounter, we keep spears (just sharpened poles) at camp and often hike with them. (They are also useful as staffs.) Enough protection? I don't know.

A gun may provide better defense at a camp. And it has much longer range for hunting. But, while hiking and possibly BEING HUNTED by a cougar, maybe not. A gun can't be gotten into action as quickly as can a spear, unless it is carried in hands, loaded, safety off, with finger on trigger. And, if carried thusly, it is dangerous: without hands free to grab, stumbling is more likely, and any jolt could cause discharge. Also, a gun is more delicate and needs much more care, and is expensive to buy or time-consuming to make. (A spear requires only a few minutes whittling.)

For safety at camp, see articles by Tim Leathers, Guy Hengst, and us in May 95 DP. If discovered, I suppose arrest is possible. But the usual procedure, I've read: post warning to move within a specified time (24 hours? 2 weeks?); then, if the camp remains, steal or vandalize the equipment. The campers might also be fined IF caught.

If not experienced camping, you might consider trying to make an arrangement with a private landowner and camp on some not-too-remote wooded or brushy acreage while testing your equipment and gaining skills and confidence, and so you can more easily obtain anything additional you need.

When camping (or doing anything), keep in mind the relative risks. Even if someone camps only 20 miles from a city and goes there only once a month, I suspect the biggest danger by far is from traffic during those monthly trips. B&H

How we dispose of kitchen waste in the woods.

First and foremost, at the end of each meal, we EAT every edible remnant that is too perishable to keep or too small to be worth saving. Then we wipe plates and pots with (eg) bread, or lick; then pour in a little drinking water, rub with a clean finger, and drink.

If people from another dwellingway saw us clean up, they might assume we are fanatic conservationists or else are from a land of chronic hunger. But our biggest reason: any edible remains will attract hungry creatures we would rather not have around: flies, mice, rats, bears.

Food parts we don't eat (peels, shells, bones, bad parts of apples, etc), we carry far away and place under bushes.

Relatedly, pee or wash-water containing menstral flow, we pour slowly on the ground (being careful not to splash), let it soak in, then pour over it Bert's pee to mask any odor.

Cattail down too clumpy to be good insulation.
I read it is warmer than goose down, so I tried it.
I stripped the dry down off cattail stalks in the fall and
stored it in a tightly-closed plastic pail for a few years
until using it to repair a garment that had lost some of its
original goose down.
I tried to tease the cattail down apart with my fingers,
but it didn't separate easily. Then I used a pair of wool
cards (which are like broad wire brushes). That fluffed the
down quite well. But after filling the spaces in the garment,
the cattail down clumped together. Shaking the garment did
not unclump it. To eliminate spaces between clumps and thus
insulate effectively, would require a dense filling using
much down - and be HEAVY - undoing the advantage of down.
I also tried the cattail down as pillow stuffing but
found it relatively hard - less comfortable than cut-up small
pieces of poly foam. Julie Summers, Oregon, March

In damp cool and cold weather I prefer wool.
Keeps me more comfortable than any other fibre I know of.
And it does not lose its warmth while I rest, like the
synthetics (plastics) do. Guy Hengst, Indiana, October

Is Baja for you?
Come to Mexico only if you are interested in Mexico, love
the people, and know Spanish or are willing to learn it.
Mexico is a foreign country. Americans are guests here.
If you do not befriend Mexicans in a sincere, respectful and
generous way, you will not be able to afford to live here and
probably won't like it. Desert conditions in Baja are harsh
and services are few, which makes people all more dependent on
each other. You will be able to live simply here only with
the good-will of the locals. Anonymity is almost impossible.
The only Americans here worth associating with, are also
doing this. If you are able to do this, you will be enriched
and rewarded by the experience. If not, stay home: do not
visit Mexico - or other countries either.
If you want to leave the USA, start today by befriending
people of color and other cultures on THEIR terms.
I live far south of the border and plan to move even
further south, as does most everyone who is halfway hip.
Near the border are gringos - and the military.
I think many DP-types might be able to hack it here.
But you must scout it out and make friends and contacts. And
you can NOT make it without help from the locals. You got to
want to mix in.
You must be very healthy and totally insane to survive in
this desert during summer. I love it. It is tranquil - no
Americans. I see the tide is nearly high again so I'm off for
a swim. I got stung by a Manta the other day and temporarily
lost my desire to swim when the tide is way out.
I can't tell you how to cross the border; I haven't done
it for many years. (I recently read that officials want to
charge $15 to everyone who crosses the border more than 15
miles, but I don't recall the details.)
Yes, dental care is cheap and good. But I am astonished
that anyone would drive 1000 miles for it. Would you save
anything? (I had a pretty good experience at the dental
school in Portland in the early 1990s.)
To live cheap and simple here, you must love the people
and want to go native. Otherwise Mexico will suck you dry.
Luz, Baja, June

(Comments:) Your advice to Americans regarding Baja, sounds much like the advice to city people in back-to-land magazines: move to a settled rural area or small town in America only if you like the people there and are willing to mix and conform.

Good advice, I expect, regarding places and ways the writers have lived. But the writers tend to make sweeping generalizations, and assume everyone will live like them.

Bert and I sometimes live on the fringes of rural areas, and do so without having much or anything to do with the local settlers. Sure, a few might be congenial IF we could associate without getting involved with the others. But usually we can't, so we don't try.

This is not to disagree with you regarding where you live. I can't imagine why any American would want to go into a Baja desert merely to live in seclusion, well-hidden from the locals, when they can do that in an American desert without having to cross the border. But when you suggest that anyone who lacks your attitudes and mix-in abilities should not visit ANY PART OF Mexico - or any other country either. !?! Not even Tijuana or Mexicali? How about Mexicans - or Americans visiting San Diego or Portland? I assume you don't like those places. But should NO ONE ?

As for dentistry, millions of Americans including many DP readers live within a hundred miles of Mexico, and many more migrate to near-border areas during winter for sunshine, visiting friends, earning money, or buying things unavailable where they summer. If they need teeth repaired, why not hop over the border? Save money and time too(vs U.S. dentists).

You say the desert climate is harsh. So is most any climate to someone ill-prepared for it. (Western Oregon has mild temperatures compared to most of the U.S. But, to someone lacking equipment or improvisation skills, the long cold rains can be deadlier than the colder snows further inland, because staying dry is more difficult.)

Personally, I don't mind heat if there is some shade (or I can rig some) so I don't sunburn, and plenty of water for frequent showers (or dips or swims), and if I don't have to wear clothes. Which brings up: I've heard many Mexicans are even more hostile to nudity than are many Americans (though SOME Indians are quite different from Hispanics that way).

Local friends may help. But I expect they will respect and like someone more if s/he does not need help often. H&B

Can a trailer be protected from thieves and vandals?
I am moving to Alabama where I was offered a teaching position. Many trailer parks are there. But I've heard: no way to stop people from breaking in and destroying or stealing everything; depending, I guess, on how they feel about you or the value of your stuff.

The problem seems global: people in San Diego talk about being ripped off repeatedly. This makes me hesitate to buy a trailer. How do your readers overcome such vulnerability, especially singles who leave their trailers and vans unoccupied while they work or shop? Angela Lakwete, CA 921, May

DWELLING PORTABLY prices as of 2009: 2 samples, $2.
Future issues: big print, 3/$6; tiny print, 6/$6.
Past issues, tiny print only: 2/$2, 6/$5, 14/$10.
Postpaid to U.S. if cash or if check is $5 or more.
NEW ADDRESS: DP c/o Lisa Ahne, POB 181, Alsea OR 97324
Email via: juliesummerseatssensibly@yahoo.com

Index